WHEN I WAS SOMEONE ELSE

"Stéphane Allix has crafted a brilliantly riveting and intensely moving narrative that sheds new light on the nature of our identity and links between human lives. Beginning with an arresting and traumatic dream reliving the death of an SS officer in the Russian campaign, Stéphane telepathically receives the name Alexander Herrmann and is astonished to find that he really existed, discovering a detailed 80-page dossier of his life. His epic inner and outer journey reveals the stunning accuracy of his dream sequence while at the same time vividly re-creating the horrors of the Russian campaign. His deep humanity, moral courage, and penetrating insight shines out from this quite remarkable book with its message of ultimate redemption through the grit of our common suffering and persistent determination. I cannot recommend this book too highly."

DAVID LORIMER, EDITOR OF *PARADIGM EXPLORER* AND PROGRAM
DIRECTOR AT THE SCIENTIFIC AND MEDICAL NETWORK

"Fascinating book. Stéphane Allix's emotional research into the life and death of Alexander—although he does not share any of his ideas and beliefs—allowed him to let go of his own past that had always pursued him. This wonderful, spiritual, and even sometimes mind-blowing book may help the open-minded reader to accept the possibility of reincarnation. Highly recommended."

PIM VAN LOMMEL, M.D., CARDIOLOGIST, NDE RESEARCHER,
AUTHOR OF *CONSCIOUSNESS BEYOND LIFE*

"This riveting book will challenge you to rethink your ideas about who you are and your interconnections with other people. Allix's dramatic journey offers profound evidence of healing of psychological wounds through acknowledgment of both light and dark."

BRUCE GREYSON, M.D., CARLSON PROFESSOR EMERITUS
OF PSYCHIATRY & NEUROBEHAVIORAL SCIENCES,
UNIVERSITY OF VIRGINIA HEALTH SYSTEM

"A riveting detective story, a thriller, a harrowing journey back into the darkest days of World War II, and, most of all, the author's relentless quest for self-discovery and to fathom the nature of his identity. An absolutely stunning, unforgettable book. Five stars and more!"

KENNETH RING, PH.D., COAUTHOR OF
LESSONS FROM THE LIGHT

"In his extraordinary investigation, Stéphane Allix offers probably the strongest support for a case of reincarnation in an adult person. A remarkable and important book that can change the reader's view of reality. Must-read!"

STANISLAV GROF, M.D., AUTHOR OF *THE ULTIMATE JOURNEY*

"*When I Was Someone Else* is both an exciting detective story and an important spiritual exploration."

JIM B. TUCKER, M.D., AUTHOR OF
BEFORE: CHILDREN'S MEMORIES OF PREVIOUS LIVES

"The forensic details of Stéphane Allix's search for the SS officer he suspects he was in a former life, combined with how this search affected him at every turn, creates a fascinating study of the intermingling of the past and present in our lives. A welcome addition to the growing literature on reincarnation."

CHRISTOPHER BACHE, PH.D., AUTHOR OF
LIFECYCLES AND *LSD AND THE MIND OF THE UNIVERSE*

WHEN I WAS SOMEONE ELSE

The Incredible True Story
of Past Life Connection

STÉPHANE ALLIX

Translated by Jack Cain

Park Street Press
Rochester, Vermont

Park Street Press
One Park Street
Rochester, Vermont 05767
www.ParkStPress.com

Text stock is SFI certified

Park Street Press is a division of Inner Traditions International.

Copyright © 2017 by Mama Éditions
English translation copyright © 2021 by Inner Traditions International

Originally published in French under the title *Lorsque j'étais quelqu'un d'autre,* by
    Mama Éditions, 7 rue Pétion, 75011 Paris, France
First U.S. edition published in 2021 by Park Street Press

Cataloging-in-Publication Data for this title is available from the Library of Congress.

ISBN 978-1-64411-080-5 (print)
ISBN 978-1-64411-081-2 (ebook)

Printed and bound in the United States by Lake Book Manufacturing, Inc.
The text stock is SFI certified. The Sustainable Forestry Initiative® program
promotes sustainable forest management.

10 9 8 7 6 5 4 3 2 1

Text design and layout by Debbie Glogover
This book was typeset in Garamond Premier Pro with Arquitecta and Majesty
used as display fonts.

To send correspondence to the author of this book, mail a first-class letter to the
author c/o Inner Traditions • Bear & Company, One Park Street, Rochester, VT
05767, and we will forward the communication.

To the Spirits.

Contents

1

Departure

As my plane flies over the green ocean of the Amazon rainforest, I am light years away from having any idea of what awaits me. I savor a certain impatience in the last moments of a trip that began yesterday, twenty hours ago, in Paris.

A few minutes more and the flight that originated in Lima, the capital of Peru, touches down on the wet tarmac of the little tropical town of Tarapoto.

How could I have imagined that my life was going to take such an unexpected turn? The *encounter* is going to happen here, but it could just as well have been in Paris or somewhere else. It's the moment that's important, much more than the place. And the moment is special: after years of intense activity, I'm finally granting myself a break. Time out.

An opportunity to take stock of my life.

Time has been racing by unattended for much too long. I want to rediscover myself, have confirmation that I'm on the right path, seriously examine the wounds that I'm carrying, understand my anger, heal my darknesses. My anger does not show up in what I do, but more in a sort of almost constant inner anxiety. And healing that anxiety has become imperative, a question of health, of survival even. There are moments in a life where something isn't right and where the *urgency* for change becomes too strong. That's what's happening to me today. I can no longer back away.

◆ ◆ ◆

I'm about to discover that when we ask for help from the universe, destiny comes to our aid. Even though it's difficult at times to realize that, it is *always* the case.

Walking beside death for so many years has allowed me to understand to what extent not listening to that inner quiet voice, and, beyond that, not being willing to see what part is suffering, is to risk in the end seeing your life pass you by.

When you put something off till later, it's often the case that later means too late.

My brother died before my eyes in a car accident. He had just turned thirty, and in a fraction of a second, at the peak of his vitality, he disappeared. He was one who knew how to follow his instincts and to never compromise. He did well.

I also accompanied my father, aged eighty-five, up until his last breath. When he was beginning to fail, something he said touched me very deeply. Sitting on his hospital bed, he looked at me and said in an astonished tone, "When I think of the future I see that it's over, and when I look back, I realize that life has gone by in the blink of an eye." And he accompanied these words with a crisp snap of his fingers, his expression shining with the amazement of a realization that brooked no appeal. What would he have changed if he had been able to go back? What had not been carried through when it was still possible? What would he have been able to heal? What regrets did he have in the closing days of his life?

This experience showed me how important it is to follow intuition, even when it seems to turn everything upside down. Wanting to be free means taking risks and putting oneself in question. The world is nothing but uncertainty, but is that a reason to never undertake anything when our inner being is screaming at us to act? Certainly we always find valid excuses for staying put, but how long can we put off discovering who we really are, when everything is on fire inside us? Is it caution, or reason that dissuades us? Or habit, laziness, fear? And isn't it this intentional blindness that ends up making us ill?

◆ ◆ ◆

I had been putting off the confrontation for too long, so I decided to jump ahead, whatever the price. I left in order to look at myself head on, in solitude and in meditation, without the blinders that daily life holds permanently in place. I am embarking on this retreat far from my usual world with the desire to encounter myself. And I have no idea just how true that is going to be.

I have the good fortune to be accompanied in this life by a wife who is like me. Natacha accompanied me to Charles de Gaulle Airport, north of Paris, and at the moment of saying goodbye in the airport parking lot, we embraced. Pressed against her, I understood this incredible thing: my wife is my *refuge*. She means so much to me! Breaking our embrace was a ripping apart—we were going to be separated for several weeks. I didn't want to display anything about that at the moment. Our hands let go, and I walked off to the airport and she drove away. We were both crying. This life that violently boils up in me has repercussions on us as a couple. But I experience so many extraordinary moments with Natacha that the obvious efforts we need to make to clarify our respective shadow sides is a requirement felt by both of us. Confidently and with deep mutual respect we are growing up together. It is the love that we carry in us that allows us to understand and accept this need for me to be on my own—sometimes. I am extremely grateful to her for that.

Just before getting on board, still shaken up, I received a text message from my daughter Luna saying, "Travel like before." Emotions again. Her sensitivity and the strength of her intuition never cease to surprise me. This newborn, whom I tenderly held in my arms such a short time ago, has become an impressively mature adult. How quickly time passes on the face of one's child. But what joy to see the forming of a human being. A human being for whom you would give everything without a moment's hesitation. How beautiful and unambiguous—that love.

◆ ◆ ◆

If the emotional intensity of the departure is a measure of what the voyage has in store, I'd better fasten my seat belt.

Wheels touch the ground. The fringe of trees beside the runway dances in the windows. Then the plane slows down, rolls to its parking spot, and comes to rest in front of the terminal. Passenger commotion, cell phones being turned on, baggage compartments being opened impatiently. The unlocked doors let into the cabin a moist warmth and the smell of wet earth mixed with the stink of kerosene. Before long, I'm getting off, moving into the little airport, collecting my bags, and taking the road out of town to the center that will be hosting me.

The rainy season is approaching—high altitude clouds already appear in the sky a few kilometers to the north. As I leave behind the last houses of Tarapoto, I find myself in rolling terrain with hills; fields; and a rich, hot, and noisy forest. Soon the road becomes a surface of red earth, and then, having come to a village, I leave the vehicle and cover the last stretch on foot.

The place where I arrive after a forty-five-minute walk is called Terra Nova. "New Earth." It is well named, and it is isolated. I'm sweating. I pass a few casemates, large black rocks along the esplanade, and I come to where I'll spend my first night in a hammock hung below a precarious roof. My cabin, located a good distance from the camp, hasn't quite been finished. I get to see it properly the next day at dawn: a platform of thick boards, a roof of palm leaves, and walls of mosquito netting that still have to be put up, all this built against an imposing tree, an *ojé,* says Yann Rivière, the young Frenchman who has been running the center for a short time. It is here that I will be spending the coming weeks, in a shack open to the four winds. All alone, just with myself . . . and the spirits.

A bed covered with a rectangle of foam, a thin bedsheet, a table, and a chair: introspection paradise. The toilet: a hole dug in the ground. In front of the hut, a space cleared of vegetation gives me a broad view of the sky. Everywhere else gigantic trees cast their foliage very high up.

Yann explains that it's possible to walk down toward the river situated about fifty meters farther down along a little path that I will be the only one using. There are some sort of communal showers, but I already decide that the river will be just fine. I have such a desire for solitude. As for meals, they will be brought to me twice a day. The isolation will be total. A dream.

2

Solitude

During my first day I gradually get my bearings, struggling to understand that time has just stopped. I no longer have *anything* to do. No emails to consult, no telephone calls to deal with, no articles to reread, no appointments to prepare for, no meetings to worry about . . . nothing. It's barely believable. The shock is almost too violent. I quickly find odds and ends to improve in my new quarters, and the day unfolds—hot, agreeable, unreal.

Once night completely envelops my hut, insects, frogs, and other invisible animals burst together into song—a singing that is as varied as it is noisy. Each night now, my night will be cradled by this chorus. The forest rustles, hums, whistles, vibrates, and it only ends when daylight returns. Already a lot of insects are hanging on to the outside of the mosquito netting, attracted by the lamp installed above the table. An area like a large cone is illuminated, leaving part of the place in darkness. I write a few lines on the pages of my blue notebook, recounting the details of my settling in. Time is going to be long.

I have brought only one book: *War and Peace*. Tolstoy's Russia in the Amazonian forest. I took care to buy a new pocket edition and didn't bring the annotated volumes that I had already read, so that I could burn the book without regret in case reading it became incompatible with the work of introspection that I intend to do. Indeed, in my solitude, perhaps reading will become an ultimate means of escaping and backing away again from facing myself? In that case I will destroy the book so I can be totally taken over by the richness of boredom.

Why *War and Peace*? First of all because it's a masterpiece. Then, more prosaically, because even without pushing it, it will last for my whole stay. And finally, I feel connected to my father through this text. My dead father, whom I miss and who must have read the book about *forty* times.

I turn out the light, and immediately darkness descends. During the long seconds that follow, as my eyes get used to the darkness, the vague outlines of the external vegetation begin to appear beyond the netting. I am tired from the traveling, and my mind wanders between sleep and wakefulness, rocked by the songs of nature. Quickly I slip into this improbable bed. It's hot, and I cover myself partly with a light sheet and fall asleep immediately.

I'm up at dawn in the pale light of the newborn day. A delicate praying mantis pays me a visit as I eat the contents of my bowl: cereal with soya milk. The hot dampness of the night dissipates in volutes of mist above the canopy as the sun appears. An instant coffee in a little cold water completes my breakfast. What happiness. I am dizzy with the realization of where I am.

The only thing that I want to follow in a regular and disciplined way is the program of body work and energy work that I began in Paris under the direction of Serge Augier. These are martial arts exercises made up of slow movements designed to have the body work deeply, in preparation for a more rigorous engagement. These physical exercises are going to accompany my future spiritual work. For how can you pacify and explore spirit without cleaning and fortifying the body that is a reflection of it?

Simply wearing a sarong, I begin an initial exercise that consists of working on balance and my center of gravity. Barefoot on the floor of boards, arms along the body, I bring my weight alternatively onto my heels and then onto the front of my feet. In the slow swaying that this involves, I concentrate on my vertical axis. It's a kind of body meditation. I am looking beyond my hut at the trunk of the majestic tree in front of me. My obsessive thoughts come and go. I don't manage to calm my mind. There is too much energy in me provoking almost a kind of permanent irritability. As I'm breathing slowly I concentrate on gentleness. I'm too agitated in my head and, as a result, in my body as well. I seem fat. Or rather heavy since objectively I'm not fat. But I'm obsessed by my belly—it's encumbering me. If the belly is a second brain, I wonder really *what has it not digested?* I need to lighten up. While I'm going through the exercises, I notice that I don't know how to breathe. I breathe in with abruptness, in gulps, like a fish out of its element; I'm constantly trying to find my air. No doubt it's due to this heaviness in the belly. However, I've been breathing like that since childhood. My forgotten childhood.

The morning runs on. I sweat, aware of the ocean of contractions and tensions that quarrel inside me.

I must have confidence in my body.

What's at stake on this trip is for me to let go, for me to halt the thinking machine—the machine that blames when I think things are not going right, and that has never learned to stop wanting to control everything. "Show me. I trust you. Lead me to gentle, soft."

Suddenly I feel that I'm being observed. I turn around immediately expecting to see someone, but there is no one there. Just the screen of the forest. And yet I have the feeling that something was there. Is it keeping itself invisible so as not to frighten me? What a strange sensation.

I pick up the training again, calmer, with one idea that keeps coming back: I want to encounter myself, know who I really am . . .

I feel that I've arrived at the end of the work I undertook on death that followed the death of my brother and my father. For ten years I was nourished by my study of death, and from that, I feel transformed, reoriented, and deeply calmed. But now I no longer want to head toward the dead. I want life, not death. It's life that's important—to experience life without expecting anything in particular.

The morning goes by, and the heat increases. My thighs burning and my arms in pain, I set out on the path that leads down to the river. The place is deserted and majestic. I step into the shallow water, trying not to lose my balance on the slippery stones. I move toward deeper water. The river winds through the middle of luxuriant vegetation. I am in a dream and let myself be carried by delight. I wedge myself so as not to be carried away and plunge my head below the surface. The coolness of the water caresses my body, sensuously relaxing my muscles and taking away the contractions and cramps. I feel the current brush lightly against my eyelids, the nape of my neck, my back, creeping along my legs. Above me, eagles circling.

I go back up toward my hut. A meal is left discreetly by the center's cook—a piece of grilled fish, some puree, sliced tomatoes, some grated carrot, and a few slices of cucumber. I look at the plate on my table, and I'm surprised by the puff of anxiety that rises up: Is it enough? The plate is quite full. It will nourish me amply. Why any need for more? It's as if something in me is hungry. Fear of a lack, a need to compensate for something that food does not satisfy. I am astonished by the intensity of my fear. On a daily basis, in France, here and there I nibble on a piece of chocolate or a sweet. Sugary food and chocolate in particular comfort this empty corner of mysterious origin. The cause is connected to my emotions, but having said that, I am none the wiser. And the fact of finding myself with nothing that could quell this compulsive need sets off, several times a day, waves of micropanic. A new discovery appearing in sharp outline. Whoa . . . I've got work to do!

In the afternoon it begins to rain. The dense, hot shower marks the forerunner of the rainy season that will reach the region in a few weeks. Without hesitation I walk out into it. Face held up to the sky, arms spread wide. Big drops whip my face and my shoulders. Like the water of a torrent, the drops mark the limits of my body, give me a felt sense of its contours, intensify the perceptions that I have of it, and, in a certain way, anchor me, bringing me back to the organic material of which I'm made. By flowing over my epidermis, my body's membrane, the water gives me a felt sense of the unity of my body. No longer is there my mind thinking on one side and my legs walking on another side, or my hand writing; my body becomes once again a complete totality, through the effect of the contact with the rain or through the water of the stream. I massage my shoulders, my arms, my belly, my thighs, and I feel under my palms the strength of my muscles, the warmth of my skin. I feel life in me—organic, animal.

When the shower ends I let the sun dry me off, then I return to the hut and stretch out in the hammock that is strung between two beams. In this state of relaxation I'm in a reverie. My thoughts are calmer this morning. I grab my copy of *War and Peace* and read a few pages, which provides an immediate change of scene that is quite striking. In one second, there I am close to my father. I'm right at the beginning of the book when Pierre, contrary to all expectations, is designated by his dying father as the sole heir to the rights and colossal fortune of the Bezukhov counts. Dusk falls quickly. Then night arrives with its wild threnodies.

At twilight I join Yann in the Maloca, the big palm leaf–roofed building where shamanic ceremonies are held. Yann is a young shaman trained in Shipibo medicine. This evening he's going to "open me up" to my diet. Diet is the hub of traditional shamanic medicine. It consists of a strict dietary regime known to facilitate connection with the world of spirits. This discipline, which is dietary but also psychological—sexual abstinence is fundamental, for example—makes it possible to activate in the body the subtle energies that are conducive to spiritual work. During the diet you ingest also one or several of what shamans call "teaching plants." The teaching is transmitted directly to you through visions, dreams, synchronicities, and other subtle signs. It is said then that the world of plants *opens*. After letting him know that I wanted to make an inner assessment and see my interior more clearly, Yann suggests dieting with Ajo Sacha. This teaching plant contains no psychoactive molecules, but according to the shaman, its power is well suited to what I'm seeking. The spirit of Ajo Sacha is said to manifest most particularly through dreams.

During this opening of the diet I ingest only a tiny amount of aya-huasca, not enough to engender even the slightest psychoactive effect. I let Yann know that I don't want to participate in the ceremonies.

As soon as this work is done I leave the Maloca and return happily to my hut. And without warning sleep takes me.

A new dawn, the same as yesterday's, in the happiness and certainty that a meeting is being prepared. The encounter with my body—first of all in the course of the physical exercises of the morning and then in the long walks along the river—activates and disorients the circulation of energy in me. I notice it from the second morning on. It's very subtle, but the sensation continues to increase with each passing day. I feel that my vitality is increasing. My desire as well. No doubt one of the first effects of the diet and sexual abstinence. And I vaguely perceive that the energy that is arising will be the driving force behind an important experience. I cannot guess what it could be. Threading through these energetic sensations, I have the impression that something deeper is at play, something linked to my general abilities to feel and to *see*.

Along the thread of days that tick off one by one, it is more and more obvious that the calm into which my mind is settling, the deep disconnection that I am experiencing, allied with the physical discipline that I'm following rigorously, are in the process of supporting a chan-neling of what formerly was completely dispersed in me. We're on the move. I love it.

Vaguely, I'm aware that other dimensions of my being quietly begin to manifest. They were imperceptible before, drowned out by the inces-sant mental noise of my thinking.

In the afternoons, I alternate between meditation times, periods of reverie, and walks beside the water. I am writing too—a lot—as on each one of my solitary voyages over the past almost thirty years, but even more so this time, on this stationary voyage. My journal becomes another me with whom I converse. I pour out my heart, hand over my doubts and my questioning. I determine that one of the most important things to work on will be to stop wanting to analyze everything.

And in fact, one morning, immobile and in silence, as I was looking forward to nothing in particular and having plunged into a contemplative state, I understand, following a brief instant of distraction, that my mind just stopped thinking for the space of a few seconds. During this moment, I seem to perceive my environment with an enhanced precision. A kind of pure perception of the nature of things. During the time of a blink of the eye. Too fleeting to leave anything more than a *memory*. Because as soon as I *return to myself,* my brain begins once again to run full tilt, and my thinking brain, my analytical mind, cuts me off instantly from the sensory experience. However, for a not negligible fraction of time, I *felt something new*. Beyond thought, a door swings open—partially.

My mental mechanisms stand revealed. I gradually realize that during this trip there is perhaps nothing to understand. I don't need to expect some revelation or reach some goal. I need only to live and be fully in my experiences, in the present. Without trying to reason—I being the one who's always cogitating. I see that in my life in France everything I do has a goal or a reason. Go here, do this, and so on. For not one second am I available, for not one instant is my mind doing nothing. And I'm astonished to be cut off from my deep feelings? At what moment during my day would I be available to allow the bursting forth of such subtle, such fragile manifestations when I'm always running? How to be *called* by the unexpected when I'm busy all the time? All I need to do is to provide myself a regular slice of time. Fifteen minutes a day doing nothing would be of inestimable benefit. We easily find time for so many useless things. When I return I must hold myself to these moments of meditation. The solution is there, somewhere within me.

Discipline is the key.

It's for me to follow "the way of the warrior," as the Tibetan master Chögyam Trungpa meant it—to hold myself rigorously to the possibility of an intentional and lucid confrontation with who I am. This becomes clear during an introspection engendered by a regular period of nonactivity. However, the face-to-face can be uncomfortable. Do I *really* want to know myself? I vaguely take stock of how my ceaseless activity and my mental desire to interpret everything hide a fear—the fear of this unknown person who would appear before me were I to fully open my perceptions. What or who am I afraid of? Where is it going to take me—this energy that is exploding in me? To what are they connected, these sometimes-violent impulses, desires, and emotions that rise up in me? Confronted by these innumerable questions, I begin to measure the extent to which I need to maintain the practice of a daily period of pause after my return. Follow the warrior way with confidence, goodwill, discipline, joy, clarity, bravery, and compassion.

At the end of one afternoon, as I was about to end a time of meditation, I look at my belly for a second and I see a black ocean, like crude oil. And sadness. Are my energy and my wounds becoming visible?

I've gotten into the habit of going down to walk in the river several times a day. Walking on the pebbles, taking care not to step on a snake, because I've already twice surprised one sunning himself on the round stones. I savor the pleasure of my isolation. The water is clear and pleasant, and every time I dive in is a delight. Eagles are constantly flying over this corner of the valley, carried by the currents of hot air.

One day, stretched out and floating on my back, my eyes follow one of these masters of the sky as he passes in front of the sun. I blink my eyes and allow myself to be carried by the current, suspended like a ghost below the surface, moving slowly. After a few moments, I go back and, dripping, pull myself up on a burning hot rock that dries me off. Sitting cross-legged, facing the sun, I slow my breathing and close my eyes. Hardly noticing the warm breeze and the sound of the water, I let myself be penetrated by the majesty of the moment. And something unexpected happens: motionless on my rock, suddenly I am no longer alone. *An Amazon Indian is there.* Not beside me, but—how can I say this? *In me.* The sensation is sharp—it is not my imagination. And it is very strange. As if I were perceiving an inhabitant *from before.* I open my eyes and I see nothing. But I know that my eyes can perceive only a small fragment of reality, so I'm not surprised, and I concentrate on the sensation. I'm still aware of his presence, which is very real. Also I make no move, trying to savor what is taking place. I'm sure of only one thing: I am not alone in this moment. There is an Indian here—in time, out of time, in the spot where I am. Me, the stranger who for some days now has been beginning to partly open a doorway to invisible worlds. For a few seconds our realities overlap. For a few seconds the Indian was more substantial than a spirit.

No doubt I needed this reminder that the invisible world is constantly accessible and present around us wherever we are. It is not in some distant place to be discovered. The door that gives access to it is in us—it has never been anywhere else.

I walk back up to my hut in a state of both upset and serenity. I feel strong. What an extraordinary experience! I hurry to set it down in writing in my journal. Clouds are coming in from the east accompanied by grumbling thunder at the same time that end-of-day darkness is gathering. My dinner is a kind of lentil cake with avocado, rice, and some vegetables. It's a week now that I have been living like a hermit in my little shack built in the middle of the Amazonian forest.

It's the next day that it's going to happen.

3
The Encounter

The sun is already high when the experience begins—so special, so peculiar. Eagles are making their usual circles above my head in a limpid sky. I finish my series of physical exercises before the heat gets too strong. I feel fine. I come back to the body—the sensation of the muscles working, of the energy circulating. My mind calms down. And suddenly, I have the intuition that I need to be still, stop moving, and listen to my deepest feelings. Most especially, I am seized by a strong desire to take sooner than planned a mouthful of this Ajo Sacha decoction that tastes strongly of garlic. Normally, every evening before going to bed, I am supposed to drink a really small glass of this teaching plant. But on this day, earlier than planned, I carefully pour the liquid into a little glass, bring it to my lips, and swallow the "teaching plant" respectfully.

Then I stretch out on my little wooden bed wearing a headset that is playing a recording of shamanic drumming in a quick, repetitive, and muffled rhythm, and I close my eyes. I don't know why I'm doing that. I just let myself fall into reverie. I'm lying down with my eyes closed, and my mind begins to wander. At the beginning I don't quite know what to do, and then I imagine that I'm an eagle, flying. Suddenly I think of my brother Thomas as well as my father, and I find myself on a familiar path facing them. Thomas is standing, and with a hand gesture he designates the space in front of us. I don't understand. Is there a message?

15

What is he showing me? Gradually, I'm flying again. I visualize in my thoughts the valley where I am, as if my point of view were that of a bird, one of the eagles that are certainly at this very moment above me. I can make out my little hut from high up; then I glide toward the river, as if my spirit were flying over it at a good height. At this moment I am quite aware that I am the one imagining this vision. And then something unexpected happens. An image surprises me. I didn't cobble it together, and yet it imposes itself very precisely. I'm still flying above the river, but suddenly I'm observing men moving forward—people walking in the river. From this height they are little black dots. Are they Indians who used to live in this forest? Conquistadors? So I move closer, and as I descend toward the ground the vegetation disappears, the river disappears, giving way to a landscape that is uniformly white, as if covered in snow. I'm at their level now, on the ground. It's very surprising: I see an assault tank and men advancing, protected behind it. They are soldiers. They're German. It's war. They're advancing, sheltering behind the tank. What is totally strange is that I am one of them. An SS officer. I see a face yelling at me. I'm in a demolished village, and I'm going to die, wounded in the throat from the burst of a shell that has severed my jugular. I die.

I am enthralled and stunned by the intensity of what is taking place.

I am lying down with my eyes closed but completely awake and conscious, on a pallet in Peru, and in the same moment my mind has been catapulted into another time, another place. Suddenly I know this man's name. His first name, Alexander, has just come to me out of nowhere and imprints itself on me. I can't make out his face very well, just that he has light brown hair, almost blond, that is cut very short on the sides and at the nape of the neck, but longer on top. I see him walking in this scene of desolation strewn with cadavers. Everything is white, as if covered by plaster dust, or snow. The silhouettes are black. Faces screaming. My throat is dry. He's wearing a long dark coat. He is tall, thin but well built, his muscles finely chiseled. The scene of his death repeats.

Why do I feel that it's about *me*?

This is too incredible, too powerful. It cannot be possible . . . I *ask* for an element that I could verify afterward, and I see appear what seems to be an identity card written in Gothic script. I can make out "Herman" where the family name is written. He's called Herman, Alexander Herman. In the same way that I *knew* that his first name was Alexander, I *know* what his officer rank is. Obersturmführer sprang into my mind. And I don't speak one word of German. Plus I am assailed by several other visions—like scenes of life that come crashing in behind my closed eyes. Some scenes of his civilian life. I see a playful little girl—blonde, smiling, joyful. She must be between two and three years old. He is with her. Is she his daughter? And then once again death, screaming faces, and suddenly he is near a lake in the countryside, and it is summer. He has his shirt off, and another man is lying on his stomach beside him—a man a little older whose face I can make out quite clearly. There is a strong connection between them. Are they lovers? I see "25" tattooed on the inside of Alexander's left forearm. Once again, a ruined town or village and the feeling that it's named Bagneux or Bayeux—actually neither of those two names but a name like that. And then the little girl is there again in the countryside scene in the company of Alexander and this other man. The little girl's blonde hair is in a square-cut hairstyle. After that, I see Alexander in Paris, on the upper part of Gay-Lussac Street in the fifth arrondissement where the street turns into Claude-Bernard Street, as if he was moving through this area. Then he is walking in the Luxembourg Gardens, which are quite near . . . He turns around and looks at me with a certain mischievousness in his eyes, as if he's amused by my astonishment. I can see his face then quite distinctly. Then I see him once again collapsing, blood spurting from his throat, pouring over his collar and out onto the ground. He holds his neck. His life is slipping away. His look flickers out. The white dust covers him. The earth is pulverized by explosions that throw out snow and fire, fury and cold. He is dead. He is me. His body is my body.

◆ ◆ ◆

When the drum recording stops, the vision comes to an end. A half hour has gone by, and I am blown away. The experience is totally unexpected, incomprehensible, and stunningly powerful. Did I imagine all that? But why? Who is this man? What just happened?

Later in the day, and the next day, the images of this German man do not manage to fade. He appeared out of the depths of darkness, he penetrated into my reality, and he's still there as if he were *living in me*. Once again I see the sinister landscape, the death, the violence, his look . . . but not for one second do I imagine the explosion that was coming after my return to France.

When I discover that this man really existed.

4

Confirmation

In the course of the following days, in spite of the emotionally gripping character of the experience, I end up telling myself that there really must be a rational explanation. Also, even before my Amazonian adventure began winding down, I set the experience aside at a certain distance. The face of the man who had appeared in my vision continues to be present in my thoughts, but the strange character of the episode gradually fades into a psychological interpretation, even though its message still remains mysterious.

I just simply cannot believe that this man is real. That would be too incredible, too disturbing. No, the source of these images must be in my mind. It has to be my imagination that constructed this scenario. No doubt Herman is a name that I spontaneously invented, like Günter or Helmut, if someone asked me to imagine a German-sounding surname. And as for the given name Alexander, I wrote a book on Alexander the Great with Michel de Grèce. This Macedonian figure has fascinated me since my first trips to the Middle East. And as for the rank of Obersturmführer, I must have heard it in a movie, or I maybe came across it in a book such as *Les Bienveillantes* (*The Kindly Ones*), for example, this masterful text by Jonathan Littell, who won the Prix Goncourt in 2006, which tells the icy tale of an SS officer. Reading that book affected me deeply. And other details of the vision? I don't know . . . So really, as unique as this *encounter* was, I don't see why it would be anything other than the strange product of a few unconscious processes. Once back in France, when I would again have access to the internet, I promise myself nevertheless to do a Google search. Just to see.

The day of my departure, the skies open and let loose; finally, the Dantesque seasonal rains that had been long in coming. Rarely have I seen that: masses of water literally knocking down the forest. The dirt road becomes a torrent, my shoes are drowned, and in spite of the poncho that I had the bright idea to cover myself with when the first drops fell, by the time I make it to the village on foot, I'm soaked to the skin.

A car is waiting for me there. Squeezed in with villagers in a wheezing taxi with mud-covered windows, I reach downtown Tarapoto feeling that I'd traveled boxed up in a rattletrap toy car. In town the downpour has calmed down, and I'm able to change before making it to the airport.

I'm always happy to set out on a trip, and this same happiness wells up in me once again when the moment comes for me to return home. I will be back with people I love—me, the solitary one who can't live without the sweetness of those close to me.

This paradox is my life.

Having left the world for a few weeks, I return with the intuition that seeking to find balance all alone, far from the turpitude of life in society, is only part of the solution. True inner peace will be born when I manage to no longer be shaken by the ups and downs of daily life as I'm completely immersed in it. I would like to escape, flee; but confronted by this anger in myself, I realize that I won't manage to reach lasting healing by cutting myself off from society permanently, even if that's what I dream of doing. On the contrary, it's by confronting what sets off this irritability, rather than trying to protect myself from it that I will succeed in understanding its source and bring healing to it.

My retreat has opened doors within me, but nevertheless I'm not coming home having magically resolved my problems. During the weeks of this time away, I opened to the invisible, I gained energy and allowed intuitions to bloom, but the work must be engaged in here, in life, in the challenges, in the day-to-day.

It's up to me now to not let what has been awakened to fall asleep again. But in this context, what meaning could there be in my story of that German man?

Out of curiosity, the day after my return, I type his name into the search engine on my computer, attaching to him those two terrible letters: SS. I try "Herman," writing it with a single "r," then two; with two "n"s or a single "n." I repeat my searches with "Alexander" or "Alexandre." In just a few minutes, I find two Alexander Herrmanns in what appears to be lists of SS officers compiled in Polish and accessible online. Minutes turn into hours, and I don't find out much more than what I found at the beginning: two SS officers with the name of Alexander Herrmann.

One of the two had the rank of Obersturmführer.

This is a strange moment.

It's as if I'm poised on a narrow beam over a dark void.

I don't know if I was expecting it. I am upset, certainly, but very sincerely cannot come to see anything in it other than a coincidence.

In my depths I do not dare envision any other hypotheses.

Because, objectively, how could I? Yes, the coincidence is incredible, but what conclusion does it allow me to draw? If I want to remain rational—no conclusion. It's a mystery, a comical enigma. It can be a strange randomness, or a more disturbing fact. In reality I'm incapable of taking it further. Since I have been a journalist, when I find myself confronted with a disturbing fact, I spontaneously give precedence to the most rational explanation. In this story it has to be a case of something a little bizarre situated between randomness and synchronicity. I do feel that something happened, but based on that, I'm not in the habit of piecing together nebulous scenarios.

In my experience, war and violence are central elements. Looking at my life, it's obvious that such things have their importance for someone like me, who became a war reporter so young and who is both invaded and fascinated by the violence of the world.

And just as a particular dream is capable of having a central role in psychotherapy work, I have a sense that the meaning of this elaborate vision is probably to be found in the recesses of the world of my mind. The key, if there is a key, will emerge through psychotherapy rather than in Google.

In fact, even though I am just the same thrown off track by this discovery, it would be more toward psychology that my intuition would take me than toward anything else. The discovery in these lists of hundreds of thousands of officers of a name identical to the one in my vision seems to me to be due to convergence of significant circumstances.

But just the same there did exist an Obersturmführer Alexander Herrmann.

5

An Unexpected Emotion

After a few hours I have the impression that I've exhausted my search options on the Web, and I don't know how to find any more pieces, if in fact that's even possible. I don't speak a word of German. I'm not a historian. No, really, I have no idea how to do more. I don't think I'm up to throwing more light on this experience.

Yes, no doubt the explanation has something to do with a fascination about war, and more specifically about the Second World War. It's a fact that I am obsessed with this tragic period of our recent history. Whatever the case, I close down my computer and move on to something else. Soon, Parisian life and my activities reengage, and I allow this experience to join the cohort of "bizarre oddities" that have happened to me. At this moment of my life, I want to give myself the means to pursue effectively this inner work that got underway during my retreat. This is my priority, and it is what appears to be necessary and useful. Rather than exploring a pseudopath that emerged during a waking dream that was ambiguous and imaginary.

I decide to seek help. I have long imagined that I can make do on my own, manage life's problems myself. No doubt it's a masculine shortcoming, but it's a mistake. After the death of my brother, it took the quiet insistence of my wife to push me into undertaking several sessions of body-mind therapy and by doing so to bring healing to the real wound that followed the accident. I turned myself inside out trying to deny the existence of that wound. Certainly inner resources are an indisputable force in self-healing, but sometimes the help of a third person can be critical in their activation. I understood in observing this in myself—and in those near me—that even when we're aware of what efforts to undertake, we are perhaps unable to set them in motion because we are blocked by a particular emotional knot or a particular unconscious obstacle. And sometimes a simple word from someone else, a treatment, a brief therapy, a single look by someone other than oneself can bring down the invisible wall that inexplicably keeps us from healing. But for that it is necessary to ask for help and have the humility to accept it. It was Natacha who allowed me to see fully what that was going to take.

A few weeks after my return, I make an appointment with Marie-Pierre Dillenseger. Marie-Pierre is a feng shui master, a Chinese discipline that consists of decoding influences in terms of temporal and spatial energy. Centered on the practice of Chinese astrology, her approach takes into account an analysis of the geographic location where the person's life takes place. It is not about "decoration," which is what feng shui is most often associated with in the West. In addition, she makes an analysis of the individual's potential and of the moment that contained the questioning leading to the appointment. Natacha discovered Marie-Pierre during the filming of the second season of *Enquêtes extraordinaires* (Extraordinary inquiries) that she produced for the French television channel M6, and in which there was a presentation on the practice of feng shui. Having seen the relevance of Marie-Pierre's analyses and, in addition, knowing the richness of astrology—my mother had been trained in humanistic astrology when my brothers and I were children—I regularly call on her at turning points in my life. It was, by the way, with the help of her advice that I departed for the period of isolation in Peru. Her recommendations are still present in my mind: "You are not starting from zero. Remember that you are not at level zero of a learning experience. You have an accumulation of strength and not just from the life here . . . You are supported by your brother and your father. You are surging ahead in terms of opening to the world of energies. Therefore, don't consider the coming retreat as an experience of serious vulnerability. On the contrary, this retreat will bring you face to face with your strength. The question is not about fear, it's about strength. That is your learning experience. You mustn't put it off. You have been attacked in a major way but the real dangers are now behind you. You are protected, you are bloody well accompanied, you are not going to be all alone."

"This retreat will bring you face to face with your strength."

Marie-Pierre, who lives much of the time in the United States, receives me in the pied-à-terre that she and her husband have in Paris. The appointment is very enriching, bringing to my intuitive insights the kind of coherent overview that offers a cyclic view of energies and forces. We speak of the lessons that I believe I have learned from my recent stay in Peru, and in passing, toward the end of the session, I get around to speaking about the experience with Alexander Herrmann.

"I need to speak to you about a very strange thing that happened toward the end of my retreat. One day, while I was doing my physical exercises, I felt strongly the need to lie down and let myself drift into a kind of meditation or waking dream—I don't quite know what it was. At the beginning, I had my eyes closed, and I imagined myself as a bird, an eagle, flying above the valley where I was staying. And then the experience began to become strange."

I then recount for her my "encounter" with Alexander Herrmann in all its detail. Marie-Pierre watches me silently, and when I come to the scene of the death of this man, mortally wounded in the throat, I see her shiver.

"I have goose bumps . . . You saw him die?" she asks me.

"Yes . . . It was very precise, and this scene where he's dying is repeated several times."

I continue my story. I mention the vision of the little girl, the other man, the different locations that were glimpsed: the ruined village near where the man died, the Paris streets that I see him strolling along. And as I'm recounting my experience, it's the memory of the energy that I felt deeply that strikes me. In fact, as the visions unfolded behind my closed eyes, waves of energy had *physically* moved through me. Energy, impulses, and again this sensation, almost a desire, as if the suddenness and the unaccustomed side of such an energetic activity in me abso-lutely unhinged all my internal *settings*. I try to describe this to Marie-Pierre, fumbling for the right words.

"During the whole experience, I felt an enormous energy moving through my body. It was almost . . . frenetic—yes, that's the word: frenetic. I was literally shaken by it. This energy stirred up a lot of emotions too. And therefore, on my return, I searched the Web and found two Alexander Herrmanns, one of whom had the rank of Obersturmführer. Well, I don't quite know what that means. But my vision had such force! That's what really affected me deeply. What do you think?"

"What comes to me, most obviously, is that it's a matter of 'mate-rial' for study. Forces that are bringing messages," said Marie-Pierre confidently. "These forces of darkness are allies. If there's one thing to understand it's that . . . "

"An SS officer an ally?"

"Yes . . . He is dead, but perhaps he had the time to realize what he was in the process of doing? Go and find out. That doesn't make you into an SS officer, or someone who would have that particular energy. But isn't it someone who really has run with horror that can afterward labor so that he has it no more? In any case . . . "

This last sentence has the effect of a blow to the head. I am literally knocked out. My emotion is so brutal, so unexpected that I am com-pletely disoriented. I lower my head, my throat is suddenly in a knot. I bring my hand in front of my eyes, repressing the desire, the imperious need to scream and let my sobs burst out. "Isn't it someone who really has run with horror that can afterward labor so that he has it no more?"

Marie-Pierre hasn't realized yet the effect of these apparently harmless words on me.

She ends by saying, "These are allied forces."

I'm not able to say a word—a ball of emotion has exploded in me. The amazement and the agitation sweep away my thought as well as my discernment. No longer does any question come to me. I'm stunned. However, what her words reflect is *accurate*. Isn't my reaction the proof of that? What is happening? What am I feeling? Why such an inner agitation? What is happening to me? I want to understand, feel, know. So I cling to this vertigo as if it held all the answers. I want to let myself fall into this infinitesimal crack that tears up the tranquil reality of this apartment that is bathed in sunlight. And at the same time I want to keep control, not lose everything. I'm afraid. I pull myself together, I regain the mastery of my awareness, but then I have this sensation of see-ing disappear into the distance a piece of truth, one that had been given for me to see in the space of one blink of the eyes. There—the link is gone, like a dream absorbed by the night. I no longer know why I reacted like that. I look at Marie-Pierre as I attempt to regain my composure.

"Excuse me. That shook me up—what you just said. An emotion rose up . . . "

"An emotion of fear?"

"No, no. Of pain . . . I wanted to cry."

"Pain for that man?"

"I don't know," I said sincerely.

And it's true that I don't know what just happened. Such a power-ful agitation and at the same time so subtle, so fragile. This echo of the invisible world dissolves into the density of the real.

"You see," she continued. "It's life you feel in the moment; it's a mat-ter of forces that are present, forces that are fundamentally allied. You must let them come . . . You must make room for these energies. What story does this man have to relate to you? And then what is the connec-tion with you? . . . Have a good cry, if you want," she tells me, seeing that I'm still shocked.

"No, thanks, it's OK; I'm feeling better."

Am I really better? I'm still unable to think, and I'm not too inclined to continue our discussion. Not for one instant have I stopped reacting to what she just said. I'm speechless. Marie-Pierre continues by linking this last episode to the ensemble of what we spoke of before in our previous appointment about my life in general.

"Cry if you feel the need. There is a link to loss in this story—the loss of the other person. It is linked to this energy that you are carrying. Don't stuff it into the depths of your memory! It's palpable . . . You must succeed in opening in yourself the 'receptive mode,' so you are better able to perceive and understand these memories. Ask for help by addressing your army of darkness . . . "

"What does she mean by 'my army of darkness'?" I'm so beside myself I don't have the presence of mind to ask her that question. Does she mean "shadow" in the Jungian sense? This hidden, unconscious part of the human being that can emerge in dreams for example? Everything comes crashing down in my head. I choose to walk home, even though I live a good distance away. An SS officer, an allied darkness? *Because you have to have known the worst in order to know that you don't want it anymore?* I cannot understand that. How could the artisan of the most unnameable horror that humanity has ever known be an ally? I must have misunderstood. I obviously got it all backward.

6

Understanding Horror

Never in my life have I felt the slightest attraction for Germany, the slightest desire to go there, and even less to learn the language. During all of my adolescence I had a kind of antipathy for this country without there being any logical reason for it. In high school I studied Russian as my first foreign language, then English. Do I need to make clear that everything the Nazi regime represents is for me the most despicable thing that ever was? And although I have this ambiguous attraction for the period of the Second World War, I experience before all else an unutterable compassion for the indescribable suffering of the victims of the Holocaust. How could such a thing have happened? How could millions of men, women, and children have seen such an abomination inflicted on them? It's so absurd. So distant from us—and at the same time so recent. My father was seventeen at the end of the war.

As I am walking, still stunned, through the streets of the fourteenth arrondissement, memories jostle and emerge in the form of images. Scenes of violence that I witnessed in Afghanistan and elsewhere, stupid deaths, mutilated cadavers, dead eyes. A thousand thoughts lead me back years into the past, when, emerging from adolescence, I had only one obsession: to become a war photographer. What motivated such a strong aspiration in me? Why would I want to "see" war, destruction? Why was fear totally absent from the equation? The answer is very clear, and it has always been in my awareness: I wanted to understand evil.

That's why I became a journalist.

It's even the sole reason: the desire to understand.

To understand how someone can kill. To understand someone who kills, someone who becomes the executioner. How is one able to shoot at another man? Even more if he's unarmed, not to mention a child? How could anybody continue to live after consciously putting a child to death? A whole family? Civilians who have done nothing, asked for nothing? What kind of a man are you when you've committed such acts? How do you look at the world? Who are these men who, by the millions, committed the Holocaust?

And in this disgusting desire to want to look at the face of evil, the SS represents the most abominable armed force that humanity has ever borne. Unfathomable beings, and yet so *close* in time and space. Europeans from less than eighty years ago.

I'm reeling under the Paris sun. As far back as my memories go, this open question has been alive in me like a loathsome wound. How is it that, in moments, man can stray so far from his humanity? This question is an open wound gaping within my life, an obsession, and for thirty years now the answer again and again eludes me. I sought for it through the kindly eyes of Samuel Pisar, one of the youngest survivors of the Holocaust, deported to Auschwitz at the age of thirteen. He agreed to see me to speak about his life. He who untiringly asked me to come back to see him in his paneled office in order to adjust a word, correct a phrase. In preparing for the meeting, I had underlined this sentence in his book *Of Blood and Hope*, struck by the horror of what it revealed: "Life, normal life, continued a few meters away from these railway cars, while behind their doors, always locked, thousands of piled up human beings were dying in absolute despair."[1]

I am someone decent. I am a tolerant man educated by parents who inculcated in their children the most noble moral values. Equality for all. I abhor all extremism, and I am intimately convinced that nonviolence, as much in the private sphere as on the scale of nations, is the only, the sole, lasting way toward resolving conflict. The idea of race is a nameless absurdity. Racial inequality a nonsense. And I have infinite compassion, in each one of my little cells, for the victims of all the injustices that gangrene our world, and above all for the injustices of the extermination camps of Nazi Germany.

However, I also have in me this obsession to want to understand the executioners.

It's this obsession that oriented my life when I threw myself into international journalism. A little more than forty years after the end of the Second World War, the question of evil that blanketed Europe and then the world reappeared once again in quite a few other places. In the 1980s, it was the Khmer Rouge regime, and the genocide that they perpetrated in Cambodia between 1975 and 1979, that symbolized the most recent manifestation to date of the absolute horror that man is capable of. Although I left school very early, I pieced together all sorts of plans to make my way to this southeast Asian country. With a great deal of naivete, I wanted to throw myself into looking for Pol Pot, the Khmer Rouge leader who had gone underground since the end of the regime, and, looking him in the eyes, ask him this one question: "How were you able to do that?"

But I must have been seventeen at the time, and without any experience. Also, when I plunged in, at the age of nineteen, southeast Asia was out of fashion in the media and it was the Afghan Freedom Fighters that I finally joined. It was 1988, and their unconquerable country was still occupied by the Soviets. Hundreds of thousands of deaths, millions of refugees, a human drama the consequences of which continue to affect us directly still today. And always within me this desire to see war up close.

I saw it.

But I doubt that this was the only explanation for my emotion on hearing Marie-Pierre's question, "Isn't it someone who really has run with horror that can afterward labor so that he has it no more?" The unsettling conclusion of this session with her leaves me wary. There has to be some denial in the rapidity with which I set it aside. Not intentionally, but I'm not doing anything in particular to go beyond it. What more is there to do?

"Alexander" cannot be a priority.

The vision is an accident, a randomness, a *strange blip*.

As for the rest of my life . . . the desire to continue pursuing work on myself is intact, and with that aim in mind, there is another woman I want to meet. When I present myself a few weeks later at the office of the healer Agnès Stevenin, it was not still about rummaging around in the story of some German man, but asking her to accompany me in working on the physical, mental, and emotional cleansing that I had already begun. I had just read the admirable book that Agnès was readying for publication and in which she speaks about her own developmental journey.[2] I had the intuition that I needed to ask her for a healing session.

7

An Ancient Suffering

S he has me sit beside her on a little sofa and asks me several questions about my reasons for being there. I explain to her in general terms the feeling of having come to a moment of transition. As I'm providing the details of my deep feelings in the body, I'm a little disconcerted to see her nodding her head while she's looking *around* me. In fact, as we're having our conversation, her eyes are not part of the discussion but are following an invisible ballet that is unfolding all around my person. It's unnerving. She comes back, sets down her gentle eyes into mine; then, as I'm speaking, her look slips toward empty space to the left of my head, behind, or then to the right, as if I had become a completely transparent being for her. I really feel she isn't listening to me. Or that my words are definitely of no importance, that her diagnosis is being shaped otherwise, with the help of information coming from me but that is not information I am expressing verbally.

And while this operation is underway, Agnès emanates a pervasive gentleness. Her eyes, her skin, her hair, her hands—her whole being overflows with maternal love.

The session itself, her work, is done on the floor, on a thick and comfortable mattress. Once I've stretched out, she puts a blanket over me. I'm fully dressed, and I'm wrapped in a cocoon of warm wool. At first, Agnès positions herself, kneeling, near my feet. She picks up that my energy body is shifted left, completely beside my physical body. She's going to try to realign them. I don't ask any questions to know what she's talking about. I trust her. Then she positions herself carefully to my right and begins her treatment by placing her hand above me at the level of my chest. I prefer to close my eyes in order to make myself completely available, and soon I feel her place her hand on my solar plexus. She moves her hand only imperceptibly as information continues to come to her.

No big movements, no agitation, but a treatment that stirs the depths without anything visible happening is how she proceeds.

My mind lets go.

She tells me I'm a good man. That's cool. Then her hand descends to my belly, and with very slow movements, pressing down, she palpates with curiosity. Her fingers tap as if they were reading a message written in braille on the blanket covering my stomach. And indeed, her hand seems to pick up information. A hand like an antenna. And she announces suddenly that she is perceiving things.

"I see blackness, images of destruction, of pain . . . of horror," she explains to me.

She speaks of a volcano, an upside-down cone moving up from the ground. Explosions that shoot up. Colossal destruction, smoke, but she doesn't manage to identify either a place or a time period.

"You have known this gigantic destruction."

It's an affirmation. And while she's delivering these first words, images of the Second World War immediately enter my mind. But I keep silent.

"You have known gigantic destruction, but it does not date from your present life . . . "

In a voice made hesitant by the state of relaxation into which I have plunged, I invite her to describe for me what she is picking up. It is then that she begins to yawn compulsively. I had read in her book that she does that when many things to clean and discard are passing through her.

"I see a man, in white, standing, contemplating the destruction . . . There is also a man who is crawling on the ground beside him."

In the short discussion at the beginning, I had spoken to Agnès of my taste for and my search for solitude, and of the difficulty to reach such moments in my active life. This point comes back, in a new light.

"The solitude," she says to me, "is also that of this man witnessing such a great horror, as if he was the sole survivor in a world destroyed. Also," she adds, "in a certain way if your desire for solitude is thwarted in the present, no doubt it is because something is protecting you by keeping you at a distance from this ancient suffering."

I remain silent, unnerved. Something is *rising up* in me. She continues.

"In being alone, you would risk being caught up by this ancient suffering."

The face of the German man makes a sudden, thunderous irruption behind my closed eyes. As if Agnès's words have just woken him up. Or have allowed him to appear before me a second time. I'm witnessing another occurrence of worlds brushing against each other. The reality that Agnès and I are in is so close to a reality that is *other*. Barriers of time and space are abolished. I am transported. My being is in two universes at the same time. My vision, my waking dream from Peru, engages once again with excess.

"Your whole being does not want this destruction to happen again," she continues.

Emotion is there—intense and unnerving.

The vision of the SS officer submerges me. "Your whole being does not want this destruction to happen again" echoes what Marie-Pierre said: "Isn't it someone who really has run with horror that can after-ward labor so that he has it no more?" I am seized with amazement. As when we solve a problem that has occupied the mind for a long time. In this moment I am caught up, disconcerted—my entire soul is catapulted *elsewhere*. Up against this other man. In the proximity of his flesh. His face is stuck to mine as if we were cheek to cheek. He's a soldier. He's wearing an officer's cap, and he is covered with white dust; and blood. I can make out another man, lying. He too is dead. Of the dead there are too many, tangled in the dust and in a landscape of destruction, of a town destroyed, razed. The power and the similarity of the scene with the one in Peru sweeps away the slightest doubt: it's the same SS officer. And while Agnès continues her work, silently now, and as emotion washes through me, the thought comes to me: he didn't know! He was not aware of the extent of the Holocaust. He never went to an extermination camp. And just as I'm having these intuitions, I can't help asking myself: is it possible that an SS officer never knew? Never had knowledge of the extent of the Holocaust? That seems to me very unlikely. Because now I'm having contradictory, but very precise, sensations that give me his major personality traits. I feel that he is experiencing immense pride in belonging to an elite corps, and at the same time he is struck by fright as he understands *after his death* what he participated in.

Then the vision fades. Inner silence returns, as if the scenes appearing in this sort of dream were accompanied by din and furor. Agnès is still motionless to my right, her breathing continues to be calm now. She continues to work on my belly. Gently.

How precise these impressions are! And so strange. But is that not my mind that is projecting, imagining, constructing an epic and unwholesome scenario?

My brain is already setting out to reason and to try to bring back a semblance of order to my head.

Obviously, only historical research would allow me to move forward on this track of an officer by the name of Alexander Herrmann and to bring a little light to our *relationship*. But how to set about that? From what angle to begin? I will see about that later, but I have to work in that direction, and I allow myself to be taken once again by the calm that emanates from Agnès.

While I am still stretched out on my back and while she is seated beside me, her hand still on my torso, I gradually feel energy rise up from my heart as well as from my belly. I *see* threads of light, splashes, fine sparkling serpents that rise along her arm. There are so many of these bright threads that they form sheaves, explosions. Then this new perception fades.

Agnès finishes her treatment. Eyes closed, I am in a state between waking and sleep, perfectly relaxed. With sensitivity, she tells me that I can get up when I like, which I do after a few seconds.

I retain only fragments of what she shared with me about her treatment. I am still too steeped in what happened and a little groggy. She told me she removed a black, misshapen ball from my belly. That I remember because I have the memory of having seen myself a *black thing* on my belly in Peru. Agnès thinks she has managed to rid me of a good part of this darkness. She tells me also that I am in the process of molting, of changing my skin, and of reconnecting to my soul. My head has already made it through, she announces, and my body is heavy, weighed down, but that will be taken care of shortly.

"Your head was already in the light; it is emanating an immense light."

Her eyes are looking at me directly now. Laughing eyes that breathe gentleness.

Night has fallen in western Paris. I am a little out of it, at some distance from the agitated, noisy crowd running from one store to another, from one activity to another. The lights are lively, colorful. I find my car and slip in. Once the door is closed, the commotion of the city is slightly dulled, accentuating the unreality of the moment. I am fine; almost a little drunk. Both happy and calmed but just the same still very intrigued by what appeared in the middle of the session—the reactivation of my vision of the war and of that German man. I take out my little notebook and make very detailed notes. And I don't know why, once the facts are clearly laid out on the first pages, I allow the flow of my thoughts to carry on. And I write down, "Why does the memory of our lives disappear almost entirely in the next one? Because in reality the memory is there, both accessible and yet impenetrable as long as one is not connected to oneself, to the 'person' that we are beyond successive personalities."

Why did I write that?

8
The Specialist

These two episodes distill in me the strange and unsettling idea that this story extends its roots down into the heart of what I am. The idea that seemed to me the memory of a former life runs through my mind, of course, but I want to be able to verify the hypotheses that I put forward, and in the present case, how can they be verified?

After my session with Agnès, weeks went by, then months, in the course of which the German man was recalled episodically. I accustom myself gradually to the idea that it involves a manifestation of an undeniable facet of my personality, a personification of the darkness I carry within me. Of my shadow. I integrate its existence, accepting it as an archetype: an unconscious personality trait. That of violence, of war, and of anger. Because these elements are in me. Because certain of my dreams are dreams of combat and murder. So it seems natural to me that this dark part of me, if it springs up sometimes in the recesses of my nights, may just as well be manifested in a kind of waking dream, in Peru.

And then one day, I pass through to a new stage in this strange, introspective journey. In vain, I have tried to remember why precisely on March 17, was I impelled once again to enter "SS Alexander Herrmann" in the Google search box, but I am unable to find the reason. That day, sitting in front of my computer, I did not know that I was opening Pandora's box, opening it wide. After that, it was no longer possible to close it. No doubt I had to be ready. And I was.

On the morning of March 17, although I had several meetings set up during the day, destiny pushed me to pick up the research that I thought I had carried out with all the great thoroughness I know I am capable of. And indeed, the first results proposed by Google are familiar. Soon, I once again put my hands on the listings of SS officers written in Polish. Then pages of homonyms file by having nothing to do with my search, links to various sites, clearly false leads, but I follow the orientations proposed to me, and from link to link, my research extends to the SS in general. I'm not very comfortable, and also I remain attentive that my exploration is confined to sites where the historical perspective predominates. Sites of universities, historians, encyclopedias of the Second World War online—I navigate blindly but cautiously.

And it's in this way that I pull up several times the name Charles Trang. Clearly, this man is the author of books on the German army and, more specifically, on the Waffen-SS, the military branch of the Nazi Party's SS organization. I refocus my research on him and learn that he is not, properly speaking, a historian, but that he is termed a specialist on several reference sites and presents himself as a passionate student of the Second World War. In the twenty or so books that he has authored, the majority are devoted to the Waffen-SS, but he has also written about the American Marines and works with a publisher specialized in military history: Éditions Heimdal. He edited several illustrated works, and I discover his authorship of numerous articles on the Second World War in magazines of military history. The idea comes to me that I should ask for his help. No doubt he would have access to more elements than these summary lists—more detailed information, perhaps?

With that tenfold energy that comes suddenly when you follow an intuition that you think is meaningful, I undertake to find his contact information. Which doesn't take me very long. But what will I say to him? It is not in my character to lie. During all my life as a journalist I have favored sincerity and frankness, so I am going to tell him about my waking dream, ardently hoping he will listen to me without hanging up on me.

At first the man is reserved but quickly shows himself to be curious and willing to help. So I convey to him details of my dream, describing the scenes I saw, the name of Alexander Herrmann, his rank. I hide nothing from him. He accepts all this in a positive way in spite of the incongruity of my experience. I'm delighted to have come upon a man with this openness of mind. No judgment. He is somewhat taken aback—as I am myself.

It only took a few minutes for Charles Trang to find traces of the two Alexander Herrmanns in his archives, including the one with the rank of Obersturmführer. He has access to the same listings as those I had discovered a few pieces of, but his are more complete, and he knows how to interpret the information they contain. He confirms what I had already found—that there was no other Alexander Herrmann besides those two who were in the SS, no matter how the name is spelled. Charles Trang shares this information with me as he finds it. I imagine him in front of his computer screen, scrutinizing his archival files.

"Obersturmführer Alexander Herrmann bore the number SS 122 211. He was born August 21, 1916, and died October 20, 1941," he tells me.

"And the other one?"

"In his case, I have found him in a document listing officer promotions for all ranks and for all branches of the SS dated January 1940. It mentions a Dr. Alexander Herrmann bearing the number SS 292 024 who was promoted to the rank of Untersturmführer. I don't have a birth date for him . . . "

"What is Untersturmführer?"

"The SS had their own ranking designations; this would be the equivalent of sublieutenant."

"And Obersturmführer?"

"It's the next rank up and corresponds more or less to that of lieutenant in the army."

"Do you have any more detail on this Dr. Alexander Herrmann?"

"I see that he was assigned to the Allgemeine-SS, Regiment 67, based in Erfurt. So he was a doctor attached to that division of the SS. Taking into account his number, he must have entered the SS as a subordinate officer earlier, say in the 1930s. What's clear is that he was not an officer in the Waffen-SS."

"What does that mean?"

"The Waffen-SS was the combat unit of the SS, different from the Allgemeine-SS. The status of this man was either that of a doctor attached full-time to the SS medical unit, but that's unlikely since full-time SS doctors were attached to more important units. Or he was an independent or hospital doctor conducting his field training, and no doubt an honorary member of the SS. And then he was Untersturmführer, whereas you say that you had the information that your man was Obersturmführer. Besides, the war scene that you describe would suggest that he belonged to a combat unit, which is the case for Obersturmführer Alexander Herrmann, who bore the number SS 122 211."

"Yes, I'm leaning toward him too since he bore the rank that I perceived in my dream. Do you know what he did?"

I fear hearing the worst . . .

"No, except that he died in Russia, so he participated in the eastern campaign. He died . . . at Sukhaya Niva, from what I see, in the region of Valdai, which it seems to me is in the Ukraine."

My hair bristled. The Holocaust began to take on an unprecedented scope with the invasion of the USSR by German forces. Notably in the Ukraine, from the summer of 1941 on. SS extermination groups, the sinister Einsatzgruppen, massacred hundreds of thousands of Jews there in what historians have called the "Holocaust by bullets." Because, in fact, it was bullets that were used to execute, one by one, hundreds of thousands of men, women, and children well before the extermination camps. This was done beside common trenches dug for the occasion or in natural valleys when the numbers were too great, as was the case on

September 29 and 30, 1941, near the city of Kiev when 33,771 Jews were assassinated by the Nazis and their Ukrainian auxiliaries in the Babi Yar ravine.

Abominable reality.

What did I expect?

The telephone exchange with this specialist plunges me into the most-raw reality of the Nazi regime. We're no longer dealing with the abstract but with a reality that is concrete, sad, and terrifying. But the door is now ajar, and from now on I have to find out. Everything that I can clarify must be clarified. I question Charles Trang.

"Do you think that the first Alexander Herrmann, the one bearing the number 122 211 who was Obersturmführer, could have been part of the extermination groups in the Ukraine?"

"I don't know what he took part in. I would have to do more research in my archives."

"I can call you later if you like."

"Yes, I'm going to see if I have more particulars. Can you phone me this evening?"

"Of course," I say, only too happy that he has given me an appointment so quickly.

However, hesitating to hang up, he continues:

"He died relatively early in the Russian campaign. The Germans invaded the USSR on June 22, 1941, and he was killed on October 20, scarcely four months later. August 1916, October 1941, he died at the age of . . . twenty-five years," Charles Trang quickly does the math.

"Yes, that's right, twenty-five years."

I am unable to ward off a shiver that runs down my spine as we're bringing our conversation to a close. Twenty-five is the figure that I had seen tattooed on Alexander's arm during my dream in Peru.

9

The Military Folder

This story of mine is of concern. It's not an accident. I have an intuition about it that is stronger every day. Since my return from Peru, I know in my depths that my experience did not happen randomly. Nevertheless, no doubt because of apprehension, up to now I have avoided giving too much weight to extraordinary hypotheses, confining my reflections to psychology, in spite of the discovery of the actual existence of an Obersturmführer Alexander Herrmann.

However, I really have to admit that the reality of this man has been even more reinforced today by my discussion with the French specialist Charles Trang. Hearing someone else speak this name, Alexander Herrmann, and describe his life, even briefly, makes him a little more tangible, more real. And that increases even more the mystery of my connection with him.

So I take myself in hand and more seriously entertain a theory that my rational mind—and no doubt also an unconscious discomfort—prevented me from considering since returning from my trip: the theory of reincarnation. Past lives. Wouldn't I be acting irrationally were I to put all my effort into refusing to investigate this lead? Or course, examining my *encounter* with Alexander Herrmann from the perspective of past lives is upsetting. He was a Nazi.

How to accept that?

How to not hate such a being? If this man turns out to be *me before*, how to have proof of that first of all, but then how to live with this idea? Having a part of me in horror? How to live with the guilt of bearing the imprint of such a personage? When forgiveness in the face of such an abomination is inconceivable, how to admit being a kind of echo of him?

How to love what I can only detest?

These questions remained purely theoretical before; from now on they are palpable. Am I the reincarnation of this man? And is that why scenes of his life have appeared to me? Because I really have to admit that this personage existed.

This is not about some exotic enigma. We're not talking about a king, a hero, or an old sage. This Alexander is not a half-mythic figure from some distant past; he's an SS lieutenant killed when my father was fourteen years old!

It's no longer possible for me to distance myself from the abyss.

Beyond his despicable thinking and his adhesion to a regime that inspires the greatest disgust in me, I cannot prevent my mind from beginning to make some connections between certain of my traits and those which could have also been his traits. How can I say that? In fact, I question myself about what would be able to pass from one life to another. Memories? There are none. But what about emotions? Impulses? Trauma? Phobias? The images that appear in my dreams? All those things which, although they are unconscious, have been shown to be present in me?

What could my psychological tendencies be that show that I am not *indifferent* to this personage and to what he went through? What comes into my head immediately is the obsession during all of my adolescence, the fascination that led me to want to become an international reporter and that I spoke about earlier. Obviously, I was an adolescent obsessed by death, blood, violence, and horror. This is not the case, so far as I know, with all adolescents. I was excessive in this area. My brothers, for example, did not display the same disposition, although we had nevertheless received the same education. Where did these black impulses come from in me?

With me, violence is an ancient mystery.

Then, in the course of my adolescence, my quest transformed into a desire for confrontation with the violence of the world. A confrontation to decode, grasp the motivations, the reasons for the existence of this evil that is so widespread on our planet. The path of journalism—wanting to understand and explain—showed up quickly in me at an age when the majority of my friends in college were looking to find themselves only very lightly. I left college very early, before graduating. I had decided not to sit for the final exams, so strongly was I called by an imperious intuition. Whereas boys and girls of my age thought only of amusing themselves and taking advantage of their youth in a carefree way, in my case I was living in a maid's room in Paris taking photos of the street demonstrations and having myself dream that I was at the heart of danger when they turned into confrontations with the police. Then, at nineteen, I joined the Afghan Freedom Fighters (the Mujahedin), real war, as if it had been clear forever that I was going to learn about this experience, hiding it even from my parents, who thought I was in safety in Pakistan.

I plunged myself into the Afghan conflict, and that changed my life.

Not having graduated from any journalism school, I benefited both from the advantages and the inconveniences of this lack of training. Besides my naivete and my total lack of experience, I had in my favor my innocence, my intense desire for discovering everything, and my ability to listen without any preestablished preconception or judgment.

The enemy of the Mujahedin with whom I shared day-to-day life was the Soviets. They occupied Afghanistan for nine years. I can no longer ignore this connection: Alexander Herrmann died battling . . . the Soviets. Of course, the situation was different. In his case he was the invader, whereas in Afghanistan it was the Soviets who swept over the country. And then, more importantly, the Soviets were not *my* enemy. I was a journalist.

But to be completely honest, things were not all that clear. I was young, inexperienced, and, more importantly, not yet molded by the practice of a profession and its ethical rules. I was free, a crazy dude, still stirred up by all my impulses. During my first weeks spent in the very center of the freedom fighters, as I was discovering the slowness of the passage of time in a country at war and as I was developing strong ties with the men, a totally unexpected question got presented to me when one of the combatants handed me his weapon. As I grasped the cold metal of his Kalashnikov, he suggested, only half joking, that I should fight alongside them on the next patrol. For these idle Mujahedin, it was playing a game that was a bit provocative. What was deeply disturbing for me was that I needed a few seconds before responding. A few seconds too long.

After all, why wouldn't I participate in their battle? It was right. These men were struggling against an implacable invader and were called "freedom fighters" in the West. And I was already with them, equipped only with my photo bags, running the same risks as they did when I approached the Russian lines in silence with an attack group, when I was sweating bullets passing through a minefield, when I was subjected to the umpteenth bombardment that would almost blow your head off. So why not grab a Kalashnikov right then and there and take part in the fight for freedom? I felt I didn't especially want to. But the Mujahedin's question planted confusion in me for a brief moment because in Afghanistan I had the *right* to do it.

I could.

Here, I had the right to kill if I wanted to.

The Mujahedin would have found it really great—for me to be firing along with them. Other foreigners coming from throughout the Muslim world, and even from Europe, didn't hesitate to do so. Their participation was praised by the resistance forces.

How upsetting to discover that if this question had never been asked of me in France—Why don't I kill?—it was not because the reply was obvious, because it wasn't! But because I was living in a country at peace where the circumstances and the law hadn't ever allowed me to have to ask myself that. And then, suddenly, at the age of nineteen, I had to discover in myself a *real reason* for not wanting to kill a man.

I am brought to the edge of a precipice. Facing a choice that seems so completely able to proceed on its own but that, the moment it's asked, provokes in my body a rush of venom and covers my eyes in darkness.

Of course I did not hesitate for long. But there was a period of time, a handful of seconds of questioning.

And this hesitation is terrifying.

Is this a connection to Alexander Herrmann? Is it because he and I share *something* that I experienced this questioning that most normal people wouldn't dream of asking? Do I kill? In the scorched hillsides of Afghanistan, in the danger of a war that enveloped me, I see once again my agitation. In the space of an instant nothing distinguished me from these men around me. These men, full of courage and arrogance, went to war, these men who defiantly put themselves in the way of bullets. These men who were going to kill, perhaps without hesitation, a detested enemy. In a space outside of time, I held this inert weapon in my hands, hands baked by sun and caked in dust, my eyes staring out into empty space.

How can one man kill another? What's more, this question did not disappear in me, in spite of all that my eyes witnessed afterward. The vision of the death of Alexander Herrmann is, in this sense, a *familiar* vision.

The question of one's own *capacity to kill*, to which it is so difficult to respond when you haven't faced it, is at the heart of Jonathan Littell's book *Les Bienveillantes* (*The Kindly Ones*). Rarely, perhaps never, has a book had such an effect on me. Perhaps because from the first pages on he pushes the reader into a questioning of personal limits just as the Mujahedin man had done in such a disturbing way by handing me his weapon. And Littell has a talent for putting such questions bluntly: "If you were born in a country or at a time where not only no one came to kill your wife, your children, but also where no one came to ask you to kill someone else's wife and children, praise God and go in peace. But always keep this thought in mind: you have had perhaps more good fortune than I, but you are not better. Because if you have the arrogance to think that you are . . . that's where the danger begins."[1] In fact, what would we do, confronted with such a choice?

Jonathan Littell's book is a novel, but it was lauded upon its release for its impressive erudition, at well as for its profoundly disturbing character. The author in fact speaks to us through the words of an SS adherent and, as this man moves through the war, the author has us follow the history of the Nazi regime, seen from the inside, up to the collapse of the Third Reich. It's a dense book of more than a thousand pages.

I read it twice. On the third reading, I stopped in the middle because I was so *sucked in* by it. It was Natacha, alarmed by the dreadful state into which these pages threw me, who made me aware that the book was *physically* carrying me toward death.

This text seemed to awaken something in me.

Black impulses.

A noxious atmosphere spread through our apartment, arising from my inner shadowy depths. It was the reading of these pages of the thick volume that brought this atmosphere to life. Why was the story told in this book having such an effect on me?

Is my meeting with Alexander Herrmann going to help me heal what has been drawing me into the shadows for so many years? This hope wins out over my initial fears and legitimizes seeing myself associated, one way or another, with this sad personage.

At the end of the afternoon, waiting for the appointment time of my second phone call with Charles Trang, I try to locate the Valdai region in the Ukraine. Without success. I enter all possible spellings, but I am always led toward a lake area hundreds of kilometers outside the Ukraine, somewhere in the north of modern-day Russia, halfway between Moscow and Saint Petersburg. When the telephone rings a little later, this is the first point I bring up.

"Excuse me but I can't manage to find any trace of Sukhaya Niva or of the Valdai region in the Ukraine," I tell Charles Trang.

"Yes, excuse me, but in fact Valdai is a region located to the south of Lake Ilmen, and not at all in the Ukraine as I mistakenly told you."

"It's in the north of Russia then?"

"Yes, south of the region of Novgorod. The town of Valdai is about three hundred kilometers southeast of Saint Petersburg."

"Have you found what activities Herrmann was involved in? Do you know if he could have been part of the extermination groups, the Einsatzgruppen that were to the rear of the front lines?"

"I don't think so. The division to which he belonged must have been integrated into Army Group North, which was headed toward Saint Petersburg, and your Alexander died in a zone where the battle was fierce during this initial phase of Operation Barbarossa . . . He must have participated in front line combat."

"Operation Barbarossa?"

"This is the name the Germans gave to their campaign in the USSR. Several million German soldiers participated in it. It began June 22, 1941, and your man was part of it."

I make a note to myself to once again plunge into the history books and to round out my knowledge of this period of the Second World War.

"How is it possible to find out Alexander's role?"

"It's hard to say, but perhaps there's an officer folder about him. Have you done any research in the German archives?"

"No. I didn't know that was possible."

"Numerous administrative documents about SS officers are still accessible, and if you're lucky perhaps there would be something about Alexander Herrmann."

"That's amazing! How can we find out? And how do you get access?"

"These documents are held in the Bundesarchiv in Berlin, but copies of the same documents are accessible in the U.S. National

Archives, which are located near Washington, D.C., in College Park, Maryland. I know a French doctoral student who's working there right now on his thesis, and he is probably consulting these archives on a daily basis."

"Do you think I could ask him for help?"

"Yes. If you offer him a little compensation for the time he would spend, I think he wouldn't find it so hard to do this research. His name is Antonin Dehays . . . Just a minute. I'll give you his email."

Our conversation scarcely ended, without delay I write to this man: "Dear Sir, Charles Trang has just given me your contact information. As part of some personal research, I would like to obtain the maximum amount of documents and information on Alexander Herrmann, born August 21, 1916, SS number 122 211, died October 20, 1941 at Sukhaya Niva (in the region of Valdai). Besides, in order to expand my research, I would be extremely interested in any documentation or information on any other officer or sub-officer of the SS bearing the name Alexander Herrmann, in all possible spellings (Herman, Herrman, etc.). Looking forward with impatience to hear back from you . . ."

A folder. And if a folder existed? This would be well nigh unbelievable. It would allow me to understand perhaps the nature of our encounter. And if it contained a photo? I dare not imagine that I might discover the face of this man at the border of an immaterial world. His face. Like a confirmation that this episode was truly real. I dare not hope for too much, but inexplicably, I am confident.

And the reply was not slow in coming. The historian replies from the United States the same evening: "Dear Sir, Alexander Herrmann's folder is available on microfilm. It seems fairly complete (eighty pages). I have not found any other Alexander Herrmann (or Herman or Herrman . . .). I am sending you the folder as soon as I have reworked the images."

◆ ◆ ◆

It's unreal. I have a lot of trouble controlling my impatience. The next three days are going to be very long. And March 23, at 2:43 p.m., I receive an email from Antonin Dehays including a link to download seventy-eight pages of documents preserved on microfilm for a half century.

The life of Obersturmführer Alexander Herrmann.

10

Shock

It's unimaginable the frustration that not mastering a language can lead to. As I look into the documents sent by Antonin Dehays, documents consisting of seventy-eight pages of military files copied from archives preserved on microfilm, I am terribly disappointed. Obviously everything is written in German. And I don't speak three words of German.

I send the link on to Charles Trang, who kindly offers to skim through them and give me a synthesis later in the day.

And, besides, this is a special day. March 23 is my brother Thomas's birthday. He died in Afghanistan years ago. My brother, who appeared to me at the beginning of my waking dream and who, gesturing to the space before us, guided me in a certain way toward Alexander. Another chance occurrence? That it would be exactly today that I receive this folder in which I'm going to discover one of the keys to my experience gives me the sensation that *someone* is playing with me. This isn't necessarily upsetting. Just impressive.

While waiting for the call back from Charles Trang, I open all the files one by one, spending an infinite amount of time on each page trying to decode the Gothic script which, in places, complicates the whole business even more. With the help of an online dictionary, I patiently force myself to extract a few scraps of information.

I find incomprehensible administrative pages that look like listings of allocations, evaluations, information questionnaires, too many numbers and abbreviations that are completely opaque to me. However, I do read the name Alexander Herrmann in various places, and I am thunderstruck. It's scarcely believable, when I think of it, to suddenly have access to so much raw data on the life of a man whose acquaintance I made in a kind of waking dream, months before.

Several pages are handwritten. This is *his* writing, his hand traced these lines less than eighty years ago. He touched these pages, applied himself to it. I manage to read the beginning: *Ich, Alexander Herrmann, wurde am 21. Aug. 1916 . . .* , "I, Alexander Herrmann, born August 21, 1916 . . . " It looks like the beginning of a kind of CV. "I, Alexander Herrmann," written with his pen. The lines are fine, the letters slanted to the right and difficult to read. A scrawl a little like my own . . . It's disconcerting.

When later I'm on the phone again with Charles Trang, I have the impression of not having gotten very far. Even though there is a sensation of familiarity that emanates from this document, only a tiny part has so far been revealed to me.

In a calm voice, Charles Trang passes on to me the elements that seemed important to him.

"On document three," he said to me, "I see that Alexander Herrmann belonged to a unit charged with guarding the camp at Dachau. This unit served as the nucleus for building the famous SS-Totenkopf Division."

"Dachau! . . . Was he a concentration camp guard? Dachau is written there? He was at Dachau?"

This name is so marked with infamy, is it possible that this man . . . ?

"I don't know, but I see that before the war he was part of the SS-Brandenburg Regiment, which later constituted the SS-Totenkopf Division. The regiments of this division were stationed in several camps, of which Dachau was one. Dachau was at the time an internment camp where the Nazi regime imprisoned political opponents, but it was also a barracks where SS regiments lived; therefore, he wasn't necessarily assigned to guard duty as such. I'll have to look in more detail because, in fact, I don't know what he was doing there . . . But in any case, he couldn't have been a softie: he was a member of the SS-Totenkopf Division—the 'Death's Head Division.'"

"I don't know what that means."

"The SS-Totenkopf Division was an armed division of the Waffen-SS, which notably participated in the French campaign. In combat it acquired a reputation for harshness and roughness. Going on, in document eight we learn that he was at the SS officer's training school at Bad Tölz in 1937 and 1938."

"Is there anything special about that school?"

"That is where the elite of the SS administration were groomed. They learned the art of warfare there, and the political indoctrination was especially rigorous. It was located south of Munich in Bavaria. In document twelve, you would be interested to know that Alexander married a certain Luise Miller. They were married May 10, 1940 . . ."

I'm suddenly very impatient, as if I were a few seconds away from a revelation. If he was married, could it be that they had a child? A little girl, as in my vision?

"Does it mention a child?" I ask hurriedly.

"I haven't seen that, but I'm far from having gone through everything. Ah, the document right in front of me is a death notice, no doubt published by the family."

At the same time as we are speaking on the phone, I'm opening on my computer each file mentioned by Charles. I am moved, astounded. I enlarge number eleven, which is a poor-quality photo in the notice: *In höchster Erfüllung . . .*

"What is it saying?"

" . . . *In höchster Erfüllung* . . . 'Fulfilling the ultimate accomplishment of his life as a soldier, Alex, my beloved son, died in the East, during major combat, October 20, 1941, while leading his courageous company . . .'"

"Who ordered this notice? His mother? But I see that it has the name of his wife at the bottom . . . "

"Exactly. It is signed by his widow, Luise Herrmann, in the name of the whole family. But clearly it's his mother writing it. She speaks of her son. This notice dating from November 1941, so a few weeks after his death, tells us that at the moment of his death he had the rank of SS-Ostuf and that he was head of a company. He was twenty-five years old at the time."

"What does Ostuf mean? It's his rank? I thought he was Obersturmführer?"

"It's the same thing: SS-Ostuf is the diminutive of SS-Obersturmführer. In document twenty-four, there is an 'evaluation.' His superiors describe Alexander as a man who is open, upright, zealous, aware of his responsibilities . . . having a sense of honor, loving order . . . No apparent faults, your fellow!"

"It's very formal, in fact . . . "

A mother who calls her son Alex. In the chill of these few lines in a death notice from so many years ago, suddenly there appears the beginning of an intimacy. Alex. Here we have a man that was up to now abstract, with an abominable life path, turning into a beloved son, an "Alex." I imagine a woman's voice, delicate and shy, speaking to her child gently. Alex. I can't stop myself from making the connection between the family name that I bear, and with which my school friends used to call me—"Hey, Allix!"—and this diminutive form rising up out of the darkness. Alex. Charles Trang, at the other end of the line, has no idea of the emotions that are coursing through me.

"In number thirty-two there's another evaluation. This one is more military. It says that Alexander was steadfast and loved by his men. Camaraderie was a principle that was raised to the level of an institution at the heart of the SS."

Thanks to Charles Trang, I discover there's a story here that I know nothing about. Our conversation winds down after he suggests that I spend time on several specific pages. It would take us hours if not days to get through the whole folder. I am terribly frustrated to have to depend on someone, even though Charles Trang is not keeping track of his time since our first contact took place. He tells me that several documents are redundant. In spite of everything, I would like to translate every line in minute detail so as to be sure not to miss any information, no matter how unimportant it may seem. An important confirmation could be hiding in a single insignificant word or annotation. A quantity of sensations and images emerged into my dream. For example, does this other man whom I saw in Alexander's company exist? And the little girl, so lively? She must be there on one of these pages, hidden among the undecipherable lines. And this village where I saw him fall, this white ground, this tank, these men falling all around, this furor of combat?

After hanging up from the call, I can't stop examining these pages. I am hypnotized, still finding it hard to understand that I am holding in my hands the garbled telling of the life of a real man.

Over the hours that pass, it becomes clear to me that it's not simply a matter of translating words. In addition, it is necessary to understand the context and the particular military language made up of a never-ending stream of specific terms and abbreviations. What would be ideal would be to convince Charles Trang for us to review together all the pages in an exhaustive way. He lives in the foothills of the Pyrenees. Could I perhaps suggest to him that I would go there to meet up with him so we could do that together? I'm going to raise that idea with him.

Secrets are hidden in this folder. I can feel it.

Alone in front of the light from my computer screen, I'm looking for lost words in unreadable pages. I now know that Alexander married Luise Miller. Does he have brothers? Sisters? Who are his parents? What did they do? Was this little girl his? My eyes tire from the rough black-letter Gothic writing. I have trouble deciphering the innumerable words, and I stop over seals that accompany the signatures of officers and officials at the end of numerous pages: official stamps sometimes half missing, sometimes clear and glacial. One sign having become the mark of this period so close to our own, where darkness threatened to engulf all of Europe:

An eagle above a swastika.

After a long overview of the seventy-eight files, I return to a document of several pages entitled: *Personal Nachweis für Führer der Waffen-SS*, that Charles advised me to examine. It amounts to a sort of official document summarizing his career within the Waffen-SS. Following the identity data and the civil status, there appears a list of dates and what seems to me to be the names of units and functions. On the third page, astonished, I discover the activities of Alexander's unit, almost day by day, after the entry of German troops into France in May 1940. Above this list of lines, I recognize the name of the city of Arras: *19.5 -20.5.40 Durchbruch über Arras* . . . ("From May 19 to 20, 1940, breakthrough into Arras"), followed by other familiar place names: Cambrai, Béthune, Artois, Gravelines. These names mark the bloody advance of German forces into France.

On the first page of this *Personal Nachweis*, I learn that Alexander was born in the town of Plauen. Google Maps tells me that it is located in eastern Germany near the Czech border—in Saxony precisely, in the region of Vogtland, equidistant from Dresden to the northeast and Nuremberg to the southwest. I zoom in on the satellite image, clicking on the blurred streets of this unknown burg as if I were going to have some response appear.

Hours pass, and night has fallen when suddenly a signal on my messenger service announces that I have a new email. It is coming in from Charles Trang. He too has continued the decoding on his side. He has translated several passages and, in a short message, telegraphic style, he passes on to me in summary fashion what new things he's discovered. When I read the last sentence, time stops. "The second-to-last document details the reason for his death: Alexander was hit by an exploding shell in the chest and in the neck."

Hit by an exploding shell in the chest and in the neck.

In the silence of the night, I am in a state of shock: the wound to his throat is the vision I had of his death.

11

Why?

How to describe what I'm feeling? I being the one who for ten years has been conducting, with an implacable rational discipline, investigations on extraordinary subjects. Suddenly, I can no longer ignore the incontestable character of this last element: Alexander died as I saw him die!

Right now I feel caught in the boxing ring ropes.

Unable to reason, my head spinning, feeling like I want to cry, wanting to understand as well, but it's amazement that predominates. Fear too. What does all this mean? What's happening to me? Because it's a fact: the most intense element, the one most charged with emotion from my waking dream, is precisely the death scene of this Alexander Herrmann.

I saw him, I repeatedly saw him, hit in the throat by a bursting shell, collapsing, losing blood.

The memory of this scene has not left my mind. It is sharp, perfectly clear, since the sequence of his death was repeated several times during my experience in Peru. And repeated again in Paris in the office of the healer Agnès Stevenin.

I grab my journal and open it to the page where I had originally written the sequence of this experience, only a few minutes after I experienced it. And I read: "An SS officer. I see a face yelling at me. I'm in a demolished village and I'm going to die, wounded in the throat from the burst of a shell that has severed my jugular. I die."

And farther down, again: "Then I see him once again collapsing, blood spurting from his throat, pouring over his collar and out onto the ground. He holds his neck. His life is slipping away. His look flickers out. The white dust covers him. The earth is pulverized by explosions that throw out snow and fire, fury and cold. He is dead." Trembling with emotion I tap away on my computer keyboard opening the second-to-last document mentioned by Charles Trang. Now I have it. The microfilm photo of a simple little yellow sheet in A5 format. As a header there is typewritten: *Verlustmeldung d. SS- T. division,* which Charles translates for me as "Report on Losses in the SS-Totenkopf Division." The form is dated November 11, 1941, which is twenty-two days after Alexander's death. And actually all the details are there: surname, given name, Alexander Herrmann's rank, birth and death dates, place of death, and on the line for cause of death is typed: *Brust-u. Halsschuss (I.G.).*

I still want a verification, and I consult several online translation sites that actually all give something like "shot in the chest and the neck." Further research informs me that "*I.G.*" means *Infanterie-Geschütz,* which is "infantry cannon"—a small cannon.

SS-Obersturmführer Alexander Herrmann died when hit in the chest and in the neck by an exploding shell.

I "dreamed" of an SS-Obersturmführer Alexander Herrmann dead when hit in the neck by an exploding shell.

I can no longer fight with the evidence. From now on it is impossible for me to go on believing that it could have been coming from my imagination, or chance, and that the established fact that an SS-Obersturmführer Alexander Herrmann really existed was really only just a strange coincidence. Because I now have the indisputable confirmation that this faraway man died exactly as happened in my vision. No, from now on, I can only admit that I encountered a real person on the other side of horror, years, and death, and that I have a mysterious link with that person. I could not have invented so many exact details. It would be absurd and irrational to still hang on to the idea that I could have. I am shocked by this news, delivered the evening of the anniversary of the death of my brother Thomas.

From now on, going forward, the question that arises is: why?

Why have I been connected to him?

Who is he in relation to me?

A ghost passing through and that I might have "captured," God knows why and how? Or perhaps it's the memory of a previous life?

But what would the ghost of a German soldier, who died in 1941 on the Eastern Front, be doing in a remote hamlet in the Peruvian Amazon some fifteen thousand kilometers away from Russia? Or am I to conclude that *I was* Alexander?

Strange day.

Let's be methodical. An initial conclusion is unavoidable: we are linked. *Something* is connecting me, through some mystery I have no idea about, to this young SS lieutenant who died twenty-six years, nine months, and twelve days before my birth. SS-Ostuf Alexander Herrmann, killed at the age of twenty-five, on the morning of October 20, 1941, as his men were preparing to take the village of Sukhaya Niva, a remote little hamlet three hundred kilometers south of Leningrad, in a landscape covered in snow, after being hit in the throat. To say that I'm unnerved is a euphemism. I am . . . troubled.

With all objectivity, the idea of having become acquainted with an earlier life has just gained a certain weight. But why him? And especially why now? I need answers. From now on these questions haunt me. Because the existence of this Alexander also throws light on my present life from a new angle: my fascination with war, the unbearable desire to want to approach evil, observe it, feel it, find out what sets it in motion. My relationship with the Holocaust, this infernal moment of our history, which I feel has always *concerned* me—from the beginning.

Is my encounter with Alexander proof that reincarnation well and truly does exist? Is it the explanation I have sought all these years in order to understand my inner suffering, the melancholy, the dreams that are not totally my own and that nevertheless impact my life, feeding my emotions, enlivening my fears, and participating in an unconscious part of my personality?

If such is the case . . . how to live with this legacy, this abscess from history buried in my own flesh? Because I have no memory at all of this man's life. Except for my vision, I don't know his face, I don't speak his language, I don't know his family. He's another man, another individual. If he is my life from before, what is it that has passed from him to me? Because I do not share any of his ideas and beliefs. This upsetting confirmation that he and I have something in common, far from closing down my questioning, opens up a field of questioning that makes my head spin.

I have to find other traces. I must go to Germany and try to discover if members of his family are still alive. And to Russia too. In this moment I know that, come what may, I will be at Sukhaya Niva, this forgotten hamlet in the glacial north of Russia, on October 20, for the anniversary of his death. In seven months. From now until then, I'm going to pursue this inquiry, one of the most essential inquiries of my whole life.

12

Company Commander

The next day, I open up and speak with Charles Trang from my emotions.

"I'm really upset. After receiving your email yesterday evening, I reread the transcription of the waking dream I had in Peru, which I wrote immediately after the experience. And in it I found all the identical details corresponding to the real Alexander Herrmann: his surname and given name, the same rank, the same age, and last night, then, the same cause of death: a wound in the neck. I can assure you it was quite a shock."

I read him the passage in question.

"Indeed, it's astonishing," he admits, with some reserve.

I'm quite aware that I'm pushing this passionate researcher of military history into a strange universe, but he gives me the feeling of being as intrigued as I am by this affair and wanting to hear my hypotheses. Also, while he is providing an irreplaceable assistance in the analysis of raw documents received from the American archives, I am drawn into sharing with him my personal feelings, as well as the progress in my thinking. A certain trust is being established between us.

"Yes, for the age, I no longer know if I told you that too, but I saw the figure twenty-five tattooed on the inside of his left forearm in my dream. And as if by chance, he died at age twenty-five. I heard that the SS had a tattoo on their arms . . ."

"Yes, but it was their blood type," he informs me.

"It's upsetting just the same that he died at the age of twenty-five and then I see this tattoo . . . It's not an element that alone would convince me but added to everything else, it begins to make . . ."

"Certainly."

I continue by asking him to go back to the Report on Losses.

"Anyway, in which document did you see that he died at Sukhaya Niva? In the Report on Losses, which mentions his mortal wound in the chest and neck, several place names are indicated, and I don't understand what they refer to. Kirillowtschina, for example, or also '*Orstausgang Mirochny, Grad Nr. 50*,' following where it says 'Grablage'?"

"Grablage means tomb," Charles tells me. "This line indicates that he is buried in position number 50, on the way out of the village of Mirochny."

"His tomb?! Would it be possible that he's still there?"

"Impossible to know . . . Orstausgang means 'on the way out of town' and Mirochny, as with Kirillowtschina, is another place situated in the same area as Sukhaya Niva. All these places must be little villages. When we speak of the place mentioned in the Report on Losses, it's probably in Kirillowtschina, that the headquarters of his battalion must have been located; also this was the name used in the Report on Losses. But on this date, fighting took place around the locality of Sukhaya Niva."

"How do you know that he died there? In my waking dream Alexander was moving forward on foot, wearing a long coat, in a desolate terrain full of corpses. The German tanks were advancing in the same direction that he was . . . then he is hit and collapses."

"I discovered Alexander's precise posting, and besides, I know, thanks to my archives, where his battalion was located. Although he was part of an infantry division, there weren't any tanks. From the end of the summer on, the Totenkopf Division was engaged in intense fighting in this region situated to the east of the town of Demyansk. Your Alexander died there at the beginning of the winter. I saw in my notes that in the autumn of 1941 the cold came rather early. At the beginning of October it snowed and the ground was already frozen. You speak of a white landscape. That's another element of similarity. I could send you the text that I wrote on this military campaign. You can see if other details evoke something."

"I ordered yesterday your book *Totenkopf Archives*. Is your text from that book?"

"No, I was thinking of the description I wrote for my book on the Barbarossa operation."

"I would be delighted to read what you're offering to send me. I know next to nothing about this period and even less about the Totenkopf Division."

Here again is one of the curious twists of fate in this story. It seems that Alexander spent his whole career with the SS-Totenkopf Division, and the one and only person that I contact, Charles Trang, turns out to be . . . the French specialist on this division! I will see the extent to which this is true in the following months as I amass documentation relentlessly, reading and contacting all the historians specializing in Germany and the SS: Charles Trang's work is unanimously hailed by these historians as a reference.

Who pushed me to contact this man—him and only him? *Someone* is pulling the strings in this story and had me call the right person. Absolutely incredible.

"I can send it to you by email," he offers. "You will see, I report with a certain precision the progress of the fighting by the Totenkopf Division. As well, in the same Report on Losses, as I told you, Alexander's specific posting is indicated. Look at the document opposite '*vom*' . . . "

I open the folder again, run my eyes over it . . . "vom" . . .

"I'm reading . . . 2 . . . wow! It's hard to make out: 2./SS-T.-inf.Rgt.1."

"That's it. It's saying that he was in the 2nd Company of the 1st Battalion of the 1st SS-Totenkopf Infantry Regiment."

"Ah. Can you explain that a bit?"

"An infantry division, like the Totenkopf Division, was made up specifically of three regiments."

"Okay . . . But 'infantry'—what does that mean exactly?"

"Historically, infantry designates the combat troops that attack on foot."

"Right."

"So each infantry regiment is made up of three battalions."

"OK."

"Each battalion has four companies."

"So to put in the order, it's division, then regiment, then battalion, and companies at the end?"

"Exactly."

"How many men are we talking about in these various groups?"

"A regiment has about 3,000 men, a battalion about 800, and a company about 180 to 200 men."

"That doesn't add up. If a regiment of three thousand men is made up of three battalions of eight hundred men, where are the remaining six hundred?"

"Good question. These figures are general. Of three thousand men making up a regiment, besides the combat forces (eight hundred per battalion), you have to also add logistical services, operational staff, headquarters staff, etc. When I say eight hundred men per battalion, I'm counting just the men available for combat."

"So the second company in which Alexander served included 180 to 200 men?"

"Yes, he was commanding it! He was a company commander in Russia. Remember it was mentioned in the death notice. And besides I found confirmation in my archives, in a table of manpower numbers of the Totenkopf Division dating from the beginning of Operation Barbarossa."

In spite of his age, Alexander had under his command close to two hundred men, which suggests he had gained a certain expertise. I let Charles continue.

"However, two hundred men in a company is a full complement. In full operation, counting the wounded, deaths, turnover, it is probably only half that who were participating in the fighting, especially after several months of a murderous campaign."

"Your help is invaluable, Charles. I have no idea how to thank you. And besides, my story must seem so strange to you . . . "

"Yes, it's true. But you know, I'm one of those people who believe that not everything can be explained . . . "

"I would really like to speak about all that with you. I'm a bit far away, but if you would agree, perhaps we might be able to discuss this in person. I don't want to impose on you or take your time, but it seems to me that this subject intrigues you as much as me. No? . . ."

"Why not. It would be a pleasure."

I hang up the call with a feeling of having made enormous progress even though so many pages are still to be explored. Alexander commanded a company. He was the head of more than one hundred men in combat. And at the time of his death, he had been in the SS close to nine years.

In fact, another file informs us more about his progress. This man entered the SS, or Schutzstaffel, meaning literally "protection squadron," at the age of sixteen-and-a-half, at the beginning of the month of April 1933, after having been a member of Hitler Youth even before Hitler came to power at the end of January 1933.

He passionately wanted this involvement. It's chilling.

Nevertheless, with the elements at our disposal, it would not seem that Alexander Herrmann found himself in a position where he would have participated in the darkest pages of the Second World War. At least in the last months of his life, during the eastern offensive, his role seems to be identical to that of millions of other soldiers in the regular German army: that of combatant. But unlike conscripts to the Wehrmacht, Alexander demonstrates his own total ideological adherence to the Nazi regime and to the person of the Führer—entering the SS was a voluntary act and necessitated a demonstration of motivation and an implacable will. He was the willing arm of the monster and was full of enthusiasm. Not for one second can I forget that.

My desire to understand will never be a desire to absolve.

But I want to discover why this young German, like so many others, got involved in an unthinkable adventure. Why, in a boy like him, does there suddenly appear this desire to dance with the devil?

The following night I had a dream of a familiar scenario but one I thought was behind me. A dream where I am killing. It just comes back, arising out of darkness. I begin to understand why my nights are haunted by such scenes. It's *not me*. These are not *my* dreams.

In this dream I am seated on the steps of a house in the company of several people, including children, it seems to me. Suddenly, two cars pass by in the street and their occupants open fire on us. Two individuals beside me die riddled with bullets. However, I remain calm. A man seated with us is involved in the shooting, I don't know how. No doubt he's in league with the passengers in the cars. In the confusion of the dream, I remember simply needing to get rid of him. Then, with a confident move, I bury a sharp knife in the base of his neck, cutting through the vein to the left of his throat. Very calmly. The man gets up making fun of me; no doubt he thinks I missed my target. Blood is flowing abundantly, and I point this out to him, adding that he has only a few minutes to live. When he sees that I'm right, he seems, in the end, to be delighted to die, and he continues to speak to me until he loses consciousness and dies.

This dream wakes me up in the middle of the night, sweating and troubled. It has been several months that I have not killed someone in my nightly wanderings . . . but each time it's the same scenario: armed with a knife or a firearm, I am always calm, detached, and not in the least affected by what I'm preparing to do. Without anger, without passion, very mechanically.

A cold being, stripped of the slightest empathy.

13

Artillery Fire

I am now immersed in Alexander's story, and it's no longer possible to turn back. I have no other choice but to follow this encounter to its end. Like an appointment set up long ago with the Black Order—the other name of the SS. Because that's what it is—an appointment beyond death, a wished-for meeting, arising in another time and space, but which henceforth is part of my life and that of my family. An appointment with another being—or another me?

Whether at work, during an appointment, or even at home, as soon as my mind breaks away, however little it might be from the task at hand, I think of him. Of Alexander. Who can he be? A monster, a victim of his times, a ghost, *me* before, a parasite, a memory, one of my faces? He is there. Mysterious and inaccessible. Imposed by a force that goes beyond us.

Superimposed on my waking dream there are now new images, given life in the previous weeks as a result of my reading: pages from his military folder, books, and all the historical documentation that I'm devouring.

Two questions cycle around obsessively: What does he look like? Does he have the same face as the man I saw? An oval shape, a little thin, with blond, thick hair combed back and cut very close at the sides, and this mischievous look, provocative, as if he had returned from a thousand battles still retaining the capacity to be amused at my amazement.

And did he have a daughter? I'm also looking for this child, impatiently, since if all that I have been able to verify from my waking dream has been confirmed, she too really must be real. Otherwise why would she have appeared to me? Could she possibly still be alive?

Charles Trang has found more information on the exact location of the place of Alexander's death and on the circumstances leading up to his death. One morning he sends me a copy of the map of the area that he unearthed in a military book in German, accompanied by a summary paragraph about the fighting on that day, October 20, 1941. The map was drawn up by the information service of the Totenkopf Division on October 23, so three days after Alexander's death. I am flabbergasted by the number of documents available to us. Charles tells me that the military positions described on the map are those that ended up being set after the fighting of October 20. Little pennants and numbers designate the Red Army units and their exact positions, which were determined through the interrogation of prisoners. The Soviet artillery positions are shown as well. Sukhaya Niva is directly on the front line. Charles reminds me that Alexander was killed during an attack by his battalion as it was advancing in a sort of valley following the little stream that passes slightly south of Sukhaya Niva. His battalion formed the point of attack of the Totenkopf Division east of Sukhaya Niva, coming from a village called Cholmy. At 8:00 a.m., after an easy advance forward, the battalion came up against strong resistance a few kilometers from their goal as they reached the road connecting Sukhaya Niva to Cholmy. It was only toward 9:30 a.m. that the battalion surrounded the village, which was taken after violent fighting. A half hour later, the battalion besieged and captured a height of land that sheltered a Soviet defense post five hundred meters southwest of Sukhaya Niva. By then they were beyond the edge of the village. Charles writes to me that we don't know at what moment Alexander was killed, but it was in this area that it happened in the first hours of the day. Is it at the time of the advance along the little road between Cholmy and Sukhaya Niva? Or perhaps in the illusory shelter of the vegetation and undergrowth? Or along this river that is marked by a simple line on the layout map? Charles makes clear that it was cold during this period of time. Snow had fallen, according to survivor reports.

Charles ends without being aware that there was a new little revelation. On that day, Alexander's infantry battalion had received the reinforcement of Sturmgeschützen—assault guns. The SS-Totenkopf had about ten of these big armored vehicles. The assault guns, Charles makes clear, looked like tanks except that they did not have turrets. They served as mobile artillery during major offensives. The reality, one more time, corresponds to my vision. In fact, in my dream, Alexander and the other soldiers were advancing by sheltering themselves behind what I took to be tanks. In the fighting that took place in the taking of Sukhaya Niva that morning, the SS of the 1st Battalion were advancing under the cover of the division's assault guns! A situation that was far from being the usual rules of engagement.

But precisely on that particular day, the day of Alexander's death, and as in my dream, he and his men were advancing under the shelter of what looked like a tank.

Following the given name, the surname, the rank, the age, the mortal wound in the neck, a sixth point in common between my *dream* and reality. Once again this twinge in the belly. Something I'm not able to get used to.

The succinct and cold report covering the fighting on the morning of October 20, 1941, gives rise in me to very sharp and evocative images, as if I *knew* how things had unfolded. I see the attack led by Alexander's company, with him at its head, under the precarious shelter of this assault gun, the enemy artillery that starts firing . . .

And that awakens other memories in me. This time, memories that really do belong to me. A situation experienced in 1998 in the north of Afghanistan and that could be mistaken for—I realize only at this moment—the circumstances of Alexander's death. On that day I was with my friend Ludovic Place near the Tajik border, at the last positions held by Commander Massoud. Ludovic and I were making a film for the

European Culture TV channel ARTE on this legendary commander.

In the extreme north of Afghanistan, on the shores of the Oxus, there is this ancient Greek city of Ai-Khanoum, literally "Lady Moon." A mysterious city, rediscovered by French archaeologists in the 1960s and erected there in the decades following the passage through the area by Alexander the Great in the fourth century before our era.

It's precisely to this place so charged with history that Massoud had been forced to fall back. At the spot where there was the ancient citadel, on the plateau overlooking the lower town, trenches had been dug and several artillery positions installed. Opposite, invisible a few hundred meters away, on the other side of the Kokcha River, which merges with the Oxus not much farther along, the Taliban had similarly fortified their positions. Ludovic wanted to advance to the front line in order to do some filming. I wasn't keen about it, but I followed him.

We had taken our places in a Russian jeep driven by Massoud's men, and we were driving slowly along the shores of the Kokcha, in the direction of the defensive lines. As we were approaching the slope that would lead up toward the upper town and the citadel, which was transformed into a battlefield and disfigured by trenches, the jeep broke down.

Out in the open, in the middle of the remains of a village in ruins.

In the silence and the crushing heat, the driver struggled to get the motor going again. Suddenly, a violent explosion resounded behind us. I turned around, staring wide-eyed and without understanding. There, on the spot where we had been a few seconds before, a dust cloud was billowing up. I didn't grasp in that moment what had just happened; however, something in me screamed to jump from the vehicle and take off as quickly as possible. But as my mind was hesitating, the jeep finally started and lurched forward, taking us as quickly as possible out of this trap: we had been targeted by the Taliban, who were only too happy to see an enemy vehicle halted within range of their firing. Thank God, their aim was a little clumsy. Our driver had the motor screaming, and a few seconds later we rejoined the fighters on the plateau. A bare and dry stretch of land, covered in dust, and a few joking men with bloodshot eyes, dead tired from sleepless nights. Faces that terrified me.

The men decided to return the Taliban fire that had missed us by so little.

A first shot, dull and heavy, raised dust and hammered my head as it sped toward the enemy. Then a second, and a third, shot this time from an old tank, dug in on the front line twenty meters ahead.

It was at that point that I panicked. I wanted to flee—immediately. While Ludovic was filming, with Massoud's men casually opening fire, I looked for cover, wild with panic, convinced that our shots were going to let loose new return shots on the part of the Taliban. Wide-eyed, mouth open so that my eardrums didn't burst in case of a close hit, I was seized by an atrocious feeling of helplessness. The sky was immaculate and blue, but death was hiding in it. I expected to see an enemy shell merge invisibly with the blue and be too fast for me to be aware of it. The terror that I was experiencing was intense. I didn't give a damn about the amused looks from the fighters watching this journalist desperately looking for a hole, a crevice. I slipped into a hollow, flattening myself against the earth, literally gluing myself to the ground, my mouth dry. Everything was flying around in bursts, the blasts sending explosions and stones on me, and I was screaming at Ludo to hurry up so we could get the hell out of there as soon as possible. Reminding him, sharply, of the first commandment of a war photographer: "The best photo is the one . . . that you bring back alive. We don't need these images, Ludo! We're not going to get ourselves killed for them." Not listening to me, he continued to film calmly. And no shots were fired from the Taliban lines. When he finished filming, we, safe and sound, left this handful of men who were already dead and just waiting for their deliverance.

I was afraid on numerous occasions, under aerial bombardment in Afghanistan or in other situations in war zones, but never had I experienced this paralyzing fright that prevents all movement and leaves you like a tiny, powerless being, swept away by the blast of an infernal tempest. Other combat situations that I had known had provoked spurts of fear, but never such a feeling of terror.

To be caught under enemy artillery fire terrified me to an unimaginable degree.

Alexander encountered death in rigorously identical circumstances, caught under the fire of Russian artillery, when an explosion ripped through his throat.

I understood in this inquiry that I had to pay particular attention to my sensations without immediately trying to judge them. Because interpreting them can make me lose contact with them. Certain keys in my relationship with Alexander will emerge if I manage to allow my perceptions to arise. Although I am someone who has always been a thinking being, I am beginning to gauge the importance of opening myself to my sixth sense. After all, that's what allowed the initial contact with Alexander! One must find the right dosage—the balance between intuition and reflection.

The story of the assault that Charles Trang brought caused a spontaneous recall of this memory of terror experienced when I came under Taliban fire on the citadel of Ai-Khanoum. That means something.

14

The Photo

Over the following days, the moment of Alexander's death circles around in my head. At night, my dreams are colored by scenes of confrontation. I don't systematically retain a memory of that upon awakening, but war is present constantly in my mind. War but also German words, which surge up like ridiculous thoughts. And I notice even nonhabitual movements of my body.

Energy is moving.

My body is like a stage where the agitation of my unconscious is acted out.

I notice too that my mood has been changing for some time. What is causing that? Life is strange. Sometimes it seems to be of such great clarity—limpid, coherent—and at other moments, I feel only grief and solitude. And today I am invaded by sadness. I see myself embarking on an implacable river of time that flows and brings us back to what has been offered to us. My childhood was not difficult—on the contrary, we had a good time, with my brothers—we were happy. Our parents loved us and inspired us. Dad in his style that could be a little distant, and Mum with her extraordinary talent for listening and her kindliness. But where has this joyous world gone now that two of our family have passed to the world of the dead? Two whom we miss.

◆ ◆ ◆

Melancholy slips into the spaces left vacant and I find myself assailed by the blackness of the world. Current affairs are terrible and resonate in a sinister way with all these documents on Nazi Germany that I have accumulated for my inquiry. How frightening it is to realize the ease with which one of the most cultivated countries in Europe let itself be dragged into the suicidal madness of the Third Reich. How could a man like Hitler have been elected by millions of Germans who saw in him a solution to their problems?

My head begins to swim as I realize that the social resentment in Germany at the beginning of the 1930s is a lot like what today is affecting France and, more broadly, the Western world. "Never again," they proclaimed. Really? Are you really so sure? What are you doing so that doesn't happen again, outside of pretty speeches? The West is affected by the same troubles today as Europe was toward the end of the 1920s: financial crisis, loss of credibility in the traditional political structures, the rise of extremist popular speeches, community retrenchment, unease, increasing social fear, terrorist threats . . .

It scares me. Current affairs drag me toward the dark and discouragement. Facing the theater of the world, I am tempted to allow myself to believe that, in the end, it's hopeless. We are too blind, unconscious, lazy; *it's going to start up again.*

Despair envelops me.

At the same time, deep down, hope does not manage to be snuffed out.

The shadow and the light confront each other and thrash it out in my body.

Tear me up, wound me; ever since I was a child.

Child of a brutal and unjust world.

Inheritor of a blood-stained Europe.

A feather on a knife blade, constantly swinging between sadness and hope.

Hope is confidence that adversity will not reach us in our values and our ethics, regardless of what it imposes on the everyday. Hope is the certainty that life's difficulties can make us better and that it is in managing to be better in painful circumstances that we will improve the world. Hope is confidence. Confidence in life, and in the invisible forces that act on the destiny of man on Earth. The certitude that our future will be constructed based on what we do in the present.

The shadow is fear of losing our riches, our comfort. It is the ease with which we accommodate ourselves to the suffering of others, *who are far away*. We close our eyes. The shadow consists of speeches full of hatred and retrenchment—the belief that if you shut yourself up you are protecting yourself and all will go better. That being realistic is to think only of oneself—being egotistical and having a clear conscience.

However, hope also is realistic, for it is based on the clear evidence of changes in our world and on the power of each individual's action. Hope does not veil its eyes when faced with the difficulties that await us. Yes, it is realistic to be optimistic in our world that is confronted by so many challenges and threats. For to be inhabited by hope is to accept to bring oneself into question. It is voluntary, clear, and generous.

The shadow and hell are constantly around us. They are in us like seeds waiting to germinate—in each woman, in each man, in each child, fear, egoism, stupidity, and torpor can at any instant bud and grow. Strength, confidence, determination, kindliness, and love—especially love—are necessary for man not to slip naturally toward the darkest slopes. Because giving up is easy. Very easy even. It's a natural movement, restful for the mind. The human being spontaneously leans toward the dark when he decides that his life ought to be easy and comfortable, before all else. Constant and daily efforts are what bring us closer to the light.

But why make these efforts? I wonder sometimes.

Yes, why does one choose to be a good man rather than the opposite? After all, isn't crushing others, being the stronger one, going to make me happier?

Why *must we* do good?

Is this question my own? In any case, it's drowning me, penetrating my throat, squeezing my heart, and veiling my vision. Fortunately, my wife is luminous and leads me back each time to life. Yes, hope looks at things as does the woman I love. Without her, the shadow would doubtless have already won.

Charles Trang has gotten himself involved in a way I never could have imagined. He searched through very many documents in the archives at his disposal in order to see if he could put his hands on a photo of Alexander. He has access to a quantity of visual documents dating from the various campaigns conducted by the Totenkopf Division, and he knows Alexander's precise assignment. Unfortunately, his quest has not furnished the result we were hoping for. But then he calls me to suggest a new idea.

"I've thought of something. It didn't come to mind before, but yesterday I wondered if maybe there weren't perhaps another folder on Alexander. In fact, you must realize that with the SS all marriages had to undergo an in-depth study and be approved by the very official SS Race and Settlement Main Office, the Rasse-und Siedlungshauptamt der SS, the acronym of which was RuSHA."

"Approved?"

"Yes, especially concerning the racial purity of the couple."

"Racial purity! That's crazy! How did they go about it?"

"This office was charged with controlling the ideology and racial origin of all SS members. An inquiry with questionnaires and genealogical investigations was conducted on the two families, in the case of a marriage folder, and going back up to four generations."

"And do you think that Alexander and his wife had to submit to this procedure?"

"Of course! For a member of the SS wanting to get married, it was obligatory. A folder had to have been put together, and perhaps it is still available."

"Where?"

"In the same place that you got the first military folder: in the U.S. National Archives. Unless this folder has disappeared, it ought to be held there along with hundreds of thousands of others. Take it up once again with Antonin Dehays."

The young doctoral student working in Washington replies to me with the same diligence as the first time. His message stirs up in me a state of feverishness that I'm barely able to contain. Not only does the RuSHA document for Alexander exist and it seems complete, but it contains . . . a photo!

A photo of Alexander.

A photo of the man I saw in a dream.

Waiting for the arrival of this folder takes an immense effort of patience. I can't sit still. I receive the whole thing after the few days that Antonin Dehays needed in order to process the microfilm images. I become aware of a whole new series of documents that I open page by page on the screen of my computer. Complicated forms, handwritten pages, impenetrable questionnaires—once again. It contains just about as many files as the officer folder, and each page takes quite a few seconds to open. Once again hypnotized by so many prospects of answers, my eyes get tired trying to recognize words, or in decoding one more sentence. I let myself flow into an archivist's study, my eyes discovering panoramas of a life. The name of the future spouse is visible quite frequently.

And suddenly a file opens and his face appears.

A smack, like the blow of a fist to my belly. I wasn't expecting it. Not like that; so taken as I was by trying to read the preceding texts that, in another state, I had almost forgotten that it was there, waiting for me. His photo.

The quality of the image is poor. Very dark. But it is possible to distinguish a little of the expression on this face that emerges from darkness, slightly brighter on one side. His hair is flat and combed back, with a parting line carefully made on the left side of his skull. The jaw is firm, and the head is carried intentional and proud. Alexander is a rather handsome man from what I can judge. There is poise and presence in this photo. A high, straight forehead, short nose. His lips are full, but in contrast the eyes cannot be seen clearly. They remain in fact partially invisible in the shadow because of the poor quality of the microfilm. And yet I can make out confidence. Is it in the shape of the eyebrow? Without being too light about it, in his look, penetrating into me, he is sure of himself.

But I am not sure that I recognize him.

Because the memory—so tenuous, so fragile—that I had, following my waking dream, is instantly and irremediably affected by the density, the force of the reality of the image that I'm studying. Memories are too unstable. Ones from a dream—even more so.

In spite of that, the face in this pale photo is not all that far from the vision I had of Alexander. It corresponds even in all aspects. Perhaps with the exception of the hair, which I had seen as blond and which seems darker in the photo. But could that be perhaps due to the poor quality of the document?

I feel strongly something upsetting as I look at this photo. I would like to see the eyes better, but most certainly the face *resembles* the one I saw. It could be the same man, and no element is far away from what I was contemplating. So there it is: I don't have enough details to recognize him, but nothing in this face is distant from my memory.

The marriage folder contains three photos in all. Two are passport style: the front-facing one I just discovered and a second, a profile. The third, a full body shot, shows Alexander standing. Following this, the face of Luise appears. His wife. Three photos also for her. A young face but faded, eyes no doubt slightly almond shaped. What comes across from her is a sort of formal, reserved air that is accentuated by the paleness of the bad shot. A hint of a timid smile perhaps?

I rework as best I can the brightness and contrast of the image. I try to get Alexander to stand out more, but I don't manage to improve the result much. I print the photo. The face from my dream has departed from the subtle space of my memories in order to inhabit the real world.

Rather frequently I reflect that the whole story is impossible. However, here I now have a very material face. It's so intimidating.

Summer comes. Charles Trang has accepted to receive me at his home in a few days. I am preparing myself methodically for this voyage to the Pyrenees. I've printed all the pages of the two files in order to put together two bound documents that are easy to work with and on which I'll be able to take notes as we go through them.

The day before my departure, I have a meeting with my friend, the psychologist Agnès Delevingne, who directs the network of health professionals of INREES (*Institut de Recherche sur les Expériences Extraordinaires* [Research Institute on Extraordinary Experiences]). She is one of the first to whom I relate my strange adventure. During our lunch, when I'm in the middle of my story, I see her face express shock. Very moved, Agnès looks at me and asks:

"Do you remember how Florence Lecuyer referred to you at the beginning of your collaboration?"

I don't get right away what Agnès is talking about, and then suddenly I remember. Florence Lecuyer is a talented editor who, at the time, was in charge of a department with the publisher Éditions de La Martinière. With her I created an ambitious series of books devoted to the extraordinary. We saw each other very regularly during this period, which goes back to several years ago. Florence is a person of great sensitivity, and she devoted body and soul to the project. Except that during the first months she didn't manage to call me Stéphane, and it was so systematic that we used to joke about it.

"Florence all the time called you Alexandre."

I look at Agnès, stunned and just as shocked as she.

15

Pyrenees Visit

Expressway A64 is deserted. My car speeds along like a vessel launched on a nonreturn trajectory. Toulouse is left far behind, I went past Saint Gaudens a little while ago, and I'm approaching my goal. On my left a countryside of great beauty. Some peaks of the first Pyrenean ridges graze sparse clouds. The sun remains the master, and a cobalt blue sky predominates. My mind, turned meditative by the driving, does not stop thinking of Alexander and all the revelations that followed my discovery of him over the previous several months. A ghost accompanies me now, like a memory that has its own life. Natacha feels it and begins to be alarmed by it. She watches out, both protective and at the same time uneasy. If this man is a little bit me, I don't want to hate him. And yet, everything that he represents ought to incite me to do so. What to do then? How to love what you detest in yourself? I don't want to devote years to the research work on Alexander—it's beginning to be . . . invasive. I don't want to remain in this between-two-lives. I need to get to the end of my relationship with him, heal, and cut away what needs to be cut away.

Charles Trang lives on the edge of a little village in the foothills of the Pyrenees. I arrive full of hope, totally fixated on these documents delivering to us the totality of their secrets, thanks both to Charles's mastery of German and his knowledge of historical and military terms.

I make the acquaintance of a pleasant man of Vietnamese origin, coming from a family of soldiers. He lives with his wife in a pretty house with a carefully tended garden. His own father served in the forces. Although he didn't choose that path, I understand better where his passion for military things comes from. The shelving in his office is loaded with an impressive collection of books. The passionate historian invites me to sit in his living room. I take out the copies of the files and open the military file to the first page. I've been waiting for this moment for months.

"We have already gone over these documents," I say, "but I would like us to go over them again because information that you might consider ordinary could for me be potentially important. I also need to know details that may appear insignificant in the life of this man . . . In fact, Charles, I don't know what I'm looking for, but each fragment of his journey helps me familiarize myself with him a little more. I need to understand."

"Yes, I see. We'll try to do our best. Could we go back over the family information? In the file there are several documents that provide precise information."

"For example?"

"Well, the one that begins on page fifteen, for example."

I go through the pages up to where Charles has indicated. A form dated January 1942. Charles looks over it, gliding his finger along from top to bottom.

"Here, Alexander's widow is mentioned: Luise Herrmann, maiden name Miller, born December 2, 1918, at Arolsen, married to Alexander May 10, 1940. Below there is a line 'Kinder,' meaning 'child,' with just a dash. That indicates, obviously, they didn't have a child . . . "

"Can we be sure of that?"

The little girl from my dream often comes into my mind. Along with the other man that I felt to be close to Alexander, she makes up one of the two strong elements of my experience for which I haven't yet had a confirmation. I let Charles know about that.

"Several documents were drawn up after Alexander's death and were concerned about the provision of a widow's pension to Luise. Also, if there were a child to look after, no doubt it will be mentioned. And we'll find it," said Charles, plunging once again into the printed pages.

"Look, here there is mention of Alexander's father. He was called Otto. Otto Herrmann. Here's his address: Martin Mutschmannstrasse 4, in Plauen. Alexander's mother was called Hedwig . . . Theis was her maiden name . . . Hedwig Theis. Ah. On this page there's an address beside the widow's name. You see . . . here: Luise Herrmann, Arolsen, Bahnhofstrasse 45. Arolsen is a little town in the center of Germany. I saw somewhere, on another page, the age of his parents. And look at this line, Alexander had a brother."

"A brother?"

"Yes. Alfred Herrmann. It specifies that he's twenty-seven years old . . . That makes him five years older than Alexander. A doctor, it says here . . . And during the war, he served in the Wehrmacht, the German army. Now coming back to Alexander's wife, in the marriage folder I saw other details—you have it here?"

"Yes, of course."

I hand him the volume. Charles takes it and turns the pages, looking for one in particular.

"Here we are. Luise's father was called Werner Miller and her mother, Hannah. The address is the same as that indicated for Luise in the other document . . . But no, the street is the same but not the number. The parents are at 52 while Luise lived at 45. It would be curious, but perhaps the Millers are still living there?"

The moment Charles makes this remark, I *feel* that it's the case. But my impression is so fine, so imperceptible that after having momentarily thought that I need to check it on Google, the idea flies out of my head and I forget it. Charles continues.

"Luise's father, Werner Miller, was forty-nine in 1939, and he was 'Automechaniker'; that is, a car mechanic. In the other document Luise states she met Alexander in April 1935 . . . I can't manage to decipher the two words handwritten above that."

We turn the pages slowly; sometimes silence falls. Charles reading, as I'm hanging on his words in search of a new element. The extensive and varied detail of the marriage folder is impressive. I learn that Alexander was 1.78 meters (5 feet 10 inches) tall and weighed 75.5 kilos (166 pounds). His eyes were blue, and his hair . . . hang on! Dark blond. The photo had misled me; Alexander really was blond, as in my dream! Dream in which he appeared muscular but tall and slender. This latter being the case as well.

Here we now have a seventh piece of information verified and proved correct: the color of his hair and his general physical appearance.

Luise was a woman 1.56 meters [(5 feet and 1 inch) tall weighing 49 kilos (108 pounds). Small compared to Alexander. Like him she was dark blonde, with light brown eyes. But why was Luise totally absent from my dream? Whereas the little blonde girl was so present . . .

"Ah, here is the social services document that contains the widow's pension information provided to Luise after Alexander's death. She received a widow's pension of 166.40 Reichsmarks and drew an allocation of 50 Reichsmarks. I don't know the difference between these two designations . . . But look, no other box is filled out. Here, the line 'Kinderzulage,' which means child allocation, is empty."

If a child was born from the marriage of Alexander and Luise, the child would have had the right to allocations as an orphan, and that would have appeared in this document. The little girl in my dream must not be Alexander's daughter. Officially, it seems more and more certain that Alexander did not have a child. Charles shares this conclusion, which I begin to resolve myself to as well.

"In this supporting document dated July 1942, the widow does not have a child. This is nine months after the death of her husband . . ."

"No legitimate child, that seems clear. I see that."

"On the other hand . . . wait. It seems to me I saw another document mentioning a daughter . . . Where was that?"

Charles goes through the pages and spends some time finding again what he was looking for. It was in the middle of the marriage folder in a rather long questionnaire filled out by Alexander on the family.

"Yes, here it is. On the questionnaire Alexander was replying to some genealogical questions . . . Look: opposite 'Geschwister,' which means children of the same parents, there is the symbol for a boy (a circle with an arrow above to the right) and the age, twenty-six years."

"That's his brother!"

"Yes. But here is what I was looking for: just below, on the line 'Geschwisterkinder,' there is only written the digit one with the symbol for a girl (a circle with a cross near the bottom)."

"What does Geschwisterkinder mean?"

"I'm not sure. For me it is also 'brother and sister,' but why dissociate this line from the one above, Geschwister? That's what I'm not too clear about . . . "

"What does the 'one' mean with this symbol then?" I ask suddenly, taken by a knot in the belly. The symbol is that of a girl. Is it about a sister? A half-sister?

"I don't know what to tell you," Charles replies, "but we need to dig further."

It's the first time in my life that I'm dissecting archival documents like this. With time and patience, the updating of our information is laborious but rewarding. We are going to work late into the day, as I preferred to spend the night before getting back on the road tomorrow morning at dawn, with hours of sound recordings and a thread much more complete and clearer about Alexander's life. I know now what he did, where he went. I'm just missing the "why." Why was he the only one of his family to have entered so young into the Nazi party? Neither his parents nor his older brother joined. Why, at sixteen, did he join the SS when Hitler had just been named chancellor? Why the SS and not the army? What was he looking for? What did he want? Some of these answers certainly must be found in Germany.

Once back in Paris, I take measures to try to find a journalist on the spot who might be able to help me in my research. The language barrier is a real nuisance. Just trying to consult online phone books to see if the Herrmanns are living in Plauen is laborious.

By chance my research has me discover a Dr. Alfred Herrmann in a copy of the Plauen phone book dating from the 1950s. Is this Alexander's brother? It must be the case—I can't believe there would be several doctors with the name Alfred Herrmann in such a small town! The address given is Dürerstrasse 1.

I am no further ahead. What to do with that?

The other address I have available is that of Alexander's parents: Martin Mutschmannstrasse 4. I spend a maddening amount of time before discovering that Martin Mutschmann was in fact a notorious Nazi and that the street evidently changed its name after the war to become Bärenstrasse.

Google tells me there is an art gallery at Bärenstrasse 4 in Plauen. I put my hands on a phone number and call. At the other end of the line, the person speaks as much English as I speak German. "I'm looking for a family that lived there at the beginning of the war . . . " The woman I'm speaking to doesn't understand me, and "Herrmann" doesn't seem to mean anything at all to her.

This is going to be complicated. Very complicated.

16

A Serious Lead

I'm cold. Summer is here, temperatures are high. But I'm cold. And I'm all the more astonished that Natacha is perfectly at ease just wearing a T-shirt, while I'm still wearing a wool sweater. Who's siphoning off my heat? My energy? "Guess!" exclaims Natacha. She doesn't like seeing Alexander making himself at home in my life. I have to admit that he is becoming very present, even in my dreams.

Among all the questions that overwhelm me, one niggles away at me more than the rest: how did he find me? Why would Alexander, dead in Russia in October 1941, come back in a French embryo conceived about Christmas time, 1967, in Paris? What logic is there in that? What is the connection between us? Why not be reborn in Germany? Or in Russia, near the place of his demise? Who gave him the ridiculous idea *to be reborn* to Jean-Pierre and Claude Allix, a young French couple living on Gay-Lussac Street, facing the Luxembourg Gardens? Did Alexander love his stay in France so much that he wanted *to return there*?

But an unexpected lead opens.

Once again it begins with an intuition. In the Pyrenees with Charles, I *knew* that I had to google the address of the family of Alexander's wife, in Arolsen. But I let several weeks go by before doing so, because stupidly I forgot. This adventure confirms for me the importance in having confidence in one's intuitions and following them.

It is through them that *someone* in the invisible world is assisting me.

Finally, I enter a search on Google Maps using "Arolsen, Bahnhofstrasse 52," and I discover to my great amazement an "Auto Miller" at that address: a car dealership and garage.

Luise's father, Werner Miller, was a car mechanic at Bahnhofstrasse 52 in Arolsen!

This can't be some chance coincidence.

I've found a link. I'm sure of it. It has to be the same family. Luise was born in 1918. It would be incredible if she were still alive, but it's not impossible. My brain explodes. Too many questions—I'm thrown for a loop. Obviously, I'm going to find traces of Luise. I'm feverish. I don't know what to do. I would like to phone, but who will I end up with? And how would I explain what I'm calling about?

I navigate to the website of the garage and discover confirmation that it existed before the war, and I consult biographies of those in charge. None of those mentioned on the site are named Miller, but the garage is obviously the one Luise's father owned. Are the Millers still the owners? I now have my first really serious lead. If listening to my urges I would leave immediately for Arolsen—seven hundred kilometers from here, or six hours of driving. I'm itching to go. What to do? Is this garage the one that belonged to Luise's father Werner Miller?

I'm going to phone.

Initially I make a choice of remaining evasive. I have to get some confirmation that someone in this garage knows or knew Luise, and then I'll travel there and explain everything in detail. On the phone, I'm not going to lie but say that I'm a Frenchman "related to" Luise's husband Alexander Herrmann. It's vague but not false . . .

I call. I have trouble making myself understood at the beginning, but then they pass me to one of the mechanics who speaks a little English. It's still hard going, but he understands the basics of what I'm saying.

"I'm looking for the daughter of Werner Miller."

"I'm sorry, but he's dead."

Why did he say "he" when I'm talking about a daughter? I decide to continue anyway.

"A long time ago?"

"Three years ago."

He can't be talking about Luise's father; he would have been 120 years old! Is it a son? A grandson? Or did he mean, "He died thirty years ago" instead of "He died three years ago?" Or is he just mixed up about his genders?

"Do you know his daughter?"

"No . . . "

"Luise Miller . . . "

"He is dead . . . "

But why "He is dead"? Clearly, he doesn't understand me.

"I'm looking for the children of Werner Miller. *Werner Miller kinder?*" I try in German . . .

"There weren't any. They're all dead."

There weren't any or are they all dead? I simplify my English sentences further. When I bring up the name of Luise, there is no reaction. This name doesn't seem to mean anything to him.

"And grandchildren? I'm looking for members of his family. I'm looking for the family of Werner Miller . . . Descendants."

"Why?"

"Because I have a connection with them. I am French, but I have a connection with this family, and I'm doing family research. I'm searching to contact descendants now."

"No. There's nobody here. I'm sorry."

We're not getting anywhere. I have to find some other way.

"I'll call back soon with the help of someone who speaks German."

"That would be good. Yes. Sorry," he says before hanging up.

I want to scream. It would be so easy if we were speaking the same language. Even when I was working in former Soviet republics of Central Asia on heroin trafficking it was simpler. The garage manager's name is Gunther Dittmar. The mechanic told me that he didn't speak

English either. I need to find a way to send him an email, and I ask a Swiss German friend to act as my translator. I send my French version to Sandra, who kindly sends me back the German text moments later. "Dear Sir. I am the person who phoned this morning from France. My name is Stéphane Allix and I'm looking for Mrs. Luise Miller whose husband's name was Herrmann. I have a connection with her husband. Luise Miller was born December 2, 1918 in Arolsen. She is the daughter of Werner and Hannah Miller. In 1940, she married Mr. Herrmann. I'm writing to you because Werner and Hannah Miller as well as Luise lived at Bahnhofstrasse 52 in Arolsen. I am now trying to contact Luise Miller, her descendants, or members of her family who knew her. Can you help me?"

Impatiently I await a reply! Did Luise die during the war? And if she didn't? Perhaps I will have all the keys within a few hours . . .

17

Radio Silence

Gunther Dittmar doesn't reply. Any more than did the Herrmanns of Plauen listed in the German white pages and whose email addresses I managed to find. The discovery of the garage freed up something in me. A kind of inhibition got thrown off, and after having sent my message to the owner of Auto Miller, I decided to list all the Herrmanns that I could find in Plauen or the environs and send them each an email. Based on the hypothesis that Alexander's brother survived the war, since I had found in the 1950s phone book a Dr. Alfred Herrmann, I threw myself into it, sending out calls for help like so many bottles thrown into the sea. Notably, I wrote to two women bearing the name Herrmann and listed in the directory as doctors. If Alfred survived, if he had children, if one of those children followed the same path as his father . . . In these "ifs" my immense hope is taking refuge. I'm entering a more active phase of research, and it's very exciting. "My name is Stéphane Allix and I am French. I am writing to you because I'm hoping to find close relatives of Dr. Alfred Herrmann, a doctor in Plauen. In 1940, his brother, Alexander, with whom I have a connection, married Luise Miller. I am hoping now to contact descendants of Dr. Alfred Herrmann or members of his family who knew him. Can you help me?"

But there you go. No answers. Not the next day. Not the day after that. And the month of August ends without a single sign reaching me from beyond the Rhine. I watch myself conducting my research in parallel, reading quantities of history books, and pursuing my exploratory reveries with the two archival files, finding that the town of Plauen, as is the case for all of Saxony, ended up in the Soviet zone after the fall of the Reich, then in East Germany from 1949 on. Arolsen, in contrast, was in West Germany. The town is now called Bad Arolsen. The prefix "Bad" in German designates towns with thermal spas. This designation, which is under state control, was conferred on Arolsen in 1997.

That Plauen and Arolsen ended up literally in different countries, a realization that never occurred to me before, makes me aware that the connections between Alexander's family and Luise's family must have been seriously complicated or even actually cut off completely if each family stayed in their town of origin. An ideological wall, then a very real concrete wall, in fact separated postwar Germany into two distinct entities that the Cold War kept separate for more than forty years. If we assume that Luise survived the war, did she remain in Arolsen, near her parents, which would seem most probable, or was she behind the iron curtain in Plauen, with her family of in-laws? Gunther Dittmar needs to answer me. Why doesn't he?

On August 27 I receive in the mail the commemorative work on the SS-Totenkopf Division written by a veteran and official historian of the division, Wolfgang Vopersal, entitled *Soldaten, Kämpfer, Kameraden* (Soldiers, fighters, comrades), that I ordered some weeks before from a bookstore in Düsseldorf. Published in several volumes, the large format work is in German and packed with operational details, photos, maps, and precious firsthand accounts. From the moment I open the package, time is forgotten. I turn each page, skimming diagonally all the text looking for the name Herrmann. This exercise takes me hours but ends up paying off well beyond my expectations: in the volume devoted to the campaign in France, on page 301, I come across "SS-Ostuf Hermann" under a photo showing six men. The image was taken in France in February 1941. I copy the caption text that goes with the photo into an online translator and get back the following: "Advance post at Bazas occupied by the 6th / SS-T.IR2 with members of the reinforced border surveillance service. In the photo: SS-Ostuf Hermann, fourth from the left (deceased). The purpose of the advance post is the control of the road between Savignac to the east and Grignols to the southeast of Bazas."

In spite of the spelling mistake in his name—there's an "r" missing in Herrmann—I verify in my documents that it is really him. Between his entry into France and during the months of occupation, Alexander several times changed assignment and duties, alternating between training periods and active service. The 6th Company of the 2nd Regiment is definitely the one where he served at the beginning of 1941 in France. It's him!

The fourth from the left.

He is seated and is wearing what looks like mitts; the cold was intense in February of that year, even in the southwest of France. He is in uniform, cap on his head, happy looking. I recognize the shape of his face, but once again the eyes are hidden in shadow. February 1941 is just before he leaves to take a company commander training course in Tours. He is stationed on the demarcation line as a section chief. Alexander is looking into the camera, and there is confidence in his pose . . .

This photo is one of the rare new elements from my research during the month of August. Only a single Herrmann has replied to me from Plauen, to say he has nothing to offer to my inquiry. The most painful, however, is the total silence from the Miller garage.

While waiting for the roadblock to clear, at the beginning of the school year, I turn once again to Marie-Pierre Dillenseger. Fascinated by my story since I first related it to her, she had proposed that we work together on the two astrological birth charts—are there observable correspondences between two beings from one life to another? This question interests her as much as it does me, and she devoted herself to looking into this experimental research during the summer.

18

The Guardian Angel
and the Warrior

Our session takes place at a distance. During this period, Marie-Pierre is in fact in her home on the East Coast of the United States. Right away, she lets me know that she ran into obstacles each time she began studying Alexander's energy chart.

"I feel a very unusual headache when I begin working on your . . . How to say? Your alter ego."

"How do you interpret that?"

"The pain appears at the back of the head. My skull is in a vice as soon as I let information approach. My understanding is that there needs to be less mental, less cerebral, and more 'leg.' In short, it's up to you to move out into the terrain, to get involved by asking Alexander for help."

"I'm willing, but what to begin with? Where do I go? Since I don't speak German, I'm trying to find a journalist locally to help me begin to explore the terrain . . . "

"And how is that going?"

"It keeps jamming. And it's laborious. None of the leads that my journalist friends have followed have come to anything. I don't understand it. I'm not able to find an assistant in Germany. It's always the wrong door, and everything falls through."

"It's because you have to get involved! Nobody can do this inquiry for you. The way I see it, everything will unblock if you get moving, if you go there . . . "

"Perhaps I have to throw myself into it without asking questions . . . "

"Yes! Get moving, and everything will unblock. You've got to go there! OK. Shall I give you the details of what came from my analysis nevertheless?"

"With pleasure. I can't wait . . . "

"The year we are in now, and even more the current month, is activating in him the energy of what I call the 'Celestial Noble'; that is, the energy of his guardian angel. It is precisely at this moment that you are paying attention to him. At a precise moment when his energetic fabric is associated with a protection, with the discovery of an allied force. In other words, you show up like a guardian angel, an ally for him."

"A guardian angel?"

"Yes, I know, it's a strange concept. Normally guardian angels are persons who are no longer in flesh and blood—spirits—who are watching out for the living. Now, in this case, he's the one who is dead and you are living. By setting in motion this inquiry on Alexander, even if it's connected to who you are, that makes you a protective force for this dead man. He needs you, Stéphane. He needs you in order to accomplish something."

"I don't understand. If Alexander was *me* in a former life, how can he need me to help him now? Is he *me*, or rather a spirit who is influencing me?"

"He's a part of you. But saying that he was another you seems simplistic to me. In my practice, we could say he has an energy that is coming back to you, an energy that has to be transmitted. In this present period of your life, you represent a potential help for him. A help to move forward on some unresolved issue. It's the current year that allows that to happen; you are not his guardian angel always and forever. You are being placed in a situation to play that role for him, just right now."

"So someone alive like me can be the guardian angel of a dead man. Someone alive can help someone dead?"

"Yes. Why not? He is lost. He needs your help. In my practice, the energy of the Celestial Noble is a form of protective energy. The name designates a substance that is acting; it is not an abstract concept. In you, since you began your research on him, you are moving into action. In traditional Chinese thought, you would be like an invisible ally for him, allowing him to advance. You are accompanying him."

"But you told me that I too have a guardian angel. Is it him?"

"I don't think so. The Celestial Noble appears in both of your energy charts and if, through your current actions, you embody this protective, activating energy for him, he, on the other hand, is not a guardian angel for you . . . I need to make clear that the Celestial Noble is however a little different from our Western idea of a guardian angel. The Celestial Noble is more a facilitator than a protection. It's a support, a bridge, a help, even when there is not necessarily danger but simply land to clear and work to do. Between Alexander and you, it's not a reciprocal helping. He needs you more than you need him. On the other hand, your own guardian angel is going to help you understand what Alexander has not resolved. But ultimately, in the long run, you are both in the service of something greater. In the end, the last word on your encounter, the revelatory word, will go beyond your two personal stories."

Understand what Alexander has not resolved . . .

Marie-Pierre's approach opens unexpected fields of thought and reflection. The role of the guardian angel, which I don't quite get, is a possibility that I had not envisioned.

But I am only at the beginning of my surprises.

"I'm finding also a sacred metaphysical connection between you . . . "

"Which means?"

"You both have what I call the 'metaphysical star.' Metaphysics predisposes people to question themselves on great questions of meaning—

the meaning of things, the meaning of the universe—and it provides also a particular intuition, an ability to see signs and decode them. You both carry this intuitive characteristic."

"That's funny. This is a side of myself that I am discovering and that I am more able to accept now. I have more confidence in my intuition since I began this inquiry. Besides, my encounter with Alexander happened in an intense moment of letting go on my part . . . "

"That doesn't surprise me. Another important point about it: his deep fabric is that of a fighter, a cuirassier—a metal-armored warrior—and in the month of August the energy of metal, which is very strong in him, is at its most powerful. He is born with a warrior's frame. He has to have been a good professional in his field. But also someone needing to be structured externally. He had no thirst for power for himself. He has no structural weakness, but his Achilles heel, and he does have one, is to be found in the region of the heart. Love distracts him and makes him vulnerable."

"I have the birth date of his wife, if you need it . . . "

"Ah. I didn't know he was married. Do you also have their marriage date?"

"Yes, it's May 10, 1940 . . . "

"May 10, 1940 . . . I immediately have goose bumps," Marie-Pierre tells me.

"Goose bumps?"

"Yes, they've become an internal signal confirming for me that the information that I'm identifying is relevant. It confirms for me the accuracy of my analysis indicating that one of Alexander's fragilities is to be found in the relationship within the couple."

"Hang on . . . I'm looking for her birth date."

"You can send it to me later . . . So May 10, 1940 . . . And he died in 1941—shortly after his marriage . . . "

"In October 1941, yes, fifteen months later . . . OK, here we are: his wife was born December 2, 1918."

"December 2, 1918 . . . What's her name?"

"Luise . . . Luise Miller."

Marie-Pierre remains silent for a few moments, working out her calculations as she integrates these last elements that I have just provided; then she goes on with her explanations.

"OK. I suspect that this marriage was what allowed him to be seen in a good light by his hierarchy. However, I have the feeling that this union leaves aside a woman he loved who was not the one he married. From that there arises a fragility which puts him in danger on the battlefield."

"But how are you able to see that? How do you know that he loves a person other than the one he married? Is that really in his chart?"

"In Alexander's chart, the energy corresponding to the couple is thwarted. Two forces precisely, linked respectively to his month and day of birth, are clashing, and this reveals the presence of an external influence that is shaking up the energy available for a straightforward couple relationship. This is a permanent flaw in him. This man could not have an expansive, flourishing relationship in a couple . . . and besides, his wife's date of birth confirms for me even more the unsuitability between them. Their marriage is a marriage for show . . . "

"I can perfectly well accept that you can diagnose that he's not equipped for a healthy couple relationship, but why talk about another love? How do you see that he loved someone else?"

"Because there is a strong offset between the metal of the warrior that he has and another force that inhabits him as well. This other force is very deep in his chart. The energy in question is feminine. This energy has been there for a long time and predisposes him to an affinity with someone else. An affinity that was already there at the time of his marriage."

"I must confess I find it hard to understand how you can be so precise . . . "

"I'll try to be clearer. I'm basing this on an analysis that is very subtle but at the same time very logical and deductive. Let's continue. You are acquainted with the analogy of the feminine with yin and the masculine with yang?"

"Yes."

"This other energy that is very deep in Alexander is a feminine energy. It predisposes him to the possibility of deep affinity with another person who also embodies these yin qualities—therefore feminine."

"Is it necessarily a woman? Could it be a man?"

I am really upset by the detail of Marie-Pierre's analysis, because I'm still wondering about that part of my waking dream in which I saw this man who seemed to be so close to Alexander, so intimate. Marie-Pierre replies.

"This other person embodies yin qualities, but definitely it could just as well be a woman or a man. That I have no way of knowing. This deep affinity with the feminine has existed in Alexander for a long time; it comes from very deep within him. It is not even linked to sexual maturity and could be prior to that."

"So he is drawn to a person having feminine qualities, but he is condemned to see his marriage not working?"

"In short, yes. I cannot believe that he loved the woman he married. But beyond that . . . I wonder if he didn't marry just to make his promotion more likely. Is there any connection between marriage and promotion?"

"Yes. In the SS, it was strongly recommended to marry. To make a career it was necessary to start a family. And I don't know if it's linked, but he was promoted to the rank of Obersturmführer on April 20, 1940, and he was married May 10, less than three weeks later."

"You will continue to investigate this . . . To go on with the analysis of his energetic chart, I discovered both in the month and the hour of his birth the energy of mobility, of travel, of movement. That means that he had an interest in being elsewhere . . . This energy of mobility means that he was curious about cultures other than his own, which doesn't go well with Nazi doctrine."

"To say the least . . . It's not really curiosity for other cultures that led him to Russia . . . "

"Yes, but this energy of mobility makes of him someone who,

although being profoundly a warrior, is open to others, to the foreigner. Which is certainly the opposite of Nazi thought. In fact, I began to like this man a lot when I started to work on his chart because you can see hidden aspects that his official history doesn't tell you."

"I would be curious to discover them. What I know of him now from his files does not allow me to bring light to his intimate motivations. I know that his father was a merchant . . . "

"A merchant . . . I doubt that Alex was nourished from childhood with a resentment toward Jews, for example. I can perceive, from the analysis of his energetic field, that he is someone for whom appearances cover a humanity that you cannot see from the outside."

"This is also my intuition. Besides, he was not raised in a Nazi family. His parents as well as his brother never belonged to the party. All the same, Alexander joined the SS in adolescence. To enter the SS you don't just volunteer; you have to be politically motivated. There is something like a contradiction in that . . . "

"If you dig into this time period, no doubt you will understand better what he was going through in his early years. I'm coming back to the year 1941. No doubt he is selected by his superiors in this period? But he is sent to a territory that he did not choose . . . At the beginning of the year 1941, wasn't he transferred?"

"He is in France at this period up to during the month of May 1941, it seems to me.

"At the moment of the swing from 1940 to 1941, either January or February 1941, he is annoyed about his assignment. The fact of being in a foreign country pleases him, but he undergoes a change that doesn't suit him. He follows orders nevertheless, but he is asked either to go somewhere other than where he is or somewhere he doesn't want to go."

"But how can you see that?"

"It is in his energy chart—super clear."

" . . . I don't have the information."

Is it possible that he didn't want to leave France? The region of

Bazas, where he was photographed in February 1941? He's going to spend a year in France, between May 1940 and the spring of 1941, in rather pleasant circumstances, the total opposite of what he's going to experience in Russia.

"Take note and look into it . . . I would like now to come to the day of his death, because I discovered something very curious. On October 20, 1941, he is in an energy that connects him to heaven. If he had not died that day, he would have been in a situation to move higher, to be more in phase with his soul than his body. That corresponds typically in my practice to a moment where one changes the level of consciousness. Now, on this October 20, 1941, he really does change the level of consciousness because he dies."

"Obviously . . . "

"Besides that, I can see that he did not die from an act of bravery, but because he was weakened. Three different things weakened him: not being with the person he loves, the annoyance of his current assignment, and the fact of becoming aware of what he is participating in. Was there a particular battle on that October 20?"

"I don't know. I know only that for weeks, he was conducting fierce fighting with no respite. Very violent. Very bloody . . ."

"There wasn't a particular victory or defeat?"

"I don't know. I'll look into it."

"This is a day of dawning awareness for him. And a day of stepping back. I cannot go further for the moment but one thing is certain: on the day of his death he becomes aware of the limits of what he is experiencing in this incarnation. He understands also the consequences of his former acts, the limits of his individual freedom and of what he was able to decide for himself during his life."

"Meaning?"

"He leaves with a secret. The secret of his love for someone. But it's not only that. He leaves also with the impossibility of being active in relation to what he has just become aware of and which is linked to his individual freedom. Therefore, today, he obviously needs someone to clarify something that became 'dormant' at the moment of his death. He needs someone else in order to act. He dies unfulfilled."

He dies unfulfilled.

I'm distracted for a moment, lost in unconscious thought; then I come back to myself.

"Well, fine . . . but why me, then? Why did he appear to me? Why is it up to me to play this role for him? What do we have in common? What binds us together? Is there a part of him that has been transmitted to me in my current life?"

"I don't have any answers. It is striking, however, how, in your present life, you try to totally ignore the warrior in your makeup. We have already discussed this point together several times."

"Yes, that's true. And even before I left for Peru you recommended several times that I affirm this force more strongly . . . "

"This warrior energy is present in you. Because you were a warrior in a previous life, perhaps in several lives. For me it is striking to observe how you turn yourself inside out in not wanting to use it."

"If a part of me was Alexander before, obviously I don't want to become an SS officer! That would be abominable."

"Certainly, you have chosen to no longer be what he was. But true mastery consists in never needing to use these forces while at the same time being aware that you have them. Yes, you were a warrior. Yes, you don't have to be one in the current life. But as the need arises, you have to use this energy. And if you no longer know how to fight when you really need to, you're going to have to learn how over again. And to do that you will have to set off into a series of lives in order to go through a new learning process. This force—you have it now. This warrior energy is in both of you, in Alexander and in you. I see it as an obvious link, a very clear correspondence between you. An inheritance.

♦ ♦ ♦

In a few sentences, Marie-Pierre has just made a perfect synthesis of my life: since adolescence a permanent skirting around warrior violence. War attracts me like a magnet, but I have no intention of taking part in it in spite of a few initial hesitations.

From the beginning, I have been fascinated by the fighters but incapable of using violence myself, because deep down I intimately know its ineffectiveness. I don't think I've even participated in a single fight or brawl in my whole life.

And yet a part of me dreams of being a warrior, which in my eyes means a strong man, muscled, dangerous, able to neutralize any threat at all. Not corresponding to this image is a daily disappointment. And this does not become any more resolved as I age.

However, suddenly, everything becomes clear: I am attracted by the warrior side that Alexander and I possess like an ancient heritage. And I detest—and the word is weak—this facet of my being because I am impregnated with the memory of the horror that Alexander allowed himself to be pulled into by using it. So from now on I refuse to use this force, even when I ought to. I pass on my disordered thoughts to Marie-Pierre:

"This warrior energy is at the heart of my life. The soldiers, the fighters whom I have met in various war zones fascinate me. I admire their strength, their determination, their recklessness. Even physically, not being especially into sports, I've always felt guilty about not having a more developed body, about being an intellectual . . . For me, force must be physical . . . and then sometimes I have these dreams of war scenes where I'm killing people . . . "

"You're mixing things, Stéphane. Being a warrior doesn't mean being violent. I think that this inquiry is going to give you the possibility of fully appropriating to yourself all the facets of what a warrior really is. To appropriate the strength that is available to you in this life here and now. What is a warrior? Someone who conquers a territory or defends it. But whether this territory is physical or spiritual, is it really any different? Why would the physical be better than the spiritual?

At the same time as Marie-Pierre is explaining the essence of this warrior energy in me, I can't help making a parallel with the concept of the "way of the warrior" developed by the Tibetan master Chögyam Trungpa. I make this remark to her.

"What does he say when he speaks of the 'way of the warrior'?"

"He obviously doesn't speak of physical combat, because aggression is the source of our problems rather than their solution, but of spiritual posture. He engages us to clarify the roots of our mental confusion. For him, there is a fundamental human wisdom that can help us resolve the problems of the world. This wisdom is not the prerogative of one culture or one religion any more than it is exclusively from the West or from the East. It is in us. In each one of us. The heart of the art of the warrior is to face confidently everything that life presents to us."

"You see!" exclaims Marie-Pierre. "You can be a warrior without being a soldier. Rediscovering that is one of the great challenges of your life. No doubt this inquiry is going to allow you to make a better discernment between the warrior way of darkness into which Alexander fell and the warrior way that Trungpa describes and that is nothing but light."

"What you are saying is very strong. I love the idea! It's what has troubled me since childhood."

"Alexander died as a soldier, on a battlefield, but on a very particular day when he was accessing a dimension that has to do with awakening. And you as well, everything that you are doing in this current life is also in relation to this dimension of awakening. But you are no longer a warrior on a battlefield. I can see a very distinct correspondence between the two of you regarding the way in which he departed and what you are making of your life today. Did anything 'warrior-like' happen the day of your birth?"

"The events of May 1968 in France were coming to a head . . . "

"It was in May and you were born in August? That means that during the final months of gestation, you too were on the balcony watching the street battles and the hurling of paving stones?"

"You couldn't have said it better. My parents were living in Gay-Lussac Street in Paris—the epicenter of the confrontation. My mother remained cloistered on the sixth floor for much of the latter part of her pregnancy."

"Gay-Lussac Street was right in the middle of it!"

"Yes, at the heart of the Latin Quarter in revolt."

"Good. We don't have all the answers, but it's clear there are bottlenecks."

"Also it was a forceps delivery—I don't know if that is important."

"Yes, of course that counts . . . you were born with iron . . . as for him, he dies from a wound to the throat caused by an exploding shell . . . metal . . . "

I am cautious as we bring our discussion to a close. But stirred by the resurgence—again—of this warrior energy that constantly pursues me, even though today it has a more peaceful and constructive appearance. Alexander the warrior was taken into a spiral of darkness, and as for me, within another form of combat, I am fighting against commonly accepted ideas on how we see things, especially the question of death.

Alexander, a warrior who lost his way, and I, a warrior for the light.

What am I to think about all that? Marie-Pierre's analysis is rich and brings together information of very diverse kinds. Certain aspects of this information speak to me with clarity. Other aspects are impossible to confirm or contradict given the state of what I know: Alexander couldn't have married the person he loved. He kept a secret, a secret love. Within the fanatic SS tribe an open and curious being was hiding. How to verify such assertions? I have to meet someone who knew him.

Marie-Pierre suggests, moreover, that I speak to Alexander as to a being who is present outside of me and ask him for help, as a way of getting myself going. It's true that I feel more and more that a part of him is still living *somewhere*, just as a part of Thomas or my dad is. Whether or not there is a continuity between him and me does not mean that a part of him does not continue to live independently as an individual. That seems paradoxical when you think of reincarnation as the passage of one soul from life to life, but I feel that Alexander exists outside of me. So I've gotten into the habit of speaking to him aloud. When I'm alone. "I need you to help me. Present persons to me on my path who will allow me to see more clearly at each step in our relationship. Help me, Alexander."

A few days later, on September 2, I receive the reply from the Miller garage that I had been hoping for so ardently. The owner writes me. He was on vacation, which was why he hadn't replied. Gunther Dittmar sends me this short message in English, "Hello. I am the son of Karl Dittmar and Birgit Dittmar, maiden name Miller. Luise Miller was my aunt and my mother's sister. I am the last descendant of Luise Miller. And you? Are you a descendant of Luise's husband, Herrmann?"

Following the joy I felt reading this message, how am I to reply? How is the German garage owner going to react? "Hello. I am perhaps the reincarnation of the SS husband of your aunt. You OK with that?" Terrified at the idea of committing a blunder and seeing this, barely open, extraordinary path snap shut again, I let a day go by before finally deciding to remain evasive in our exchanges.

Once I'm with him, I'll confess the nature of my link with Alexander. But first of all: get an appointment. Let's be cautious. "Dear Mr. Dittmar. I'm so grateful for your reply. Yes, I have recently discovered I have links with Alexander Herrmann and I am conducting research on him. I am planning to come to Germany in mid-September in order to visit various places, notably the town of Plauen where he was born. I also hope to come to Bad Arolsen, and would be happy to meet you. I am seeking to know more about him and his life. I'm also planning to go to Russia this October to the place where he died on October 20, 1941. Would it be possible to meet you around September 17 or 18?"

With this message, I show him that I know Alexander, that I know when and where he died, and I tell him that I will be in Germany very soon. I fervently pray to all the forces of the invisible world to ensure that this man is open to what I'm preparing to announce to him. May doing so encourage him to want to help me.

His reply came very quickly: "Dear Sir: My family and I are excited at the idea of meeting you in Bad Arolsen. I don't speak either English or French, but my son will be present and will help us by translating."

I leave immediately for Germany.

19

Bad Arolsen

During my life I have been aware of the existence of other times and other spaces. I felt in myself memories other than my own. But never before has that been so clear, so powerful, so obvious, so disturbing.

All the water in the world comes crashing down on the north of Europe when I take the opposite direction that Alexander and the Totenkopf Division followed in May 1940 coming into France. An interminable time getting out of Paris, day is breaking as I pass Compiègne, then a gray dawn slowly replaces the darkness that was hiding from my eyes the sadness of the countryside. I cross the Belgian border west of Mons in a downpour, driving carefully on a bad expressway. Charleroi, Namur, and so on. Toward Liège, traffic is heavy and the rain remains just as violent when there comes back into my memory a fragment of a dream from the night before, a night that was, as it turns out, short and troubled, punctuated by waking up numerous times. It's an image that must be part of a more detailed dream—an image of a small-sized cannon, more precisely a cannon mounting. I see the barrel, I see the shell that is placed inside it. Just at the moment that I am surprised by the memory of this dream while I'm zooming along at high speed, an ambulance passes me with all its sirens screaming.

Cannon, shell, ambulance sirens.

For several weeks now, I have the sensation of living between two times: the present time and the period between 1930 and 1940. I am reading so many things that plunge me eighty years back in time. I think constantly of Alexander, every day, every evening so that a part of my mind is carried into the past while my body, in contrast, moves around in the present. My dreams seem more vivid, and my day-to-day is colored by an increasing number of synchronicities, some lightweight like this dream fragment, some more dense and disturbing.

I am struck by a strange sensation as I leave Belgium for Germany.

I guess that I've crossed an invisible border when I notice that the language of the expressway road signs has changed. Aachen, Köln, Dortmund. This western part of the country is heavily populated, and being in traffic is tiring.

But I am happy to be on my way.

This is the first time *in my life* that I'm going to Germany.

I have traveled in Belgium, Switzerland, Holland, all around Germany, but never in Germany. I have never been interested in the language, never wanted to go to this country; it has always remained distant and unfamiliar. A guardian angel, it seems, has kept me at a distance. I wasn't *to return there* before consciously having access to this very troubling memory. I had to be prepared and strong. And today, finally, I am moving into it. I am joyful to be on this Earth. I'm looking forward enormously to the coming days. What's happening to me is incredible.

A little before Kassel, I take exit 64 and head straight south toward Bad Arolsen. In the fifteen kilometers that I still have to cover before reaching the native town of Luise Herrmann, maiden name Miller, I find myself in a countryside of rolling hills. The rain has stopped, the sun has reappeared, and the beauty of the environment impresses me with its autumn colors. In spite of being tired from driving, I am watchful for any feeling of dèjà-vu that might emerge in me, going around a bend in the road, before the appearance of such and such a field or valley, or this portion of forest with its pine branches stretching out from massive trunks. But nothing of the kind happens.

And then, here I am in Bad Arolsen. A little provincial town with farmhouses. Strange impression. I find the hotel Zum Holländer very easily, where I have a reservation for the night. It is located right in front of the magnificent baroque chateau erected at the beginning of the eighteenth century by the Prince of Waldeck. It is one of the attractions of the town.

I am tired, I have a headache, but I want to stretch my legs by wandering around the town. I put my things in my room and go out again immediately. Eyes wide, I feel both excited and touched.

Leaving the hotel, I go left in the direction of the garage, which is a short kilometer away. I really get into walking. The sky is cloudy again, the street is still very quiet. I proceed in this way a few hundred meters until I come to a small square where the town church is perched.

I cannot say that I *recognize* anything at all; nevertheless, the place, the houses don't seem foreign to me. How can I describe that? Often, when I am discovering a country or a town that I've never been to before, I experience this feeling of not being at home, an imperceptible sensation of discomfort and disorientation. But in this case, in walking to this church, I do not have this loss of orientation, this slight confusion. I'm aware that I'm not at home, I don't recognize the houses and the streets, but there is a kind of proximity, a feeling of ease. I feel comfortable here. I don't feel lost. That's it—I don't feel *lost*.

The town square and the church that was built in the middle of it break up a major straight-line thoroughfare. The eastern part that I was walking along is called Schlosstrasse. It begins a little before my hotel on a level with the chateau. To the west of the church, the street becomes Bahnhofstrasse, and the garage is located halfway along it. The church, which is built of dark red stone, is an evangelical church. Luise stated in several of the documents in the marriage folder that she was of the evangelical faith. She must then have attended this church located less than six hundred meters from her home. Luise walked on this square. She entered and prayed inside this building very many times. Did she take Alexander there? Would they have been married there? Here, right in front of me? We would then be separated by only a few meters and a few decades. So close, so far.

I feel that Alexander was here. That he breathed the air of this street, saw the worn walls of this church. Alexander was here. Proud, with Luise on his arm. It's odd—I find myself hesitating to use the term "in love." When I imagine them I do not feel a sensation of love within me. Was such a feeling unknown to him? Am I being influenced by what Marie-Pierre said to me? No—at this moment I no longer have her words in mind—I am cradled by a time and memories that are not my own. Under the sole influence of the living memory of a dead man. A man for whom love was too distant from his concerns, from his ambition, from his life. What room could there be for a woman in his existence at the service of the Black Order? Luise stirred an emotion in him, but no passion. Passion was something he kept for the war. That's what I feel—deeply.

Night is approaching, but I decide to press on to the garage. How can I wait for tomorrow when I'm a few minutes away on foot? The houses are big three-story buildings. A lot of shops. Is this prewar architecture?

And then, in the distance, there is the Miller garage. At this hour, it's already closed. The main building is modern, but the central structure is older. A provincial car dealer. It's really odd to find myself here. Facing this ordinary storefront. In this town that was still unknown a few weeks before and that now is the center of everything. A place that is foreign to me and yet so important. Night has fallen, the street is peaceful, and I am stirred by something indefinable. Alexander came here. I am sure that is the case. And it is he who has led me here. Now I just have to understand why.

Opposite the garage, on the other side of the street, is number 45, which was, according to the archival documents in my possession, Luise's residence. It's a big house identical to all the others. It must be divided up into several apartments. Did Luise live opposite her father's garage? Was this the family house?

I'm standing still—motionless in the middle of a deserted street.

A little distracted. Distressed by the turn my life has taken since my waking dream in Peru. A part of my mind in the present, looking at the closed garage and part of the street lit by the lampposts; another part in the past with Alexander, right up against him, looking through his eyes as if the time elapsed between our two lives simply no longer existed. Two lives, two realities separated by a few microns of a thin sheet of gold. Nothing separates us in this moment, and he is *reliving* this through me. In front of a garage in Germany while darkness falls around me and a few drops of rain moisten the skin on my face, I am touching a reality that is indescribable.

I slowly walk back to my hotel. Melancholy.

I don't manage to extract myself from this dissociative state that I'm now immersed in. But rather than its being a handicap or upsetting, it has the effect of having me live in a kind of heightened reality. I'm not suffering from it, nor am I frightened by it. It's a complement, a new perception that is enriching my reality. That doubles it. At moments I am literally in two time periods at the same time. I am able to be aware of it very clearly even though it is accompanied by new emotions. I am sufficiently balanced to not be submerged or to lose my concept of what is real.

I am physically in the current time period, while my mind, in frequent flashes, has access to the prewar period. In order for the power of the world of the past to appear as an overlay on my awareness, I need only let myself move a little toward reverie, keeping my gaze unfocused, and no longer fixing my attention too much on any detail in physical reality.

The two time periods then overlay each other with equally clear definition.

As if the past were becoming real, with its own sensations, its fragments of information, and scraps of memories that don't belong to me but *come back* to me as if they were mine.

I have just experienced this forcefully in the street.

The phenomenon continues in the hotel restaurant.

Seated at the back of the room, I look around at the other tables where several customers are chatting quietly. The scene is very sharp, clear, and then suddenly I imagine these same people dressed in 1930s style. The men wearing uniforms from the past. And I begin to question who they would have been in 1936, in 1940. What would have been the life of this fine-featured man with such a serious voice sitting opposite me with his two friends. Today he must be a sales representative, but I visualize him in an SS uniform. There then emanates from him something terrible and alarming. A threat. I take stock of how, in this same restaurant, at the end of the 1930s, if I had been a Jewish customer, I would amount to nothing for such a man. I would no longer be a human being in his eyes, and I would be considered to be sub-human—an Untermensch. In mortal danger. This young man, even though pleasant and apparently likable, would find nothing objectionable in having me exterminated. How is such a thing possible?

There comes back into my memory now the passage in Primo Levi's book, *If This Is a Man,* where the author evokes the moment when he finds himself face to face with a German officer, Dr. Pannwitz, while he is interned at Auschwitz. An Italian Jew facing a German officer. Two men, two Europeans who share the same profession, but who are separated by an unbridgeable gulf: "When he had finished writing, he raised his eyes and fixed his look on me. . . . His look was not that of one man to another; and if I were able to explain in depth the nature of this look, exchanged as if through the glass of an aquarium between two beings belonging to two different worlds, I would at the same time be able to explain the essence of the great madness of the Third Reich."[1]

I sense that this gulf, this threat is still present in the hotel restaurant. It is close, contemporary, even if everyone today puts on the proper face of thinking otherwise. It is there, sleeping, in every man. Next to nothing is needed to awaken the blackest tendencies, tendencies that sprang to life barely eighty years ago in so many men and women, parents and grandparents of those around me in this room. This same vile face appeared also in France in those who denounced their neighbors and who participated in the deportation of Jews with the kind of satisfaction felt by those cowards who were *respecting the law*. And it appeared too in this huge silent majority who accommodated themselves to the occupation and its retinue of persecutions, just as we can accommodate ourselves to anything so long as our immediate comfort is not threatened. These are normal people who can so easily become monsters, without even being aware of it.

Has this "silent majority"—in Bad Arolsen, Berlin, Paris, or anywhere else—drawn any lesson from history? No. The idea that the monstrosities of the past will prevent the following generations from repeating them is a comfortable modern myth. Ceaselessly, we revive the same mistakes. Hatred still sweeps away whole nations. Those who live with the sweet thought that such a drama will not happen again cradle themselves with illusion. Because serious crises have already brought to light the same demons (Cambodia, Yugoslavia, Burma, Iraq, Syria—the list is too long!). They will reappear around a conflict, and no one will be expecting it.

During our discussions, I felt that Samuel Pisar, the Auschwitz survivor I had spoken with, was anxious and alarmed at the idea that the horror that had engulfed them—he and his family—was threatening once again to reappear.

Because these monsters sleep in the hearts of men.

Pisar wrote, "A society does not have to be crazy for the leaders to engage in demented politics. The nation that gave the world Gutenberg, Beethoven, Goethe did not swing into a delirium but was only consensual when, through democratic elections, it allowed its destiny to fall into Hitler's hands, having swept away the leaders who had no power to rectify the situation."[2]

We are not so different today from 1933.

It would be dangerous to relax into any false assurance.

The vile monster is not dead.

Our political institutions are perhaps more solid, our longer experience of democracy provides us with greater confidence in our collective maturity, but we must never abandon our watchfulness. The very structure of our world is fragile, so fragile.

This evening, in this restaurant, I am fearful. Fearful because the thoughts, the prejudices, the fears, and the faces of the men I am living with on this planet are the same today as those of eighty years ago. My mind is looking at the two eras. They are so similar . . .

I fall asleep exhausted and feverish, with a stabbing pain in my head.

20

Luise's Great-Nephew

Rough night waking numerous times with the memory of a string of dream fragments. Fleeting impression that I'm being *shown things,* but once up and about it all disappears from my awareness.

I'm up early. The sun is shining brightly on Bad Arolsen. My appointment with Gunther Dittmar was set for 2:00 p.m., so I need to busy myself until then. Not easy. When so much hope is invested in a meeting, time has a tendency to slow down. I decide to wander around the town to see if other spots would awaken reminiscences in me.

Leaving the hotel, I turn right in the direction of the chateau, and then I head up under the canopy of majestic trees on the Grosse Allee. I stroll along, allowing chance to carry me through this treed part of town. Some of the oak trees that I pass have massive, solemn trunks. My footsteps resound on the asphalted walkway that runs parallel to the street. I approach one of the most imposing trees. Its trunk is vigorous, and it rises up far higher than the other trees. A need to touch it, to greet it, and to ask it for help. Given its splendor, it must have already been old even before the birth of Alexander and Luise. My hand against its bark, my eyelids close and *I imagine* the couple walking together right here where I am. Alexander is wearing his black uniform, feeling the same pride as a child dressed in his first Zorro costume. Luise is walking at his side, deferential and admiring. She is nearly twenty-five centimeters shorter than he is. Alexander can show off his vanity and contemplate the effect that his belonging to the Black Order produces in the moistening eyes of Luise. He is also pleased to detect fear mixed with respect in the eyes of the passersby. Here he fully savors his pride, accompanied by a woman a head shorter than himself, displaying his powerful uniform, clicking his heels on the pavement of the walkway: sharp sounds of his steps, the martial air, the straight back, young and already an officer in a prestigious unit, the elite of his time.

As I'm moving away from the tree, I notice that a woman is looking at me, smiling. No doubt it's not usual to see a man in a suit murmuring to a tree. I walk up to her, and we engage in a conversation in English. I emphasize the majestic nature of the place.

"It was Prince Georg Friedrich who had these trees planted," she tells me.

"Prince Georg Friedrich?"

"Prince Georg Friedrich of Waldeck. In 1670, he had 880 oak trees planted in the alignment that you see here. The Grosse Allee is 1.6 kilometers long. It is the most beautiful avenue in the town."

"Very impressive. Thank you."

The lady walks on, and I continue my stroll in this welcoming spot. I don't feel lost. A man who had 880 oak trees planted has to have been a goodly man.

I am in front of the garage before 2:00 p.m.. I walk around for a while, and precisely at the appointed time I enter the reception area. I speak to the man behind the counter, telling him that I have an appointment with Gunther Dittmar. He gives me a strange look. Clearly he doesn't understand English, and he invites me to take a seat while he dives back into the clutter on his desk. Behind me the mechanics are returning from their lunch break and are getting back to work. After about twenty minutes, I tell myself that something is amiss. Did I get the address wrong? Or the time? When I question the man at reception again, he decides to make a phone call. Is it to Gunther? I don't know. He hangs up and motions me to wait. I sit down again, more and more frustrated.

Time ticks by some more, and then a woman accompanied by a young man comes through the garage door and, seeing me, approaches with a big smile. The young man speaks to me in English.

"Hello. I am Gunther Dittmar's son, and this is my mother."

Full of joy, I greet them.

"My father is not here today because your appointment was for October 17 . . . "

"October 17? That's not possible . . . "

Today is September 17.

I open my portable computer to check my email exchanges with Gunther, and actually in his last reply to me, he says that he is expecting me on . . . October 17 at 2:00 p.m. It's clear. In the previous email I told him that I would be in Germany on September 16 and 17, but I didn't even notice the change of month in his response. Besides, in mid-October I would be in Russia, so I thought it was clear that the appointment must be in September. I am very embarrassed. What a blunder! But Gunther's son is reassuring.

"I've just spoken to my father on the phone. He will cut short his appointment and be with us here in less than an hour."

"I'm really mixed up . . . For me it was so clear that I had written I was coming in September. I just didn't pay enough attention . . . "

I close my laptop, and the mother and son have the sensitivity to not heighten my embarrassment. However, I have no choice but to begin to recount my story before Gunther's arrival. His son and his wife seem impatient. Probably they are expecting an extraordinary tale, but a conventional one. How could it be anything else? For them, I have to have been the product of an adulterous affair of Alexander's in France. He would have met someone, would have had an illegitimate and secret child, and I am that son. Or grandson.

When I begin to recount how I had a waking dream on my trip to Peru . . . I see appear on their faces a kind of odd but polite reserve. Behind their eyes I imagine their two brains in full revolt. Even though I took care to relate beforehand my professional experience, which they clearly had the time to check out on the internet, they must be thinking that even though this French journalist seems quite respectable, what he's telling us makes no sense. I imagine the various scenarios that the son and Gunther's wife are probably in the process of developing at this very moment in order to bring some rational logic to my experience.

Speaking of out-of-the-ordinary phenomena with people who have never been interested in such things is always delicate. Having been deeply involved in it for so many years, I tend to forget that. We live in a society where the mind-set is very, very limited and where only a personal search allows certain individuals to discover a larger reality. Such questioning, which leads to a putting in question of the vision of the world acquired since childhood, is, in general, sparked by an "accident." An unexpected event in life that suddenly and quite simply makes the model within which existence has been flowing until then unsatisfactory. The loss of someone close to us that makes us question death and the meaning of life; a serious illness affecting a family member or ourselves and that leads to the same questioning.

In posing questions, you run the risk of getting answers. And the responses are capable of having us put our way of living into question.

Also, most people refrain from such questioning. Or only when they are forced and constrained to do so. The vast majority proceed through life without making waves, always putting off till later a study of the great existential enigmas. It's amazing, when you think about it, but it's the result of the conditioning in which we've all been raised. We are fearful beings, terrified of freedom.

Paradoxically, in spite of his youth, the son displays a certain inability to imagine that my story has even a tiny speck of reality. In contrast, his mother, Gunther's wife, in her fifties, offers a sincere smile and sparkling eyes. No doubt for the first time in her life she finds herself at the edge of an unknown world, and she is honestly intrigued. Here is a story that really does go beyond the ordinary. Why not? She listens to my words that her son translates for her, and soon both of them know the details of what happened to me in the Amazonian forest and what my inquiry has produced.

Now it's their turn to enlighten me. The son begins.

"Luise was my father's aunt, which he no doubt told you. She died of cancer in 1975."

Something gives way inside of me: 1975, more than forty years ago!

"Were you acquainted with her?" I ask of the mother.

"No. I was only ten years old at the time, and obviously I had not yet met Gunther."

I do the math. Luise died at fifty-seven. We continue our discussion, but it rapidly becomes clear that neither Gunther's wife nor son knows much more about this lady who died so many years ago, and even less about her husband Alexander. We engage in chitchat while waiting for Gunther to join us. Time lags, and embarrassed pauses punctuate our exchanges. Finally, Gunther arrives after more than an hour. Well into his fifties, the man is very jovial and outgoing. I let his son provide a summary of my story. He doesn't seem too surprised, but even so he doesn't take what I'm telling him to be hard facts either.

"You're a journalist," he asks me.

"Yes . . ."

"I recognize your face. We did some searches on internet and I saw your photo. Why are you here?"

"As your son must have told you, it's concerning a personal investigation. Following a dream in which I received all this information about Alexander Herrmann, I engaged in an inquiry and discovered that he had existed and that he had married Luise Miller, your aunt. And now I'm following up on these leads . . ."

"When did Alexander Herrmann die?"

"In 1941."

"Obviously, I never knew him," he said. "But I knew Luise."

"Really? What was she like?"

"She was a very elegant woman. Pretty, delicate, and always extremely well dressed. Careful of her personal appearance. She was extremely kind to me and my sister because she had no children of her own."

"I suspected that she actually had no children with Alexander," I say to him.

"She never had children, no, but she was married three times."

"Three times?"

"Yes, two other husbands after Alexander, but never any children."

"Did she sometimes speak about Alexander?"

"No . . . Well, I don't know much about it. You know, I was only fifteen when she died, and she was my aunt. Why would I have spoken to her about that? I only knew her third husband. She never spoke of Alexander Herrmann in my presence, and why would she have? When were they married?"

"May 10, 1940. I don't really know where. Did Luise live all her life in Bad Arolsen? In the documents that I have, mention is made of an address opposite the garage, number 45 on Bahnhofstrasse."

"Her apartment was there. She took up residence there during the war, probably after her marriage to Mr. Herrmann. I know that at one time she lived above the garage with her parents. No doubt that was before. She always worked in the garage. She even managed it after the death of her father, Werner."

"Do you have any contact with the Herrmann family in Plauen?"

"No. None at all."

"Do you know how Luise would have met Alexander?"

"No, I don't know. But there was an SS barracks in Bad Arolsen. Maybe he was there."

"During the year 1936, it is noted in his military folder that indeed he belonged to the SS-Germania Division. This was a purely military SS unit and an antecedent of the Waffen-SS. And in that year, he was stationed in Arolsen. But you don't know anything more about that?"

"No, but it's very likely that Alexander and Luise met at that time," Gunther suggests.

"In the marriage folder, Luise states that she met Alexander in

April 1935, and I don't know where Alexander was at that time. Where is the barracks located?"

"It's now a shopping center. The barracks no longer exist."

I begin to realize that, among the four of us, I no doubt know the most about Alexander. I don't know what I was expecting, but I had hoped it would be more than that. Photos, letters, information, personal effects? Answers . . .

"I would really like to see a photo of Luise and Alexander," I say.

"I seem to remember seeing a photo of Alexander in uniform," Gunther replies. "We must have a few photos of Luise, perhaps even one of Alexander. I'll have to look—they must be at home. But I have no idea where—you know how it is—family photos. Luise died in 1975, and her sister, my mother, in 1982. So where could we have put that away?"

"That would be terrific. When do you think you could take a look?"

Gunther doesn't hear my question since he's speaking with his wife. I don't dare interrupt their tête-à-tête. I feel that they want to help me by trying to find a lead, an image, something. After a while he turns toward me.

"Luise had a cousin who is still alive—she might know more."

"Can I meet her? I can stay longer in Bad Arolsen if necessary."

"She is very old," Gunther replies after a moment of hesitation. "We will have to ask her ourselves, and we'll keep you informed by email."

Having understood that they were going to undertake this little family investigation on their side, I present them with my deepest concerns on the matter.

"It seems to me that Luise, being widowed, must have received Alexander's personal effects. No doubt she would have kept letters. Things that belonged to him. Do you have an idea of who would have inherited that after her death?"

Gunther looks at me with a certain aggravation. He wants to dissuade me from having too much hope.

"I don't know if any such things could still be in the family today.

She died in 1975, you know . . . I think that we might perhaps have one or two photos but not much else. Everything else has disappeared. Perhaps you should check the Plauen phone book. No doubt members of his family are still living there."

"I'm going to Plauen tomorrow, but I had hoped that with Luise . . . I'm looking for more personal information on Alexander, items from his family life . . . "

"I understand, but we can't help you much more. We will look for photos and keep you updated by email."

We take our leave following what was a very pleasant and courteous meeting, but clearly this lead, on which I had placed so much hope, expired decades ago. As Natacha told me before my departure for Germany, I am the one today who has the most direct access to the memory of Alexander and his life. It's up to me to find *in myself* the answers that I'm looking for. But I'm still hopeful, and I take my leave of the Dittmar family with the feeling that they will help me if they can.

As I leave the city of the princes of Waldeck, Alexander is still guarding his mysteries. Apart from my deep feelings, I did not obtain any clear confirmation here. Did he come to Bad Arolsen to marry Luise? Did he live in the town with her? Why did they not have children? On this point, the fact that Luise never became a mother in spite of three marriages would lead one to think that she was unable to have children. That doesn't explain, however, why Luise did not appear in my waking dream whereas it was so rich in other details. Such as the little blonde-haired girl whose image is becoming more and more haunting. Who is she?

I leave disappointed, even though the tension that gripped me in Paris has calmed down. I had expected more sharing of private information: photos, letters, intimate details, and bits of his life. And I came up against a wall of silence and oblivion. I have to recognize that, for the Dittmar family, this uncle by marriage, an SS member who died in

1941, and this aunt Luise, who died forty years ago, are ancient history. But for me, they are present at my side on a daily basis. They are contemporary. They are alive. I have lightly touched their presences . . .

Departure at dawn. The road signs announce three hundred kilometers (3.5 hours) to Plauen.

21

Plauen

The Miller garage was my only somewhat tangible lead. As for Plauen, Alexander's town of birth, I have no plan, no idea. Just a printed list made before my departure from the German white pages website with listings for nine "Herrmanns" in the area of the town. And I also have the address of Alexander's parents before the war. Pretty thin. But I am confident. I'll go door to door if necessary. The goal: find a descendant, even a distant one.

I arrive at Plauen at lunchtime. As I leave the countryside behind and the first buildings of the town appear, I straighten my seat back and slow down, watchful and full of hope. Will I have a flash as I pick out a familiar spot? These first minutes in the town are so crucial: here is where Alexander was born! I don't want to miss a thing. The avenue I'm moving along is wide and has a double tramway track in the middle. The buildings on either side are elegant and well constructed—seven or eight stories—but every other one is abandoned. Doors and windows boarded up, broken windowpanes, sidewalks askew, decorative moldings crumbling, storefronts covered in graffiti. And few people on the streets. Even though it's Friday. The atmosphere throws me back into the last century. As if time had stopped before the German reunification and the town still bore the stamp of former Eastern Bloc countries. Apartment blocks devoid of signs or color, sad, dark facades of gray community living. Warmly dressed passersby move along like shadows. I feel a strong emotion. Here I am, after so many months, in the hometown of the ghost that I am harboring. My eyes, which have never before seen Plauen, recognize nothing, but in my heart and in the depths of my awareness, the town sparks a certain emotion. Which tells me that it's my dream that is leading me here.

The downtown area is more cheerful and alive. As if the whole population had assembled there.

My hotel is situated below city hall. I drive down and park in the parking garage and walk back up to reception. I immediately address myself to the young woman at reception because I don't want to waste these last few hours before the weekend.

"Can you help me?"

"Of course, go ahead," she replies.

"I'm a French journalist, and I've come to Plauen because I'm doing historical research on a man who lived here. Unfortunately, I don't speak German, and I need to hire someone to help me—a translator. Do you know of anyone?"

"What do you need?"

"I have a list of nine people to contact in order to find out if they belong to the family of the man that I'm researching."

The young woman says that she can think of several translators, but in the short term she offers to phone the Herrmanns that I have identified. What a good idea. I dig through my files and quickly hand her a copy of my list with the phone numbers.

"What should I say to them?" she asks.

"I'm looking for a man who died during the war and who was called Alexander Herrmann. He was born in Plauen."

"Alexander Herrmann?"

"Yes. With two r's and two n's. Let me write it out for you on the list. There you are. As well, this gentleman had a brother by the name of Alfred. I have good reason to believe that Alfred, who was a doctor, had a practice here in the 1950s. And therefore, I would like to know if one of these nine individuals on my list has a connection with Alexander or Alfred Herrmann. A descendant, even a distant one, is fine."

"As soon as I have a free moment I'll try to call. And I'll see about translators that I know . . . "

"Thank you. That's very kind of you. I'm going to get a bite to eat, and I'll return right after."

"When you come back after your lunch, perhaps I'll have some answers."

An inn is open just one hundred meters from the hotel. The Handelshaus guesthouse. As I walk into the beautiful dining room with its vaulted ceiling, I'm almost euphoric: how *easy* the entry into Plauen has been. Local décor: even the waitresses are in traditional attire. Wide skirts of heavy fabric, white cotton blouses with the sleeves turned up to reveal delicate forearms, period aprons tied at thin waists. I am once again catapulted into history in a new way. Thank God the menu has English translations. *Das ist gut!*

I take a seat at the only small table in the tavern. Thick white-washed columns support the whole building, which is several stories high. Between the columns there are big tables for whole families. On the walls a collection of random objects shares space with faded paintings, etchings, and old portraits representing people from the past. An ancient past before this terrible interlude that would be the Third Reich from 1933 to 1945. Scarcely thirteen years of an unspeakable plunge into horror. In this guesthouse, German history, from ancient times until today, quivers on the faces of those seated here to dine. But there was this breach, this brief moment with its terrifying consequences. This inn where I am now existed then, and perhaps Alexander came here to have a drink. Where is this part of history camouflaged? In what way is it still present in minds and memories? It will impregnate forever the history of Europe, and yet it is so unthinkable that it's as if we have all collectively forgotten the way in which we all ended up there.

It starts up again. Barely am I seated when I begin to imagine these jovial families, handsome couples who were chubby mites a few decades before, in the summer of 1941, for example. The German troops soar from victory to victory, and the Soviets are soon destroyed. The German Reich is at the peak of its power, and its territorial expansion seems impossible to stop. Who would be who? Who would do what? How many of these young men now eating would be in uniform? How many in the SS? These men, these women, happy in a prosperous country, would they be nothing more than just anxious to see their Führer engage in such a broad front? No. They would be proud. How could they say otherwise?

Here I am then, finally in Alexander's hometown. Where he was born and grew up. I can hardly believe it, but it really is the case. Plauen, in the Vogtland region. It was within the walls of this burg, twenty kilometers from the Czech border, that he lived, went to school, had friends, and enjoyed exciting times. It is here that the idea came to him to enter the SS. With other young men his own age he marched in these streets, full of high spirits, no doubt. Motivated, vengeful. So young in the springtime sun, whereas the future that was originally destined for him did not make him dream. All right, Alexander. I'm here. I'm in your hometown. Tell me why.

Back at the hotel, the young woman at reception had time to make three calls, but no one answered. Rather than waiting I decide to go immediately to see where Alexander's parents lived. Using the map provided by the hotel, I easily find my way. I have to go back up toward city hall and then follow the tramway tracks that cut across in the direction of the station, near the theater. One hundred meters farther, the avenue goes back up, and I follow it on the left, through a maze of little streets that climb up; the town is hilly.

And Bärenstrasse is there.

Alexander's street.

The street is very steep where it begins. I'm out of breath. Grand old properties with gardens line both sides. A deserted street. I arrive on the right-hand sidewalk, near number 2. I come to the following house, a massive three-story edifice in red brick. Number 4. Bärenstrasse number 4, formerly Martin Mutschmannstrasse 4, at the time of the Nazi regime.

Alexander's home.

The home of the man from my dream. It looks a little decrepit. The walls of red brick are worn, some bricks are broken. There must be several apartments on each floor. I am standing still in front of it, taking it in while waiting for something to emerge, a somersault out of memory. Nothing.

Having looked at each window, I walk to the entrance and ring several buzzers. The nameplate for the art gallery that I called, unsuccessfully, from Paris is attached to the right of the entrance. Unfortunately, the only two persons who answer don't speak English and refuse to open for me. What a bother to not speak this language! Silence, a light breeze on my burning face, and the door remains shut. Blood hammers away in my temples. I try a different buzzer. This time the caretaker answers. The lock clicks, and I push the door open and find myself in front of a glass door of a lodging being held ajar by some good woman with a suspicious air. Behind, her husband checks me out. I try English . . .

"Good day. I'm a French journalist. Didn't this street used to be called Martin Mutschmannstrasse?"

"*Nein* . . . "

She doesn't understand me.

"Martin Mutschmannstrasse?"

"*Nein* . . . "

I try something else, a name . . .

"*Herr . . . Herrmann? Otto und Hedwig Herrmann?*"

She doesn't blink. Her unfeigned lack of reaction shows that the name Herrmann means nothing to her. A string of incomprehensible sentences. But using gestures, I grasp that the lady is inviting me to ask at the workshop on the ground floor. I go back out onto the street, walk around the building, and discover that the entrance to a ceramic workshop is actually there but . . . closed. Looking up, I notice the fold of a curtain move behind the window above. The caretaker, taking care.

Back on the street I try my luck with each passerby. But they are few and far between. A young woman actually comes to number 4. She lets me know that the old woman who runs the ceramics shop has been living there for fifty years. And as for herself, neither Mutschmannstrasse nor Herrmann mean anything at all to her. She's too young and hasn't been there long.

I'll spend whatever time it takes, but I will make it into this house. I have come from so far.

I decide to bathe in the atmosphere of the place, and I walk back up the whole length of the street, which extends in a straight line for almost five hundred meters. At first there are other grand old buildings that look like Alexander's house, then some apartment blocks, and finally more modern buildings at the end of the street.

As I'm coming to the end and I turn back, suddenly I feel strange.

I am invaded by sadness, whereas I wasn't sad at all just ten minutes before. I feel that I've come to a dead end. I have no way of explaining this melancholy that is as sudden as it is unexpected.

My heart is blanketed in sadness.

The surroundings are *closed*. Heavy. Silence weighs down on the street. The place is not welcoming; in fact, I feel like crying. I hold back my tears. It's an emotion from the place itself, an emotion that lives there and that filters into my meridians. I have the feeling of penetrating into a depth. An ending. Without understanding why, this street fills me with sadness. I am not discouraged, no. I am struck down by a hurt that haunts this place. It's as if *it's all over, it's all finished.*

I walk back down the whole length of the street and then sit on a parapet, opposite Alexander's home. I take a few notes, trying to recapture the sensations that surprised me and whose meaning I want to understand. After a few minutes, a young woman parks beside me. As she's locking her car I approach and ask:

"Excuse me, do you speak English or French?"

"English, yes."

"I'm a journalist and I'm trying to find out what this street used to be called. During the war."

"I'm sorry. I don't know."

She walks toward the entrance to her building, the house facing Alexander's, and then stops.

"Well, I don't know, but the owners of my building might know."

"They reside here?"

"Yes. An elderly couple. They live on the ground floor. Wait a moment—I'll see if they're there."

The young woman returns in a moment, accompanied by the couple in question. The elderly man is thin but has a sporting energy about him. He and his wife are immediately very friendly. They are chuckling and even speak a little French.

"Yes, this street actually was Martin Mutschmannstrasse before," the man confirms for me.

They invite me into their place for a few minutes. Their kindness is touching, and soon I am telling them the broad outlines of my story. I feel right away that I can trust them. And my dream, my inquiry, my link with Alexander immediately fascinates them.

"My name is Claus Weisbach and this is my wife, Monika. You can trust that I believe you. I know strange things are possible. My grandfather had a dream that a bomb was going to fall on our house. This was well before the war, and no one took him seriously. However, during the Second World War, a bomb actually did crash into the house . . . and did not explode. Was it a premonitory dream? In any case, your dream with this Alexander Herrmann does not shock me."

Claus and Monika are caught up by the game. They want to help me.

"We know the owner well at number 4. Her name is Ilda, and she has lived there a long time. No doubt she knew the Herrmanns. She's close to ninety."

"Do you think I could see her now?"

"I was just about to leave for my exercise class," Claus tells me.

"It will only take a few minutes," his wife whispers.

So we leave their building and cross the street to Alexander's house. However, no response to the owner's buzzer. Ilda, the owner, is not answering.

"She is often in her garden, which is another part of town," Monika tells me.

And Claus adds, "We will try to reach her and will phone you once we have an appointment set up."

"That would be wonderful. I'm at the Hotel Am Strassberger Tor."

We return to their handsome, bright apartment so I can give them the hotel phone number. Claus puts his exercise equipment together, and I move toward the door with him. I don't want to overstay my welcome.

"Have you been living here since childhood?" I ask Claus.

"Yes, but I left East Germany in 1948 at the age of seventeen. My mother lived in this house since her birth in 1902. She always lived here."

"You were born in 1931!"

"Yes, I was a child during that whole period. I was very young when your Alexander lived there, and I have no memory of him or the occupants of number 4."

A living witness? He *could have run into* Alexander in the street!

"You or your mother obviously could have run into Alexander in the street," I remark.

"It's possible . . . I came back to Plauen only in 1995. I'm an architect. And can you imagine—I had to buy back my mother's house at city hall for ten times the price it had been sold to her for."

We agree to call each other a little later. Claus and Monika are exceedingly kind and obviously touched by my story. This couple are a gift; perhaps they will open for me what is closed. I go back toward downtown with a lighter heart. My sadness has flown away as if by magic. For not one second do I imagine the tempest I have set off in the red brick house at number 4.

22

The Tempest

It is still early, so I will continue my exploration of the town. But first a quick stop at the hotel to see how the receptionist is making out. Among the Herrmanns no one has replied. She confirms that this is not unusual—people are not necessarily home in the middle of the day. As well though, she gives me the names of three translators that she has dug up. I decide to call them in the evening if her further attempts continue to not bear fruit. Then I go out again immediately, having thanked her very warmly. I have one other address to visit: Dürerstrasse number 1. The address I found in the 1950 phone book for Dr. Alfred Herrmann.

The town of Plauen is not huge, and my hotel map shows me that Dürerstrasse is a little farther down from the hotel. I walk for barely a few minutes and arrive in front of a block of apartments that is entirely derelict. As if the area had been deserted by its inhabitants a long time before. The building at Dürerstrasse number 1 has four floors. It must have been a luxury building like most of those on the street, but now it is unoccupied and in a sorry state. Access from the street is blocked, and "Fuck" is scrawled on the door. The empty, tumbledown building is at the end of the street, at an intersection, like the prow of a dead ship. It smells of piss. No one comes here anymore, and Alexander's brother, if he really did live at this address, departed long ago.

I go back up toward the hotel, once again full of bitterness. My mood has been decidedly off since my arrival in Plauen. The slightest bump on my path affects me, like right now the dilapidated state of this building. Something is heavy here. Brutal. The atmosphere is dense. As much as Bad Arolsen was light and welcoming, in contrast Plauen is heavy. Plauen is a place you want to leave.

But this sensation is not mine.

It's an impression, a message, an indication, a measure sent by Alexander.

Alexander wanted to leave this place.

In Arolsen he was carried along and was happy. He could be expansive. Suddenly other questions well up. What role did Alexander's father Otto play in his departure for the SS? Was he fleeing from his father? Was it hard for him to be around his father? The sensation of freedom and expansiveness that I sensed yesterday in Bad Arolsen is no longer present here. In Plauen I feel the weight of the looks of others, judgment, and disapproval.

These thoughts crowd into my mind as I walk through streets that are more and more deserted. Dusk is approaching, and the inhabitants are hurrying home, as if the byways of the town had to be turned over to a number of beings, invisible and feared. Fragments of forgotten memories that are still alive, perhaps?

The young lady at reception left for the day without being able to reach anyone on my list. I have a quick dinner and retreat to my room to make an assessment of my day. As I'm putting my notes in order, the telephone rings.

"Good evening. I'm told you might be looking for a translator?"

A woman's voice. She's one of the three people recommended by the young woman at reception and has called me before I can call her.

"Yes. Thank you for calling."

I explain succinctly why I am here.

"Unfortunately, I'm not available this weekend, and if it's urgent for you, it's going to be complicated for me at the beginning of the week."

"I'm only in Plauen for a few days."

"I've been reserving this weekend for a long time . . . a birthday party."

"I understand. It's really very kind of you to have called . . . "

"I know a man who's a French teacher."

"Don't worry. I've been given other names besides yours."

"I know this man well, and his wife specializes in researching information on people."

"Really? That sounds like a good idea. How do I reach them?"

"His name is André Harnisch, but I don't have his number."

"What did you say the name was?"

"Harnisch. They must be in the phone book. I hope so . . . His wife's name is Andréa."

"Really? André and Andréa," I ask, not sure I had understood.

"Yes. That's it: André and Andréa Harnisch."

How considerate. This lady calls me to give me a helpful solution even though she's not available herself. I'm touched. I set out right away to find André Harnisch's number, but to my great distress, I can't find it on the internet. After fifteen minutes of fruitless attempts, I give up and tell myself that I have two other possible interpreters thanks to the receptionist. I will call them tomorrow morning.

Since my arrival, I have the impression both of being helped in an incredible way and, at the same time, being confronted with unaccustomed obstacles. As if the energies were heightened. On the one hand, this elderly couple who bend over backward for me; or this translator who takes the trouble to call a stranger in order to suggest a solution because she's not available herself; and, on the other hand, doors that close inexplicably, this brutal melancholy that knocks me down at certain moments . . . As if by approaching closer and closer to the goal, things tighten up, become strained. I feel very clearly two opposing forces. A force of inertia and a force of helping and opening. I need to stick with it, and be more watchful than I usually am so that I am not pulled down by discouragement.

And besides, I continue to feel the interweaving of eras. The 1930s are here, invisible, *present* in the current moment. As if linear time was no longer what was linking one event to another, but that these events were harmonized *differently*. By feeling, by awareness, I don't know . . . a link stronger than time. Walking around Plauen today, I was very aware that another era was accessible—Alexander's era . . .

As I'm getting ready for bed, I receive an email from Monika. She informs me that she and Claus still have not managed to contact Ilda, the owner of the red brick house. Their phone calls remain unanswered. What's even more odd, exclaims Monika, is that from their window they can see that there is a light on in Ilda's place. Monika concludes that she and Claus will try again tomorrow morning, and if Ilda still isn't answering, they will go and knock on her door.

It's so strange. Why doesn't this lady answer her phone when the lights are on in her place? I'm taken by some anxiety. I hope nothing has happened to her.

In the morning, Claus phones to let me know that Ilda has finally spoken to Monika and . . . she is refusing any contact with me. "Come to the house; I need to explain . . . "

On leaving the hotel, a new receptionist informs me that I had a call at 3:00 a.m., but the person asked to just leave a message so as not to wake me. I take the note and discover the phone number of André Harnisch that I was unable to find the day before. The message was left to me by this unavailable translator who gave me the name of the Harnischs last night. I cannot believe it. This woman is really knocking herself out for me.

"We were really upset that Ilda was not responding," Claus tells me.

At 10:00 a.m. I am once again in the large sunny living room in Claus and Monika's home.

"Tell me about it," I say.

"Ilda finally had a discussion with Monika this morning, and she doesn't want to meet you."

"That's odd. Do you know why?"

I'm rather annoyed. A promising new lead fading away. In fact, my only lead. Claus and Monika tell me that they didn't understand at first. They've known her for twenty years. And then the light dawned on them.

"This lady, Ilda, rented rooms to Helmut Rauca in this house. Have you heard this name before?"

"No. Who is he?"

"A Nazi war criminal involved in the massacres in the ghetto of Kaunas, in Lithuania. This man was originally from Plauen and, after the war, he lived in her house. Ilda confided in me this morning that when you rang her apartment yesterday, since she didn't know what you were saying, she thought you were tracking Rauca."

Helmut Rauca is indeed a sad personage. In October 1941 he was responsible for the massacre of more than eleven thousand Jews in the city of Kaunas, in Lithuania. He emigrated to Canada in 1950 and obtained citizenship in 1956. As a war criminal sought by West Germany, he was extradited in May 1983 and died in a Kassel prison, before his case came to trial in November of that year. My arrival at the house where he took refuge during the years following the war caused a welling up in this old lady of a period she thought was over, but the fears of which still haunted her. Claus confided in me that she spent the whole day shut away, not daring to answer the phone, her mind over-whelmed by a tempest of panic.

"Ilda belonged to Hitler Youth before the war," Claus noted.

The past lives on. It oozes through. It is here. Nauseatingly.

"I remember them marching in the streets at the time. She was an adolescent while I was still a child," Claus adds.

"Ilda has never acted like this since I have known her," declares Monika.

I understand now that this old lady took Rauca in for reasons I would prefer to not know about, but which I believe leave a web of sus-picion and paranoia today, so many years later, when death is approach-ing. The time of reckoning.

While we are discussing this, seated at their kitchen table, the telephone rings. Monika gets up to answer. I see a stunned expression on her face. She looks at her husband and hands him the receiver. As she sits down she says to me in a low voice, "It's Ilda."

The owner of the red brick house knows that I am with Claus and Monika. I came by car and parked right in front of their house. Suddenly an immense hope dawns anew. Has she changed her mind? In the thick of an animated discussion with her, Claus' eyes crinkle, impatient to share something with me. The phone call goes on and on. Monika and I remain silent, hanging on Claus's every word—and of which I understand not one bloody word. Finally, he hangs up and looks at me.

"She has just told me that there has never been an Otto Herrmann in her house."

"How can that be?"

"She lived there during the war and has never known a Herrmann in her building. But that's not all, Stéphane. She looked in an old phone book that she has and discovered that the Herrmanns lived at Martin Mutschmannstrasse 48a. And not at number 4."

Could this be possible? I take out my computer, open the folder containing Alexander's military files, select page number fifteen entitled "Bericht," on which there is a lot of data, including the name and address of Alexander's father. On this line I read, "Otto Herrmann, Plauen i.Vgt, Martin Mutschmannstrasse 4" But the "4" is right at the edge of the page. Has an "8a" been erased? Even enlarging to the maximum, nothing more becomes distinguishable. However, if this address is in a phone book it has to be the right one.

"In the file that I have, it is definitely 4 but perhaps there's a mistake—a typing error. Where is 48a on the street, Claus?"

"Much higher up, but all that part of the town was destroyed by Allied bombardment at the end of the war. None of the buildings from that period remain."

Claus opens several large drawers of architectural drawings and finally puts his hands on what he is looking for: a map of the city dating from 1939. He spreads it out on the kitchen table.

"You see, starting here, everything was razed."

His finger draws a circle into which a large part of the street disappears.

After having warmly thanked them for their help and having promised to keep them updated, I leave to do my own exploring. I walk back up the street until I encounter modern buildings. After that, there is a narrower walkway, then the street continues and ends along a little wooded hill. Above, a metal tower serves as a lookout point, and right behind, my map shows the location of the train station. In front of me, spanning a rapid transit track constructed on the rubble of a whole neighborhood that was swept away in a few hours, there is a kind of vacant lot: the site of 48a. Even though I had felt nothing in front of the red brick house, at least it had the advantage that it did exist. Here there is only abandoned land and parking spots. As I find myself at the end of Bärenstrasse, I remember that yesterday it was precisely here that I had been invaded by sadness, and I found myself almost on the edge of tears.

The spot where the *real* home was located.

My body had experienced a mysterious and untranslatable hurt when I passed by that spot, and then I went back toward a building that in the end had nothing to do with Alexander.

My body knows what my mind does not.

Taken by a sudden inspiration, standing in the street, I dial the phone number of André Harnisch, the French translator, a number that I had written on a scrap of paper and stuffed carelessly in my pocket. He picks up after three rings. Very considerately, he tells me that he's available this weekend. We agree to meet at the hotel thirty minutes later. He's coming with his wife.

23

Andréa and André

I'm in the lobby of the hotel for about five minutes when I see a couple in their sixties come through the glass door and look around as if trying to find someone. I wave my hand.

André comes across with gusto; his wife is more reserved. He speaks an excellent French—a language that he has taught during his career here in Plauen. She understands French but prefers to speak English. A francophone and a specialist in genealogical research—how could I have done any better than that!

Once again, I pass on the strange reasons that impelled me to come all the way here, noticing their reaction. She is respectful. André's eyes widen. Andréa puts on a smile that I have trouble interpreting, but they are both touched by my sincerity. Who's going to invent such a story?

André immediately proposes that we proceed methodically. He takes charge.

"You say you have a list of Herrmanns living in Plauen?"

"Yes, I have it here . . . "

Addressing us both, he continues.

"Andréa can try calling them now. We're looking for a descendant of . . . "

"Best to start with Alexander's brother Alfred . . . "

"Fine."

With my list in hand, he explains to Andréa what we just said.

143

Impatient, she tells him that she has already understood and is dialing the first number. André is very didactic and extremely efficient. They both correspond perfectly to the image I have of East Germany. An image no doubt loaded with somewhat silly prejudices. I'm aware, however, of their sincere desire to help me move forward.

The first person answers, Andréa asks several questions, then hangs up.

"False lead. The person has no connection for you. I'm calling the second."

Within a few minutes, several names on my list can be eliminated.

During this time, I take out my computer and show André the pages from Alexander's military folder, explaining that his parents lived in a part of the former Martin Mutschmannstrasse that was bombarded.

"Close to 75 percent of Plauen was destroyed at the end of the war," he tells me.

"Under what circumstances? When the Russians were advancing or during aerial bombardments?"

"The great majority of the destruction happened during a single unique enormous bombardment carried out by American and English planes. It was during the night on April 9 and 10, 1945. Plauen was razed to the ground that night. The town had been bombarded before but never to that extent.

"Seventy-five percent of the town?"

"The upper part of what today is Bärenstrasse is located near the train station. That's why it was especially targeted. At the end of the war Plauen had become a large production center for tanks. The Allies wanted to destroy it completely."

"OK. I've finished," Andréa interrupts us. "Five have no connection for you, and four are not answering."

Andréa seems to have an extremely smooth contact technique. I convey fully my admiration of her ease of maneuverability.

"I'm used to it from my genealogical work. You know, people are rather distrustful here. It's a holdover from Communist days."

"You're terrific. I hope that one of the numbers will come up with something. But it's possible that Alexander's parents or his brother, if they survived the war, moved to the West. That they left Plauen. That could also be the case with any possible descendants of Alfred, the brother, if there were any. What do you think?"

"That's right," Andréa interjects. "To be honest with you, I'm not very optimistic."

"Oh. Really?"

What to do? It's not only my lack of German that explains my difficulty in conducting this research. In general I am fairly gifted for this work. I have worked in difficult areas—heroin trafficking in the Middle East, for example. But with this research I am struck by my ineffectiveness. I don't know what to look for, how to continue . . .

"Show me that," asks Andréa, indicating my computer screen.

She approaches and, along with her husband, begins to read the archival pages in the military folder. Suddenly, I remember that with Charles Trang we were intrigued by the mention of a daughter in Alexander's family. We had wondered if it was Alexander's sister. I look up the page that is in the marriage folder. Locating it, I show it to Andréa.

"Yes, she was his niece," Andréa confirms immediately.

"How do you know that?"

"It has to be his brother's daughter. You see—this word Geschwisterkinder designates possible nieces or nephews. And beside the word there is a '1' with the feminine symbol. Your Alexander had a little niece."

I'm staring at the yellowed archival page. It's so easy when you're familiar with things. A big smile must have spread across my face when I raised my head and looked at Andréa.

"The '1' must be her age and the document dates from the beginning of August 1939. Alexander would then have had a one-year-old niece in August 1939?"

"Yes. She must have been born in 1938," Andréa concludes.

"And if I give you a copy of these documents, could you look through them?"

I am certain that numerous elements are still hiding in these files. With a little mischievous smile indicating she is already taken by the inquiry, Andréa takes out a USB key from her purse.

"Put them on here."

"Stéphane, here's what I would advise," André says to me. "My wife will return home with these documents and begin the research. During this time, I can tour you around the town. What do you say?"

I'm not super enthusiastic about a tourist walk through Plauen, but after all, I want to keep exploring the place, and what else is there to do? Since we're already partway through the Saturday, everything is going to close early in the afternoon, and Andréa will no doubt move ahead faster working on her own. We leave the hotel, and while Andréa catches a tram, André and I descend toward the downtown area and its historic treasures.

I am back at the hotel by the middle of the afternoon, and I discover a first email from Andréa, who is not wasting any time. At the same time as she was digging into the reading of my files, she was also conducting research using her professional resources as a genealogist, notably by consulting the town's digital archives. The results are impressive.

First of all, she confirms that the information found by the old lady in the red brick house is accurate: Otto Herrmann lived at number 48a Martin Mutschmannstrasse and not at number 4—definitive confirmation. However, he appears at this address only in 1939. Before that, in 1937, the father Otto as well as Alexander's brother Alfred—who is already referred to as a doctor—are recorded as being at a different address: Neundorfer Strasse 47. That is where they lived before the war, and that is where Alexander grew up.

It was in 1938 that Otto must have moved to Martin Mutschmannstrasse. At that date, Alexander had already been an SS member for several years and had left the family home.

In 1940 the situation is the same: Otto on Martin Mutschmannstrasse and Alfred still in the apartment on Neundorfer Strasse.

The same in 1941, the year of Alexander's death.

But surprise, from 1943 to 1944, there is only the name Hedwig, Otto's wife and Alexander's mother, who is listed as living in the apartment on Martin Mutschmannstrasse. And at this date it is noted that she is widowed. Alexander's father then must have died between 1941 and 1943.

When we move on to 1947 either Hedwig has died or she has left Plauen because there is no longer any listing for her.

In contrast, Alfred and his family then moved to Dürerstrasse number 1. They are still there in 1950, as I had discovered in Paris. Therefore, I have the confirmation that Alexander's brother and sister-in-law, whom we found was named Inge, were alive in 1950 and were living in this apartment block that is decrepit and abandoned lower down from my hotel. Alfred's medical office was located there as well.

Alfred, Inge, and their little daughter.

I can't stay put any longer, and after having looked up the location of Neundorfer Strasse, I rush out. That's where Alexander actually lived. In fact, when his parents, Otto and Hedwig, moved to Martin Mutschmannstrasse in 1939, the street that I had already visited, Alexander was in the barracks of the Black Order near Berlin. He never lived in the second location and must have been there only for a few visits to his parents. But the location where he spent his childhood and adolescence certainly was on Neundorfer Strasse.

This street is a major thoroughfare that I had already walked along. It goes down almost to city hall. Number 47 is located less than a kilometer away. I go on foot.

These addresses that get revealed as the inquiry proceeds take on an enormous importance in my eyes. Their discovery by Andréa constitutes the only really tangible elements in Plauen that link me to Alexander. I have the impression that I'm getting closer to him by discovering these biographical elements about his life and his family. Being in the area, it's possible for me to go there right away and breathe in the reality of these discoveries.

Once on the street, I walk steadily east. The road is on a slight incline upward.

I am nevertheless troubled about the discovery of the existence of this little niece. And even more troubled by the fact that in October 1941, the date of her uncle Alexander's death, she would have been the age of the child I saw in my dream.

If, as I now believe, each of the elements in the dream is important, the little girl is central because she reappeared several times with insistence, clarity, and force. Could it be Alfred and Inge's daughter that I saw? As I proceed toward the former family apartment, this intuition strengthens, and suddenly a certitude bursts into my mind: the little girl in my dream is Alexander's niece, and she is alive!

She is close to eighty, but she is still alive. Today she is somewhere in Germany. And I'm going to find her!

This lightning intuition seizes hold of me a few blocks away from where Alexander grew up.

24

Flashes

Here I am in front of number 47. Facing a five-story building with a yellow ochre facade. In places, the stucco has fallen off so the bricks underneath show through. Yet another empty and abandoned building. How sad, this town that life is leaving behind. Above the entrance doorway, the construction date is written into the white stucco coat of arms: 1908. The building must have been upscale at one time. Plaster frescoes and moldings in art nouveau style decorate the friezes above the windows. On the fourth-floor facade, on the left side of a window's frame, a beautiful winged woman runs her fingers through her hair, while on the right side of that window that she is stepping out from, a faun with cloven hooves tries to seduce her with the song of his flute. A representation of Pan and Selene.

Pan, a nature divinity, protector of shepherds and flocks, took pleasure in frightening travelers who strayed into the forest. Selene was the goddess of the moon, whom the Romans called Luna. A beautiful woman of sparkling whiteness riding through the sky on a silver chariot pulled by a pair of horses. She let herself be seduced by Pan.

The Herrmann family lived behind these windows.

On the fourth floor. They occupied the whole floor.

Was Alexander's room on the side of Selene or of Pan?

I approach the entrance door and shade my eyes trying to see something through the dark glass. I can make out a dark hallway. There is an opening toward the back. The ground is littered with dead leaves and old boxes.

Big drops of rain begin to fall. Several gray, threatening clouds scud across the blue sky blocking out the sun. I step onto the stoop and shelter myself in the doorway, my back up against the condemned door. Inexplicably, my mind keeps going back to the little girl. I am surprised by the irruption of this almost compulsive thought. I see once again the scene from the dream where Alexander is in the company of another man and this blonde child. The strength of the certainty with which I *feel* that this child is still alive surprises me.

And suddenly, it all becomes clear: this other man is his brother! It's Alfred.

In my dream, I felt that Alexander was experiencing a feeling of love toward him: "Suddenly he is near a lake in the countryside, and it is summer. He has his shirt off, and another man is lying on his stomach beside him—a man a little older whose face I can make out quite clearly. There is a strong connection between them. Are they lovers?"

However, what I had taken to be a homosexual attachment can in fact be the feeling of love for a brother. In this scene the two men are laughing, dressed only in civilian trousers and shirtless. They are on vacation near a lake. But of course! If this little blonde girl is Alexander's niece, it's suddenly obvious and clear: this other mysterious man must be his brother.

I'm going to find this little girl. I'm sure of it. She appeared because she is what connects me to Alexander. She is alive.

The short shower ends. I step off the stoop and take a few steps. I go up the street a couple of buildings more and then come back. I stand still once again in front of 47. It's odd; something holds me here. As if I don't want to leave, as if I don't want to move away. So I stay there, without forcing. Then I cross the street and stand on the other side, where I have a better overall view. On the wall of the building opposite Alexander's apartment block, there is graffiti written in French: "L'important, c'est l'amour." Nothing else but this sentence, clearly visible. No other graffiti the whole length of the street. There it is. In *French*! "What's important is love."

What's the message?

Well . . . perhaps just that: What's important is love!

I walk back across the street. Stay a while in front of the door to 47. I step back. I lift my head and examine the detail again of each frieze, Selene, Pan, and the other bas-reliefs. Is there a sign? A message waiting for me? A shadow, a movement, a gesture behind a window? After a long moment, I finally let my legs walk down the road, very slowly. I follow the sidewalk down to the first street . . . and there, instead of going on to the hotel, I turn right. Like a sleepwalker. My steps are slow. After fifty meters I arrive at a cross street. The street is called Pestalozzistrasse. And I turn right onto it, in the opposite direction to my hotel. I am in the process of circling around the whole apartment block that 47 is part of.

My steps are still slow, and as I'm moving forward, I notice a walkway on my right. It gives access to the inner gardens that are behind the buildings on Neundorfer Strasse and on Pestalozzistrasse. I walk in and discover ochre brick facades of the buildings that on the street side are coated in stucco.

These brick walls, these little courtyards, and these little gardens pull me in.

I can't take my eyes off this scene; I'm almost trembling, without understanding, magnetized by what I'm seeing.

I make my way precisely to the back of Alexander's building.

Walls of ochre brick.

Window, hallway door, weeds gone wild . . .

The back of 47.

I look. I feel deeply this visceral need to *not leave*.

Another very long moment follows where I finally am almost forced to reason with myself: "You can't stay here indefinitely!" So I return to the street, groggy, unsteady. Alexander existed, his family too. How can a dream have led me all the way here? Why? Hesitatingly, I continue back up Pestalozzistrasse. At the end of it, I turn right again and find myself once again on Neundorfer Strasse. A few more steps and once again I am in front of 47.

My little merry-go-round is about to repeat.

My reasoning orders me to return to the hotel. There is *nothing more to do* in this street! But it is as if by leaving I'm going to miss something. So I go back down once again and return to look at the backyard gardens.

No memory comes back to me. And that's normal. Why would I have kept memories? I'm not the one who lived here; it was Alexander. *Someone else.* The memories of this house are his. How would I have access to memories that belonged to him?

Here I am perceiving something else: sensations, an intimacy, and that is very different from a memory. I am even in the process of experiencing it in this very moment. It is more delicate, more incomprehensible, and unsettling.

The back of the house is *familiar.* And this is not just a light and evanescent impression. It's strong and intense enough to drag some tears of emotion out of me.

Night is falling when I finally make it back to the hotel. I have a quick dinner, then go up to turn in early, collapsing into the bed.

At dawn, I regain consciousness thinking that I heard someone knocking on my bedroom door. I know no one knocked but, with my mind still half asleep and the daylight peeping through the blinds, I did nevertheless *hear* something. Someone knocked on my door *in my dreams*.

Is it Alexander who has woken me up? It's almost 7:00 a.m., I get up. I turn on my laptop, and with one eye I watch the emails coming in while I put the kettle on to boil. Packet of instant coffee, cup, lukewarm water, plastic stirring stick, the familiar scent reaches my nostrils and warms my dry throat.

A new message from Andréa, sent at 1:50 a.m.

She's writing me a novel. It's super long and detailed. It seems she has an all-consuming passion for her calling. My good luck!

A part of the text is about the life of Alexander's parents, Otto and Hedwig. Andréa explains first that she has managed to contact the other Herrmanns on my list and none of them are connected to Alexander's family. The leads are completely cold in that direction. In contrast, Alexander's father Otto settled in Plauen in 1908. In 1910 he marries Hedwig Theis. Neither of them was originally from Plauen. Andréa is not surprised that they have no family here. Otto Herrmann comes from a little town situated 250 kilometers to the northeast of Plauen, and his wife is from Leipzig, 150 kilometers north. From 1910 to 1913 Otto and Hedwig Herrmann lived at first in an apartment. Then from 1913 to 1922 they lived at number 64 on Pestalozzistrasse. Alexander must have been born there. Then from 1922 to 1937 Otto and his whole family moved to the fourth floor of Neundorfer Strasse 47. The building that I visited yesterday.

I come back to the name of the street where they first lived. It's familiar—where have I seen it before?

I open Google Maps and locate Pestalozzistrasse 64.

Shock.

That's what I was led to like a sleepwalker the day before.

That's where, hesitatingly, I turned right instead of going left toward the hotel as I should have done.

I discover that the two addresses, Pestalozzistrasse 64 and Neundorfer Strasse 47, are located in the same block of apartment buildings, the inner gardens of which I was drawn to magnetically.

I spent time in front of the address that Andréa had initially given me and which turns out to have been where Alexander lived most of his life after the age of six. But something physically pushed me toward the back, to where he was born and would have spent the first six years of his life.

It was so clear, so obvious, to have been inexplicably led to this building. And this morning I understand why. But I cannot believe it. Leaving my coffee behind, I take a quick shower, head down to the garage, jump in my car, and end up parked in front of Pestalozzistrasse 64 five minutes later.

That's it. That's exactly where I stayed so long yesterday afternoon.

I try to recall precisely what I was feeling so deeply. The best word that comes to me is "inspired." I was inspired.

I had no memories, no images that came back to me, I had no experience of déjà vu, and there was no voice "speaking in my head." I don't feel any sufficiently convincing reminiscences for me to consciously remember places in Plauen . . . However, I realize that I am led to certain places.

I am *inspired*.

I don't know how this works, but there I was yesterday, unable to depart when I was around this group of buildings. I went around to the back of the apartment block even though there was no reason for me to do that. And it was there that Alexander spent the first years of his life.

Alexander—or I don't know who—is guiding me in such a light fashion, so subtly, that if I begin to reflect, everything stops. Yesterday, in the street, I was not reflecting, I was not thinking, and something *led* me. Pushed me. The sensation was so fragile, so imperceptible. Once again I have this surprising experience that my body knows where it needs to go.

Andréa ends her email by saying that she will try to find some record of Otto's death, no doubt in 1941 or 1942. She is also hoping to find out more about Alexander's mother.

Imperceptibly, a veil is beginning to be raised.

25

Dream

It's dark. Where am I? It takes me a few long seconds to regain consciousness. Day has not even broken yet. In my last moments of sleep, it seems that I had a dream. I had to approach a house in order to kill the occupants. Armed with a rifle and a pistol in my belt, I see myself approach the entrance to a farm building where the gate is open leading toward an inner yard. There is a dog, a Rottweiler, and two men who are no doubt guards. Behind them a whole family is assembled outside around a table. There are several women wearing shawls, and men dressed in rough clothing. Old people, young people, and children too. The thought occurs to me that I'm not going to be able to kill them all fast enough so that no one reacts. As soon as I come through the gate, after having cocked my pistol but first using the rifle, the Rottweiler runs toward me. I let him approach, and then I fire. I don't hear a shot, but I've wounded him. I've got to finish him off. The pistol is jammed, and I can't rearm it. I go through crazy moments of vain attempts. It's often the case in these dreams where I'm firing on people that each time my weapon jams and I no longer manage to fire. But this time I manage to get rid of the dog without really remembering how, and then I'm watching myself from another angle. I am standing facing a group of people around the table. Starting at this moment, everything happens very fast: I aim, I fire, and I take down everyone one by one. No one resists, no one fights back. Just a mother who holds her infant up so I can take better aim and finish it off on the first shot. Then I finish off the woman. So I execute most of those present. Then I have to escape. People are after me. I'm in a kind of village, and it's hot. Then I come to a magnificent seashore. It looks like a painting. The colors are unreal. The sea is an effervescent green, there are numerous people, the earth is a yellow-red. I run along the uneven coastline to escape my pursuers, whom I can't see. A stronger wave comes crashing over the legs of a group of women and children that I am among. I have to get away from this place. I am armed—I can force the pilot of one of the craft that are dancing on the sea swells. I look at my hands and find I have a handful of cartridges. But soon the dream slows down and halts.

I wake up without knowing where I am.

It takes a few long moments for me to regain consciousness. OK: Plauen, Germany, hotel room.

As I'm getting up, I knock off the night table Karl Marlantes's book, *What It Is Like to Go to War*, a few pages of which I had read before going to sleep the evening before. Marlantes is an American writer. After studying philosophy at Yale and Oxford, he finds himself in Vietnam with the rank of lieutenant in the prestigious Marine Corps. He returned to his country loaded with medals and deeply shocked by his experience. His book is a philosopher's view steeped in his combat experience as a Marine. On every page we cannot help being struck by the brutal sincerity and honesty with which Marlantes speaks of war. This is far from the fantasizing chatter of intellectuals who have never experienced the front lines, and even further away from the unreal moralizing condescension of philosophers.

If my nightmare had been a single occurrence, I could have imagined that it was set off by reading this book, but unfortunately, these kinds of dreams have been part of me for decades. As well, I'm noticing that they are becoming more frequent lately. It's only when I'm awake that the discomfort sets in as I measure the horror of what I've just "done."

In his book, Marlantes speaks of a recurrent nightmare that first took place in Vietnam, in 1968, and that came back periodically during his nights for the next twenty years. In this dream he is engaged in hand-to-hand combat with a North Vietnamese soldier whom he designates in the pejorative manner of 1968 as a *gook*. Karl is armed with a dagger and the North Vietnamese soldier with two razor blades. In the dream, they are fighting in the hot muddy water of a river. Karl finally buries his dagger in the man's Adam's apple, and he writes that he feels a resistance, "as if there was a carrot there." He stabs him several times. Then he continues to relate what he understands from his nightmares, and now what he writes sheds new light on what has just come once again to torment my night: "This dream has nothing to do with Vietnam. It is speaking about what took me there. I was fighting this *gook,* this inner enemy, in various forms, for a good part of my life. He represents parts of myself that I detest. Not only do I not want others to see them, I don't want to see them myself. These parts are what is weakest in me—indecisive, violent. [. . .] We all have inside ourselves this 'inner *gook*.' This is what Jung calls 'the shadow.' In those who state they have gotten rid of it, it takes up even more room."[1]

There it is again—the shadow.

And this morning, in Plauen, I begin to no longer know who is who. Am I Alexander? Am I not Alexander? Is he just the activator of my shadow side? But then, why is he leading me so smoothly to the places he lived? If, as Marie-Pierre advised me, I am his guardian angel and it's up to me to help him—why me? Nobody asked for my thoughts on the matter.

It's heavy.

Suddenly I'm fed up. Enough of playing this little game.

Sixty million human beings died in the general horror that was the Second World War. That doesn't fascinate me. Alexander participated in this conflict in the most indefensible area. That of pure shadow, despicable, negation of all thought, of all humanity.

I have nothing to do with that . . .

Three pages later Marlantes writes: "The more we deny the existence of this warrior shadow, the more we become vulnerable to it."[2]

Shit!

Laptop, instant coffee, filthy mood. Email from Andréa. According to her, there is no male descendant of Alexander's family living in Plauen. In the rest of the email, she relates the story of a popular tale from the Vogtland region that she had mentioned and promised to send me: "On the top of a hill not far from the village of Stelzen in the Vogtland region there is an old maple tree. People say that it was planted in 1430, when a shepherd was condemned to death for something he had not done. The villagers had stuck the shepherd's staff in the soil after his condemnation, swearing that the staff would take root and become a sturdy tree if the shepherd were innocent. And that's exactly what happened. Centuries later, a young and very poor peasant named Christophe fell asleep at the foot of the tree. He had big problems and didn't know how to pay his debts or feed his children. While he was sleeping, he had a dream in which a voice said to him, 'You will find your fortune on the bridge in Regensburg.' We don't know if he had this dream once or several times, but in any case, he decided to use his last pennies to go to Regensburg which was more than two hundred kilometers away. When he arrived, he found the bridge and spent the whole day on it without finding anything. A generous innkeeper offered him lodging for the night. Christophe continued to search for his fortune the next day, and a third day, looking all around him and staring at everyone on the bridge without discovering the slightest indication. The innkeeper wondered what Christophe was waiting for and asked him the reason for his stay. Quite straightforwardly Christophe told him his dream. Of course, the innkeeper started to laugh. He said to him, 'You must be completely crazy to make such a long trip because of a dream. I can't believe it. I too had a crazy dream years ago. I dreamt that someone said to me, "Go to Vogtland, on a hill near Stelzen, dig under the tree that you will find there and your dreams will be fulfilled." Thank God, I was smart enough to not go and let myself be influenced by a stupid dream.' Christophe returned to his village. Once there, he took a shovel and found under the tree a copper strongbox full of gold coins."

Andréa ended her email by writing, "Perhaps you had to make this long journey all the way to Plauen just to discover that the answer to your question is in France. In any case, for over a century this old tale has been told to the children of Vogtland in order to teach them that it's important to believe in your dreams."

It is important to believe in your dreams.

I am touched by her words—so delicate. I feel clearly that not only is Andréa passionate about my story in its purely historical aspect, but I suspect there is more than that to it. A sincere friendship is beginning to blossom between us. My story touches her.

Our meeting is so amazing and so unlikely. Her help is priceless. Marie-Pierre had told me I had to travel, that I needed to be active for things to start happening. I'm just beginning to realize how accurate her advice was.

Last evening, I confided in Andréa about my intuition: Alfred and Inge's little girl is still alive somewhere in Germany. I know that Andréa is on her trail.

Now I have to allow time for things to emerge.

May the little girl rise up toward the light.

26

Hitler Comes to Power

I get back to Andréa in the middle of the morning. Today, she and her husband André want to show me the town from its highest point. The metal tower of Bärenstein is located on a little hill overlooking the street of red brick houses where I began my inquiry in Plauen. From a height of thirty-five meters, it offers an unequaled panorama of Plauen. Right at the bottom of this hill is the vacant lot where the apartment of Alexander's parents was before it disappeared in the April 1945 bombing. From the upper platform all the locations where the Herrmann family lived are visible to the naked eye.

"You see, there was Alexander's school, the Realschulle."

Andréa points to a massive building on the right below the vacant lot. An imposing edifice with a kind of little clock on the roof and sports field beside it.

"On foot, he would have taken the bridge that you see behind it."

She extends her hand along the itinerary that Alexander would have taken to go from his school back to his home, pointing to the Friedensbrücke, the Peace Bridge, which spans the Syrabach Valley in the heart of Plauen and provides access to the south of the town. My eyes follow the route that Andréa is pointing out, and I seem able to recognize the building at Neundorfer Strasse 47, the one on which, on the fourth floor, Selene succumbs to the charms of Pan.

"Is that really Alexander's building?" I ask, pointing at a line of rooftops located a good distance from the direction of the school.

"Yes, exactly. It would have taken him about fifteen minutes, walking."

I imagine Alexander as a child: a boy quick to laugh, with a dreamer's eyes, surrounded by his school chums and running in short pants on the stone bridge as classes are letting out.

"By going through the files that you showed me, I saw that he entered this secondary school in 1927 at the age of eleven," Andréa tells me.

The beginning of the school year of 1927, in autumn; my father was born in October 1927. So far, so close.

"He went to school there up to 1933, Easter 1933," she continued.

"In 1933 he was sixteen. Did he finish his studies?"

"He obtained a certificate of school completion. But Easter 1933 is also the moment that Germany swung," she said to me with a very pointed look.

In fact, Adolph Hitler came to power on January 30, 1933. Alexander was sixteen-and-a-half and had been a member of Hitler Youth since the previous year. How did he come to that? How was he seduced by speeches of hatred that I sense distanced him from the education he had received? The answer is both simple and terrifying: the more I look into it, the more I understand that his fascination for Hitler and the Nazi party is no different from that experienced by a large segment of the German nation in that era.

And do we need to be reminded? Hitler obtained the power and the position of chancellor following democratic elections. It is chilling but important to keep this fact in mind.

Never forget it.

In order to explain this slide that Germany experienced in the 1930s, the English historian Laurence Rees tries to be humorous: "When you have gone through a time of chaos and humiliation, you welcome order and safety willingly. If the price to pay for that is a 'lesser evil,' you accommodate yourself to it. The problem is that there is no lesser evil. That reminds me of the old joke where a man asks a woman, 'Will you sleep with me for ten million pounds?' She replies, 'Yes.' And the man then says, 'Good. Now that we have an agreement in principle, let's talk about the price.' For the German people, the price to be paid for this lesser evil was going to be very high."[1]

Here we have a reality that is stunning but very real: Adolf Hitler came to power legally within the constitutional framework that was in place. Once in control, he proceeded to destroy democracy. Which he did in scarcely a few months. Let us mistrust what seems seductive, for when we allow ourselves to embark on an adventure proposed by a "savior," we give up our rationality and our critical sense.

How did a man who went on to provoke one of the greatest genocides humanity has ever known come to power through what seemed like a democratic process?

The Nazis did not come out of nowhere, like evil demons that nobody saw coming. The roots of their rise to power are to be found notably in the cataclysm of the First World War and the humiliation that resulted for a defeated Germany.

At the beginning of the 1920s, the young German democracy was hit by runaway inflation and terrible political chaos, caused by the conquerors of the First World War—principally France and Great Britain—who imposed humiliating conditions at the time of surrender and demanded exorbitant reparations. Nazism took form out of this extreme feverish state in German society at that time. It was in Munich in 1920 that there appeared a group with demagogic and racist goals, which foresaw notably the exclusion of German Jews from citizenship, the nationalization of businesses, and also the augmentation of retirement pensions. Hitler—who was not a German citizen at that time—quickly joined and made of it his Trojan horse by giving it the appearance of a society reinvigorated—proud, just, and firmly German.

The account of August von Kageneck, a young man from the old German nobility, takes us in this direction. In 1939, at the age of seventeen, he entered the military and left it only in 1955. His sincere and lucid story is one of the most remarkable accounts of the Third Reich as seen from the inside. About Hitler he wrote, "And then comes a man who promises to erase the humiliation, to restore to Germany its dignity, to lead the country back into the ranks of the great European powers from which France and England had so unjustly excluded it. How not to hear him? How not to vote for him? How not to be attracted to this intoxicating waltz of marches, flags, drums and fanfares? How to ignore the construction sites that opened everywhere, how not to see, from one day to the next, the disappearance of the pale, waiflike unemployed who were no longer lingering in the streets and around stations because they had found work."[2]

Laurence Rees cautions us that the popular success of the Nazis, however, cannot be explained solely by the electors' adhesion to a single political program: "The Führer rarely made allusion to any topic at all that was as dull as 'politics,' but instead offered a form of authority laced with visions and dreams. In doing so, he touched something deep in the human psyche. Here is how George Orwell expressed it in his famous summary of *Mein Kampf* (My struggle): 'Human beings don't only have need of comfort, safety, a short work week, hygiene, birth control, and, in a general way, common sense; they also need, at least intermittently, struggle and self-sacrifice, not forgetting the drums, the standards and marches of allegiance.'"[3] The journalist Balthazar Gibiat is more concise in explaining, regarding Hitler at the beginning of his rise, that "his speeches fitted perfectly with the mixture of anger, fear and resentment that animated the public. Simplicity and repetition were his oratory weapons."[4]

No need for a program—just kindle the embers of resentment. By the way, Hitler described it very clearly himself in *Mein Kampf*: "The art of all the great popular leaders has always consisted in concentrating the attention of the masses on a single enemy [because] the masses are blind and stupid. [. . .] The only thing that remains stable is emotion and hatred."[5]

How does that make you feel?

Jacques Lusseyran, the resistance fighter and deportee, writes, "Nazism was not a historical evil limited to one time and one country— a German evil. [. . .] Nazism was an omnipresent seed, an endemic sickness of humanity. You need only throw a few armfuls of fear to the winds in order to reap in the next season a harvest of betrayal and torture."[6]

After the trauma that follows immediately after the First World War, the Nazis profit from the political instability in the beginning of the 1920s.

But from 1925 on, the societal situation in the country improves. And as a direct consequence, even though this new prosperity was artificial, the Nazis suddenly lose most of their audience. At the end of the 1920s, the National Socialist German Workers' Party (NSDAP) no longer has much relevance in the German political landscape, and it is at the same time beset by internal tensions. An initial success linked to fear dissolves as soon as uncertainty about the future disappeared. The party receives only 2.6 percent of the vote in the 1928 elections and wins twelve seats in the Reichstag, while the left pushed ahead strongly, which does not suit President Hindenburg's taste at all.

Then comes the economic crisis of 1929, which, after beginning in the United States, spreads inexorably to the whole world. Fear surges back, and everything topples very quickly. With the stock market failure, cascading bankruptcies, and a colossal increase in unemployment, social unrest spreads once again through the country, causing the population to fear the worst.

At the beginning of the 1930s, unemployment affects more than five million in Germany. The collapse of the economy pushes an immense majority of Germans toward parties that say they will take things in hand by force: the Communist Party or the Nazis, two organizations situated at opposite poles, with one voice, accuse democracy of having failed, and they promise to overthrow it. However, it is the nationalist parties or the "center" that, because of visceral anti-Communism and fear of the Soviet Union, carry Hitler to power.

Insecurity threatens. Confrontations and disorder are skillfully maintained by hordes of strong-armed Nazis making a daily show of strength. Alexander must already be participating with the Hitlerjungend (Hitler Youth) with excitement and discipline. From 200,000 members in 1930, the NSDAP rises to 1.5 million in 1932. However, in a minority position in the presidential elections of 1932, Hitler did not lead the NSDAP to win the legislative elections. In spite of this, on January 30, 1933, the president of the German Republic designates Hitler as chancellor, impelled by a cynical strategy from the financial, nationalistic, and conservative elite, who think they will be able to use him to get rid of the powerful German left.

And it is because the elite underestimated Hitler that he was able to rapidly and apparently legally install the dictatorship he had envisioned since the creation of his party. Terror (assault troops, the Sturmabteilung [SA]) and provocation (burning of the Reichstag), arrests, arbitrary imprisonment, murders, taking control of the police; all such means are good in reducing the political opposition and paralyzing the population with fear. But also in order to galvanize the crowds and give them an escape from their frustration (a war lost, economic crisis), anti-Semitism is raised to a state policy. In a Europe that was mismanaged economically and where anti-Semitism was solidly anchored in people's minds, it was fertile ground. In Germany, conquered, humiliated, and politically unstable, it was introduced effortlessly. As an antithesis, the carefully constructed image of a German people—ideal, handsome, proud, strong, and "pure" was also not difficult to install in people's imagination. This image had been widely promulgated since the 1920s through Hitler's speeches, through the parades of his youth and paramilitary organizations, and in public meetings. The propaganda bore fruit. But the politician had also very broadly infiltrated organizations such as the police, the building trades, the university . . . When Hitler made his coup d'état he already had behind him a force ready to act for him from the moment power was taken.

He doesn't waste time: On February 27 a fire destroys the Reichstag; on February 28 a decree suspends the rights of all German citizens by authorizing their "protective custody." Newspapers are closed, Communists imprisoned and assassinated, and political gatherings outlawed, and no other sound than Goebbels's radio is heard.

Scarcely had he been named chancellor when he organizes new legislative elections, to reinforce his movement in the country. But on March 5 the Nazis, although allied with the nationalists and in a context that was favorable to them, obtain only a short majority (44 percent), which does not authorize Hitler to change the constitution. On March 23 the assembly (legislature) meets in Berlin, in the Opera building. The SA and the SS, threatening and ready to intervene, surround the building. Hitler, in SA uniform, wants a law to be voted on that gives him full powers. Refusal by ninety-four Social-Democrat members, but the centrist Catholic party, the Zentrum, which allied itself with Hitler on March 20, swings the majority in his favor. Dachau opens that same day. Full powers are voted for Chancellor Hitler. The Reichstag reforms the constitution and adopts the black, white, and red flag with its swastika (which Hitler had already designed in 1920). On March 29 basic civil liberties are abolished. On July 14 the NSDAP becomes the only party.

Bringing the German nation into line begins. A large part of the populace—nervous, and whose legitimate fears are skillfully nourished and maintained—have brought to power, full of hope, the very one who has affirmed for years that he will put an end to democracy.

In a few months tens of thousands of Communists, Social-Democrats, and Christians are sent to work camps. Political parties are banned, unions dissolved. Jews are driven from the civil service. The aim is still to force them to leave Germany.

♦ ♦ ♦

And Alexander leaves school.

During our conversations, which affected me so deeply, Holocaust survivor Samuel Pisar came back to this accession to power by Hitler and to the worries that Hitler's rise sparked in him for our current era, because of how strongly he seemed to observe today the same sliding away, the same dangers that carried his father, his mother, and his little sister to their deaths. He already confided this fear in his book, *Of Blood and Hope*: "I claim to know a specific dimension of the dramas that threaten us—it is the dimension of the connections between fear and hatred, between fear and violence. There is nothing mysterious about what derailed our civilization in the 1930s and 1940s: the economic collapse, endemic unemployment, social fragmentation, xenophobic prejudice, and, when all is said and done: fear. Everyone was afraid of losing their job, their savings, their retirement funds, their security. A society riddled by these fears and these hatreds is at the mercy of blind forces. When despair drowns our reason, madness recruits a savior. All that is needed is: for politics and morality to collapse, for well-intentioned traditional leaders to be found powerless, unable to face up to things, for the hour to be rung for demagogues, tyrants and their scapegoats. And very soon—it all falls into place."[7]

In the spring of 1933, Alexander, like millions of his compatriots, begins his dance with the devil.

27

Adolescence

Coming back down from the station side of the Bärenstein Tower, Andréa and André suggest we dine together in a little restaurant downtown. Andréa has continued her analysis of the folders and tells me she understands Alexander's developing journey better by looking at it in parallel with the history of the town. She drives. The inn is barely ten minutes away.

As soon as we're seated in the thick-walled dining room and our meals are ordered, André comes back to a preamble about the history of Plauen and his view on what led Alexander astray.

"As you know, Plauen was a flourishing town at the beginning of the twentieth century. The reason for Alexander's parents' arrival was no doubt linked to the extraordinary economic boom in the region resulting from the production of lace. This prosperity attracted tens of thousands of additional residents. In 1900 the town had already doubled its population in a few years to reach 70,000, and in 1912, at the moment of its highest point, it was at more than 125,000 inhabitants."

André asks his wife, "When exactly did Alexander's parents move here?"

"They arrived in 1908–1909."

"Yes, and they got married in 1910," I added.

"The lace industry collapsed in 1912," André continued.

"Why?"

"The industry began to decline because of changes in fashion, and then the production fell dramatically at the beginning of the First World War, two years later."

Andréa, who had worked out the comings and goings of Alexander's parents in Plauen since their arrival in the town elaborates further.

"In 1912 Otto and Hedwig were already settled. They had rented an apartment, and in 1911 their son Alfred had just been born. No doubt it was impossible for them to leave again. Where would they go? So they stayed but without having much relationship with local people. I was able to put my hands on the baptism certificates for the boys. For Alfred, in 1911, six witnesses were present, all relatives who had come from Leipzig. For Alexander, in 1916, there were only three witnesses. Times were hard. He was born in the middle of the First World War."

"Yes, the context was very different between the two brothers," I remarked.

"Exactly. Alfred was born in a wealthy era. Five years later, when Alexander arrived, the few industries that remained were slowing down. Inflation began to soar at the beginning of the 1920s. Independently of all that, I discovered that in 1921, when he was ten years old, his parents sent Alfred to a very good school, a gymnasium. In contrast, it was not possible for Alexander to attend a school of the same caliber when he reached the same age. In my view, this is linked to the family's situation."

André continued:

"Clearly, it was foreseen that Alfred would be offered studies but Alexander would not. It was costly, and in such a period of uncertainty, as Alfred must have been well on his way, he was privileged. In 1929 to 1930, if I'm not mistaken, Alfred finished secondary school and began to study to be a doctor. In fact, he plunged into his medical studies right at the beginning of the world economic crisis of 1929, a crisis that arrived in Germany in 1930 and peaked in 1931, when the country counted six million unemployed. The family invested what they had available in their elder son's education, while Alexander left school with only his high school completion certificate."

Andréa picks up the thread:

"The economic crisis was of such an amplitude in Germany that it led the family to make some difficult choices. Hedwig, his mother, did not work. Alexander's father was trying to sell textiles in a country in crisis when no one wanted them anymore. And what led me to say that Alexander left school because of his family's financial difficulties is that he immediately began to work."

"Yes, I saw that. In a curtain factory, wasn't it?"

"Yes. This is mentioned in several documents, even in the CV written in his own hand and that appears in his folder. He says he was an apprentice clerk in a curtain factory in Plauen from the spring of 1933, the date he left school, until October 15, 1935."

"Do you think he gave up school in order to work?"

"Yes."

"While his brother continued his medical studies?"

"Exactly."

"Psychologically, that must have been hard."

I wonder even how the relationship with his older brother must have been affected. Fertile ground for possible jealousy, potential frustration. Even if the brothers got along well, it's hard. André and Andréa are in complete agreement with me.

"No doubt this work is the most boring thing in the world for him. Being a clerk in a curtain factory for the rest of his days! Can you imagine anything more tedious than working in a dying industry in a town that is in decline?"

"Seen from this angle . . . "

André pushes these reflections a little further.

"The only thing that must have been exciting in the life of this young man in the middle of his adolescence was the movements flourishing at the end of the 1920s. Nearly half the Germans at this time attended one or another of the numerous youth organizations present in the country. Religious organizations and also political like Hitler Youth.

"When did Alexander join?" André asks, looking at his wife.

"In his handwritten CV, he says he joined in January 1932."

"In the middle of great social agitation. Remember, Stéphane . . . Germany had lost the war and had to pay exorbitant reparations. As a result, everything that seemed even a little luxurious wasn't selling any more—like curtains and lace: Otto and Alexander's line of business. And according to the Nazi propaganda, who are responsible for this crisis? The French, the Jews, and so on. That's what the speeches are saying in the Hitler Youth organization that Alexander attends."

André continues on. He explains to me that in these times Germany was on the edge of chaos. Hitler Youth and all the Nazi Party institutions were in demand. They provided an unequalled propaganda and mobilization domain, especially for youth having grown up in frustration and fed with vengeful speeches. They organized marches and camps where people came together around great bonfires . . . It was fertile ground for the party's propaganda. At the time, two great forces nourished the revolutionary aspirations and stirred up young Germans. Andréa explains to me the circumstances that likely pushed Alexander into Hitlerjugend rather than into Communist movements.

"Alexander came from an educated family. And he must have learned French and English at school. Even though his family was not well off, he grew up in the privileged neighborhood of the west part of Plauen. The other force that wanted at that time to change things using violence was the Communists. But they developed instead in the southern and eastern suburbs of Plauen. They came mostly from the working class, were less educated, and were boorish, known to be brawlers. There was a big difference between them and the Nazis."

"Really?"

"Yes. For middle-class people such as the Herrmanns, the Communists were perceived as troublemakers. The Nazis were not reassuring, either, but in the eyes of a young person such as Alexander they stood for order. The uniforms were impeccable, the discipline rigorous, and their marches were always impressive. The demonstrations never stopped. The Communists in rough groups and the Nazis with magisterial orchestras.

He had to have been impressed; then once he joined Hitlerjugend, brainwashing began in the summer camps . . . He couldn't step back. He had left his parents' influence. The excitement was such . . . "

Suddenly, silence falls. For a few moments each of us weighs what those years were. I *see* Alexander at sixteen, overflowing with energy, harboring so many frustrations, both those of his times, shared by millions of other Germans, and his own private ones, no doubt unconscious: his privileged brother, this sinister career that appears as the only possible thing to look forward to. While I am still lost in my reflections, Andréa puts words to my thoughts.

"From the moment of Hitler's rise to power, when Alexander leaves school to begin this work as a clerk no doubt imposed by the circumstances as much as by his parents, he leaves Hitlerjugend and joins the SS."

"But could you be in the SS and have another job?"

"Yes," André replied. "Because the SS is a civil organization. A sort of paramilitary service order, an extension of Hitlerjugend. He would have worked during the week and paraded in SS uniform on the weekend."

It was in the days following his departure from school, on April 1, 1933, that Alexander joined the 1st Century of the 7th Regiment of the SS as a candidate. This was not a combat company but a political unit, a sort of militia of the party that had nothing to do with the army. Members of the Allgemeine SS wore a black uniform and kept order in public meetings.

In December 1933 he left the status of candidate to become a full member of the SS. Fifteen days later he joins the Nazi Party (NSDAP) as number 3 288 213. He will be the only one in his family to do this. However, his joining, which took place after he was confirmed in the SS, would indicate that his motivation was more linked to prestige and to the dream that his belonging to an elite corps represented, than to a thought-out attachment to Nazi ideology. Andréa makes this clear.

"It's important to notice that by entering the SS Alexander was latching on to the only career opportunity that was available to him. He fitted perfectly the male prototype that was sought for after 1933: schooling completed, blond with blue eyes, tall, athletic."

And André added, "It was an honor to be offered such a career, and when the alternative was spending your life behind a desk . . . In 1933 it was impossible to know what was going to happen afterward. Alexander let himself be influenced by the party's frenetic propaganda without questioning it."

A career in the SS or a dull life in an office.

Today it is impossible to ignore *what happened afterward.* But in 1933 Alexander could not have suspected that his engagement and that of millions of others was going to lead to the Holocaust.

An impressionable young man who lets himself be taken by the current without asking questions. Why did he do it? How can he be reproached for not looking for another career? He had nothing else. The Nazis had just come to power. Hitler promised a glorious future. If we want to understand the motivations of these millions of young Germans, we must agree not to interpret their actions of 1933 with the measuring stick of what we now know, *afterward.* How could he have guessed that he was engaging in a direction that was going to lead to the Holocaust? At a time when no Nazi leader had even yet envisioned implementing the final solution.

"He wanted out of his sad daily life," André added.

Andréa's husband then continued, taking as an example his own experience of the former Communist East Germany.

"Anything that went wrong was the fault of the bourgeois or the fascists. I belonged to the new generation on which everything depended, and we were very fired up, ready to fight. As with Alexander less than forty years before, I was fed with a propaganda that was no doubt identical."

"Yes, but for you Communist and for him Nazi . . . "

"For sure, but essentially, isn't it the same thing? A young person always wants to change the world. For me, the former East Germany;

for Alexander, Nazi Germany of 1933. The mechanism is the same, only the direction that is proposed is different. Alexander must have sincerely thought that he was on the side of good. As I too felt myself to be."

A man born and raised in the former East Germany enlightening me about Nazi propaganda by taking as an example the Communist propaganda that he had been subjected to himself—is that not a beautiful example of lucidity? How easy it must be to arrive at committing the unspeakable when you are immersed in a context in which people are unable to see what is amoral.

28

The Black Order

Daylight sparkles behind the curtains. I am moving very slowly out of a dream, so I am able to hold on to the sensation of it. I am in a large out-of-doors space in front of two Germans in uniform. They control a checkpoint and are seated behind two little worn-down tables. I approach one of them and hand him a paper that he looks at carelessly. And then suddenly I say to them, "Do you know that I studied Second World War history?" They stare at me, cautious, but without hostility. I exclaim, "I know how it all ends." No reaction. So I ask, "What time period are we in right now?" "1942," replies the one facing me. As he's giving me this date, a thought is resonating in my head: "I come from the future." These words run through my mind as my dream begins to freeze. I come from the future. The two Germans are silent, bound to their task, without desire, like two robots winding down. All three of us are in a scene that looks like a vast central plaza of a destroyed town. I tell them nothing of what I know. Then I regain consciousness. I awaken, and I leave them there.

Do the various epochs of history exist *at the same time* in parallel dimensions? Do dreams sometimes transport us into one or another of these worlds? Of these epochs?

This morning I'm leaving Plauen. I don't know yet if I will come back, but something in my depths says, "Yes." Travel calls. My brief stay in Alexander's hometown was fruitful, and my meeting with Andréa was a real gift. These few days in the heart of Saxony have allowed me to move forward on several fronts. The most surprising was to discover how there is an active link functioning between Alexander and me. I am permeable to his inspirations. He manages to guide me physically to locations that are important to him and that initially I know nothing about. Does he do this from another world situated in a spiritual realm, or is he *in me*? I don't know. For me, being in my thoughts and intellectual, I am nevertheless discovering with astonishment my ability to perceive. My sixth sense is waking up and becoming *usable.* I am learning now to understand it and to *sort through* my feelings. I have the impression that it is stronger and stronger every day. Where is it going to lead me?

Another positive point: the discovery of all this biographical data about Alexander and the context of his childhood. The mysterious warrior who gave rise to my dream was a child like so many others, born with memories of the past, challenges to face, strengths, and weaknesses. And all that in circumstances and an era that provided no help. On a land of blood, at the beginning of a reign of darkness.

The context becomes more precise. The contours of his life become sharper. He is moving through a real landscape, with parents, an older brother, a wife, a school, an apartment, friends . . .

Last element: the existence of his niece.

That is the most troubling.

Information about her is the most unclear and yet at the same time she predominates, because in my eyes it means that the little girl from my dream existed. And added to this revelation is the inner certainty that she is still alive. The intuition is sharp, strong, and unambiguous. I'm sure about it. It is she who links me to Alexander today. Finding her is just a matter of time. And with Andréa, the genealogist who fell from the skies, I'm going to manage it. Two days, a week, one month . . . we shall see.

In the meantime, it doesn't seem necessary to stay in Plauen. As far as my inquiry is concerned, I've made my way through it, and other places now are calling. First of all, other locations in Germany where Alexander's life proceeded after he left his parents' home and joined the SS, right after his nineteenth birthday.

I am on the road early in the morning, heading due south. Three hundred and eighty kilometers. Destination: Bad Tölz, a little village in the Bavarian Alps, located not far from the Austrian border. This spa area south of Munich was, starting in 1936, a reception area and training area for future officers of the Waffen-SS: the SS-Junkerschule Bad Tölz. And for Alexander starting in October 1937.

The trip is longer than I thought and I see the first foothills of the Alps a little before nightfall.

I discover Bad Tölz with some apprehension.

This feeling dissipates as I arrive at my lodging that I found by chance online and where I reserved a room. It is located several kilometers to the south, in a valley through which there winds the Isar, an impetuous torrent of blue water. In Wackersberg to be exact. A bucolic hamlet with sturdy chalets of wood or stone. Is it because I am traveling through two epochs that Alexander's hand is on my shoulder? I am pleased with this spot immediately. It is reassuring. There is a kind of excitement in the ambient air. The roads, the villages, the hedgerows, the flowers, the hillsides; this corner of Bavaria has the good smell of youth, mountain excursions, and fraternity. Muscled athletic bodies, sweat from the efforts made, chill along the spine, young girls, blonde and impish with rosy cheeks. Barns full of hay and wood for the winter. A little withdrawn from the world, set apart, a summer camp. Once again I feel on familiar ground. I want to stay, wander through the byways, discover nature all around. Here there is safety and protection.

Impossible to dine at the Landhaus Benediktenhof—the lodging doesn't have a restaurant. It's too late to go out again, so I grab a few slices of cake, a tea, and go up to bed in my little room with its wood-paneled walls and its narrow but welcoming bed.

Light, agitated sleep. In the morning I leave the village in dawn mist. The first rays of the autumn sun are pulling the dampness from the cold earth. An enigmatic fog spreads over the hillsides still in shade and brings a shiver to the trunks of the gray pines. A few curves of the clean road, three sleepy villages, and I'm back in Bad Tölz.

Alexander spent a year here. All of his twenty-first year. From October 1937 to the summer of 1938. I can feel it—he loved this time. In this academy designed to make an officer of him. When he comes to the SS-Junkerschule Bad Tölz as an SS-Junker (candidate officer), Alexander has been an SS member for two years.

Before all this business, I didn't know much about the SS. In beginning my research work, I came across the book by Jean-Luc Leleu, who has a PhD in history and is a research fellow at the CNRS (French National Centre for Scientific Research) at the University of Caen-Basse-Normandie. His book, *La Waffen-SS: Soldats politiques en guerre* (The Waffen-SS: Political soldiers at war) is the historical reference book on the subject. Reading it allowed me to understand better this almost one-of-a-kind Nazi feature: the creation of an ideological army, alongside the regular army.

Created in the 1920s with the aim of forming a small troop in charge of protecting the Führer, the Schutzstaffel (the SS, meaning literally: "protection squadron") is an organization of the NSDAP. Heinrich Himmler takes charge of it in January 1929. At the time of Hitler's coming to power in 1933, it has a little more than fifty thousand men. After this date, the SS goes on to become the tool used by Himmler to gradually take control of all of the Reich's organizations for security and repression.

In fact, alongside the police, intelligence agencies, and even the army of the German state, various branches of the SS developed and became parallel organizations of control.

This is without precedent. A paramilitary organization of the Nazi Party, a private, ideological militia proceeds to gradually infiltrate, among others, all the police and military services of the German state.

And within this private organization of the SS, the SS-VT (SS-Verfügungstruppe) constitutes the military branch and the tool for exercising power over the Wehrmacht—the German army. The SS-VT is later renamed Waffen-SS. (Waffen-SS means literally "armed SS.") It was created officially on May 18, 1939. In this way, Himmler will almost achieve his goals: creating a private army from scratch beside the official army. An SS army made up solely of volunteer soldiers, hand-picked for their ideological motivations and their "racial purity."

This war of influence between the Waffen-SS and the Wehrmacht will reach dizzying proportions, illustrating the fanaticism of Himmler and his associates. And beyond that, it illustrates the intent that drove the Nazis to transform the entire state apparatus.

In October 1935 Alexander enters the Waffen-SS. He is a volunteer. He is taken on and has just signed a three-year contract. Initially, he is assigned to an engineering battalion stationed in Dresden, 150 kilometers northeast of Plauen. But at the beginning of April of the following year, he spends six months in the Reich Labor Service (RAD), an obligation of all young Germans.

Upon his return in October 1936, he is assigned to the SS-Germania Division and takes an initial officer training. This training takes place in Arolsen, the town where his future wife lives. During his time with the Germania Division, he receives several athletic awards. His progress in the SS is relatively ordinary at this time, and since he seems to be a good type, he is invited to become a student officer in the school SS-Junkerschule Bad Tölz.

The SS badly needs officers, and Himmler has his projects.

I am surprised that I immediately find the school, although I hadn't put its address in my GPS. Without a search, without asking anyone, I arrive in front of a cluster of buildings that formerly housed the SS-Junkerschule. Of course, the town is not huge, but this ease in driving straight to the right place leaves me with a strange impression. I saw several black and white photos of the place from the time it was active. I recognize it even though it has lost the arch between the two towers that marked the entrance. In front of me is a gigantic square made up of long and wide bands of three-story buildings and a monumental central courtyard.

I move into it, having left my car in the adjacent parking lot.

If you didn't know what this place used to be, there is nothing to give you a clue. I make the rounds of the inner enclosure.

A walkway through the courtyard, which must have been used for assemblies and which today is flanked in the middle by a large modern building. Around the square, shops. On the other side of the entrance to the site, part of the old buildings have been destroyed.

The place is unremarkable.

No *physical* sensation, no notable emotion. It's beginning to drizzle. I drive downtown. The sun comes back as I go back up Marktstrasse, a paved street bordered with pretty dollhouses climbing up the street in a row. Multicolored and golden facades, taverns, various boutiques in an affluent Bavarian town that at one time had twenty-two breweries.

During his months with the SS-Germania Division, Alexander must have displayed above average qualities for him to have been offered training as an SS-Junker. However, although the speeches were very elitist, the SS was still totally lacking in military experience. The training provided at Bad Tölz suffered from this. The young candidates who became officers before the war, like Alexander, were trained by former subofficers who had little competence.

On the front lines this was to have devastating effects.

But it was not the front lines that awaited Alexander when he left Bad Tölz to enroll in an "end of studies internship." On August 12, 1938, Walter Schmitt, head of personnel for the Chancellery of the Reichsführer-SS, signs the order nominating Alexander for the rank of Standarten-Oberjunker (the highest candidate rank). In the evaluation memo drawn up a little before and signed by the SS-Hauptsturmführer in charge of the school, it is noted: "Herrmann is a hardworking man, honest and disciplined. He has a good mind, is well-educated and talented. He makes a good soldier but is sometimes a little arrogant and boastful. Good for nomination to officer rank."

It is to Dachau that Alexander goes for his internship.

29
Dachau

I spent less than twenty-four hours in Bad Tölz. In the middle of the morning, I head off to Munich and the former concentration camp of Dachau located about twenty kilometers north of the metropolitan area. This place is visited often!

Dachau.

Created in the first months of the Nazi regime, in March 1933, the Dachau concentration camp is run by the SS. From the moment it opened, it ignored the rules of the penitentiary system and the rule of law. Thousands of people were imprisoned there without judicial review as a result of a measure called "protective custody," which allowed any acts of violence, even assassination. Himmler had at first thought of an institution for political incarceration, but it quickly expanded to racial and "undesirable" inmates such as the mentally ill. Dachau, and its violence that became a way of life, is the model on which were organized all the other camps that were the instruments of an implacable repression against "enemies of the Reich."

But when he entered the SS at almost seventeen, what did Alexander expect? What was he looking for by engaging in this parallel-police force? Economic security in a period of crisis? Social status? Respect? Satisfaction at being obeyed? Adventure? Wanting to bear arms? But in this case, why wouldn't he have chosen the army? Could he have imagined that his training would lead him a few years later into the barracks of a concentration camp? Certainly not. At that time, the future functions of the Waffen-SS were still just a project in the heads of Himmler and a rare few of his close associates. Also, by signing up for three years, Alexander probably does not have a clear and definite vision of the career he can accomplish in the SS. However, he cannot be unaware that the SS is already known and feared for its extreme violence and its action outside any legal bounds. In front of him there is a path sketched out, but no destination is indicated. It's a matter of following it by conforming to it without any departure from the imposed rule. This is a sacred obligation in the SS. The national-socialist motto of the SS is "My honor is called loyalty" (*Meine Ehre heisst Treue*). Each SS adherent takes an oath to the Black Order and to the Führer. Consequently, blind obedience is demanded. No order received from a higher officer can be questioned, whatever it may be. This oath must be taken by Alexander without reservation. No more than can any of his comrades, he cannot imagine where his engagement and his devotion to Hitler is going to take him. But he is ready to go all the way.

Arriving at Dachau August 1, 1938, he knows what this camp is for and what is going on in it. He has just finished his section chief training. He's learning to command the equivalent of a *peloton* (platoon) in the French army; that is, about thirty men.

The Dachau complex houses the concentration camp. In 1938, under the surveillance of SS members, and especially of the kapos*— often criminal prisoners—those interned there had to engage in forced labor, seven days out of seven. They are constructing an extension to the camp to accommodate more detainees. The camp is also an important barracks location where battalions of the future Waffen-SS live and are trained. Not all the SS stationed there are guards. However, if we are to believe the directives of his superiors, it is very likely that, as part of his training, Alexander would have had to divide his time between

---

*A kapo or prisoner functionary (German: Funktionshäftling) was a prisoner in a Nazi concentration camp who was assigned by the SS guards to supervise forced labor or carry out administrative tasks. —Trans.

activities linked to guarding the camp—watchtower duty, making rounds, surveillance of the forced labor detainees, and so on—and military training. Did Alexander carry out orders without compunction? No doubt. Otherwise, he would not have been able to remain and progress in the SS. We must not imagine that an SS member could do anything other than blindly obey the hierarchy. In the Nazi rhetoric that they had been fed, all prisoners were guilty regardless of why they were imprisoned. Feeling compassion for them was seen as a sign of weakness and unworthy of an SS adherent.

I am apprehensive about my visit to the camp.

I skirt around Munich gliding through heavy traffic. Then I notice directions to Dachau. It is 1:00 p.m. when I arrive. Numerous signboards provide itineraries for the historic sites that are spread over a large area. Not knowing what I'm looking for, I follow the directions to the "camp," which is where the parking lot is and where the former concentration camp is located.

I drive on a small road under a canopy of trees, and I miss the entrance. I decide to do a U-turn at the next roundabout.

Suddenly, in front of me: the enclosure and the watchtowers. Recognizable in the midst of everything else.

My surprise is total. The place grabs me. Hits hard. It's a shock. On the left my car moves along an endless concrete wall. It has barbed wire on top of it. There are watchtowers every hundred meters. I didn't expect to come upon the place so brutally.

The truth of history.

This twentieth century infamy, so unimaginable that it remains abstract for most of us. Finally it is very real. Here, before my eyes, behind these walls, scarcely seventy years ago men experienced hell. Here, right here.

I am speechless.

At the end of a long straight line, I make a U-turn and go back to the parking lot entrance. Many cars parked; tourist buses too. I head toward the reception building.

I feel heavy, oppressed.

A modern, unobtrusive building houses the visitor information office, a bookstore, and a restaurant. There are too many people. Touristy ambience, laughter, ruckus, shouts, children being called who want to be somewhere else. Something knots inside me, my belly tightens, my head hurts. I want to run from this crowd. I pick up a little French guidebook, and I leave the reception building as quickly as I entered it. A dirt walkway, people coming and going. The entrance to the prisoners' camp is located at the end of this walkway under the trees. A few hundred meters away. Like all the people here today, I am free to walk along this path. There is nothing forbidden, no danger, no threat; the air is cool, the weather is good, a mix of sun and cloud, and yet the oppression becomes stronger and stronger. I keep my head down as I move forward. A whirlwind awakens in my belly, almost cutting off my breathing at the solar plexus as if my lungs were about to explode. But nothing comes out. The pressure increases in my body, in my chest. A pressure that now extends up to my throat and dries it out instantly. My anguish provokes nausea. What should I do? Why am I here? I want to vomit, I want to weep, I want to scream.

Moving toward the entrance, I still pass people laughing. Not all.

I do not understand how anyone could laugh in this place.

I walk looking at my feet. I want to be alone. I want only one thing at this moment: find an isolated corner. I come to the entrance. So recognizable: they're the same in each location. It looks like a little train station. There's even a clock tower. But it's especially the gate. Oh my God! This iron gate. I approach it. Other visitors are moving toward it. A gullet of strangulation, the concentration camp entrance. This iron gate. More and more intense emotion. I am unable to hold back my tears.

"*Arbeit macht frei*" forged in iron. The slogan that welcomes all internees in all the Nazi camps across Europe. The expression, meaning "work makes free," is rendered in the metal of each gate at each camp.

I pass through.

And I move into a gigantic esplanade.

The Dachau concentration camp.

This place really existed. I am here. Pierced through with an unbearable emotion. I walk quickly toward the camp buildings, and I am no longer able to contain my hurt. I want to be alone, I want to sit down. So I take refuge in a space deserted by the crowd, and I address Alexander. He has to hear me. I want to go everywhere, I want to try to understand, I want to follow him, but today I am a man cast down as never before by the pain and suffering of these walls. I am not the one who worked here. I am a good man. I don't hate anybody.

"You are not going to carry me off, Alexander."

I am master of my life. And my life is at the service of the light; the darkness will never seduce me.

"Do you hear me?"

I am here in the middle of the courtyard of the Dachau camp, and I am . . . so moved. I weep, I splutter, uncontrollable . . .

"You see, Alexander, when we don't pay attention—you see where it can lead! Coming here means you participate in that! You see, Alexander, when we're not watchful, when we don't make an effort, we let ourselves be taken by the shadow. This is what you have done! This is what you participated in . . . "

I didn't think this visit was going to be so hard, so harrowing.

New waves of emotion shoot through me.

Regrets, guilt, pain.

The pain is mine. The pain of being in such a place. The pain that gives rise to my perception of memories of the suffering that still haunts this ground.

The guilt is not mine. It is not me . . . I am not guilty of anything here.

"You. You were guilty! And the regrets are also yours and are not my concern."

And yet they plow through me, tear me apart.

"Your guilt!"

I am cut in two.

A good man crying when faced with so much suffering.

A man of shadow who caused suffering.

I don't want to be associated with that.

"It is up to you to ask forgiveness, Alexander. It's up to you to hope and pray so the souls forgive you. If they are able to. You are guilty of cowardice, of stupidity, of laziness, of idleness of mind. Without noticing, you became a monster."

It's so easy to become a monster.

"I am not you.

"I am not carrying you.

"I *never* did what you did.

"If you *come back*, Alexander, above all, do not expect to get me on board once again with you. War, violence, blood . . . all that . . . Was it you? And this magnet that you slipped into my flesh from the first seconds on? This wild, untamed beast that you abandoned? This shadow that haunts you, that possessed you, here, in the courtyard of this concentration camp, at this moment right now, I swear, I free myself from it.

"All that belongs to you.

"All that is not mine.

"This inheritance, heal yourself from it. And if I can, I will help you. But not for one second will I put myself in danger. You lost yourself—not for one second will I believe otherwise. I know what suffering is. I don't want to inflict it. Cost me whatever it may, I will never inflict it. I see the price you are paying for this life in which you decided that your conscience was a weakness. But no, Alexander. Your conscience was your life buoy, your salvation. And you—excited, blind, frustrated—you didn't want to hear anything about it until exploding metal freed you and catapulted you into my life.

"But know, Alexander, that I am the master of my life."

Anger. Master your anger.

"Yes, master it!"

◆ ◆ ◆

The oxygen of the air freezes my throat. My head is spinning. I'm thirsty. I don't have any water. I remain seated alongside the building. As if I need to gather my spirits. As if it is necessary for me to find once again *my* spirit, *my* mind. My guide. My ally. My friend. My protector. In this moment there's only one thing I can do: pray. Make love spring from all my pores, hoping that this love will join that of millions of other human beings whose desire is to calm the suffering of all beings, both alive and invisible.

All the suffering of humanity is here.

It is here that it can be healed.

Some time has passed when I stand up and come to an immense open space—an esplanade of incredible proportions. Today there remain standing only two long barracks and the foundations of others. In front of each one, two poplar trees, planted during the time the camp was active, are now immense. A great alleyway of poplars.

I know what fear is.

I know what is felt deeply here.

I'm acquainted with this fear. I have already experienced it in my current life.

Stuck in dangerous situations.

Famished on a war field.

Brought up short and threatened in corners of the world where the law is as fragile as it was here.

"I have tasted in my soul what you made people undergo. With your look devoid of love that condemned." One day, a man made me crumple looking at me with such a look. He wanted me dead. He saw me only as a threat to be cut down.

I know what it is to be paralyzed by fear.

Only the concentration camp and its administrative buildings have been preserved. Of the various barracks of the Waffen-SS, nothing remains. No doubt they were torn down and reused. I find no trace of where

Alexander must have lived when he came to the camp on his departure from military school.

Platoon head in Dachau. Assigned guard duties in the camp. A young man sometimes a little arrogant and boastful, in charge of the surveillance of enemies of the Reich.

I seek out solitude and calm, approaching the enclosure wall that I had driven along earlier on the other side of it. Seated between two watchtowers with this open space before me, suddenly all is silent. A total silence. Although I can still make out people in the distance, and no doubt birds are hiding in the poplars, but suddenly, not a sound, no wind, no life. Nothing.

I spend the afternoon in the camp. My head is a theater stage for an incessant assault of images. Dachau was a concentration camp. There passed through here tens of thousands of political prisoners, then war prisoners, Jews from Bavaria, priests, homosexuals, and the mentally ill, all living in inhuman detention conditions. The camp witnessed hundreds of extrajudicial executions, from a bullet in the back of the head for "trying to escape," or from death under torture, or from beatings, or from hunger and exhaustion. It was not an extermination camp like Auschwitz or Majdanek, but death does haunt this place.

The sun descends to the horizon and dissects the barbed wire. The sky turns red. As the sun sinks, the central precinct empties. I go back through the camp entrance, just like any other free man, like everybody else present here—what an unfathomable luxury. Freedom is such a prodigious treasure.

Precious freedom.

"You no longer exist, Alexander. The flesh of your body is dead and as cold as the pebbles here on the ground. The anger that animated you no longer exists either."

Alexander was just a personage, an ignorant boy who played a game he found seductive but that today is repugnant to him, I am sure. Today this Alexander is no more real than I am. You and I, like other humans, are only the costumes that *continuums of consciousness* put on during the very brief time of passage through the terrestrial world.

"You are not the costume that you wore during the Third Reich. Do not identify yourself with him. Stop attaching yourself to this angry boy; otherwise, then, yes you will come back to life. And as for me, I feel the movement in my being of a breath that moves through you. I am wounded by it. And I am suffering, and I am your anger. Even now as I was beginning to perceive the being of light inside myself. You and I share that. A light. Remember that! Find it again!

"That is where we have a rendezvous."

Not here in this shameful place.

Alexander left Dachau on September 14, 1938, in order to enter another concentration camp—the "model" camp of Sachsenhausen, north of Berlin. There he will spend only a few weeks. He will be rejoining the SS-Brandenburg Division, which will become his definitive base unit. A combat unit. The one he will die in.

The sinister "Death's Head" Division.

30
Death's Head

Driving straight through to Paris. Being on the road is like a necessary anesthetic following this visit that knocked me down. I step on it and sometimes exceed two hundred kilometers per hour on portions of the German expressways that allow it. Flee. Get home as fast as possible. Get back to my own epoch, to the fortress of my body, under the protection of my beloved.

Something clicked into place in the courtyard at Dachau.

A break, the beginning of a healing, the beginning of the final liberation.

Dissociation between me and these memories that are sticking to me.

A process that will complete in a few weeks, on the coming October 20, when I will be in Russia at the place where Alexander died. This is what I hope for.

After leaving Bad Tölz and the training period at Dachau, Alexander is assigned to the SS-Totenkopfverbände (SS-TV) Brandenburg, where he is back in a suburb of Berlin. During this period, the various SS-Totenkopfverbände Regiments—literally "Death's Head" regiments—are guard units for the various concentration camps in the country. But the ambition of the Reichsführer-SS Heinrich Himmler and their commander-in-chief Theodor Eicke is ultimately to make them into real combat regiments whose purpose would be integrated into the military operations that Hitler plans to conduct.

When Alexander joins the gigantic barracks of Sachsenhausen in the center of the little suburban town of Oranienburg, thirty kilometers north of Berlin, history is speeding up. His regiment will immediately be deployed on the ground in Nazi Germany's first act of aggression: the Sudetenland Campaign. Nothing less than the annexation, pure and simple, of the western part of Czechoslovakia, mainly peopled by German-speaking people.

The Totenkopfverbände will be assigned to the Czech territory with the task of police reinforcement under the direct authority of Heinrich Himmler.

Hardly having arrived in Berlin, Alexander then leaves the area with his regiment in a southeasterly direction. On September 30, 1938, at the end of negotiations with Great Britain and France, the Munich Pact is signed; Germany is authorized to extend its territory. Section Chief Alexander Herrmann and his regiment are part of the German forces that invade Czechoslovakia.

The arrival of German troops foreshadows what will be a Nazi policy of territorial expansion: the setting in motion of the Führer's intention of creating a great German Reich. A program in which the SS will play a central role.

An evaluation memo in his military folder, dated October 14, 1938, confirms that on this date Alexander is section chief in the Sudetenland. Here again, his regiment commander states: "Herrmann is a hard-working person and shows himself to be suited to military affairs. However, he tends to have a certain arrogance. It would be suitable to correct this flaw with firm and appropriate authority."

As for submitting to a "firm and appropriate authority," he couldn't have found anything more suitable than the SS-Totenkopfverbände. The SS-TV constituted an elite within the elite structure of the SS. An elite with at its head one of the most feared commanders in the whole SS, a brutal man with a fiendish reputation: Theodor Eicke.

In parallel, in this same year of 1938, Germany is struck by an intensification of anti-Semite persecution, notably in the course of the summer and fall. This increase in the power of violence against German Jews reaches an unprecedented dimension in the so-called "Crystal Night" during which numerous synagogues are destroyed, thousands of businesses run by Jews are ransacked, and several hundred people are killed.

The synagogue in Plauen is destroyed on this night.

A few hours before bestial, murderous furor erupts all across Germany, during the day of November 9, 1938, Alexander is appointed to the rank of SS-Untersturmführer, effective retroactively to October 1, 1938. Strange synchronicity of events. Reaching the first officer rank (sublieutenant) for Alexander, only twenty-two years old, and Germany unleashing its power against thousands of its own citizens in a debauchery of blind hatred.

Is Alexander still in the Sudetenland during Crystal Night? How did he celebrate his much-awaited promotion to officer rank? I don't know, but there is indecency here. An indecency that colors a part of his short adult life.

November, December, January, February 1939? When Alexander leaves Czechoslovakia, he returns to the barracks of the Brandenburg Division assigned to guarding the Oranienburg-Sachsenhausen camp.

Of the Sachsenhausen camp, there remains today only the concentration camp part. As at Dachau, the place is excessively large and is located in the center of town. Standardization of the architecture of death: buildings, prisoner barracks, even to the iron gates, everything is identically designed, from Dachau to Sachsenhausen, from Auschwitz to Majdanek. The part that was used as SS officer barracks is today the head office and the school for police in the Land of Brandenburg. The offices for the general inspection of the concentration camps has become offices for the taxation division of the town of Oranienburg.

It is from Oranienburg that the overall system of Nazi concentration camps was directed. In the period when Alexander lived there, Theodor Eicke was in charge before he delegated this function in order to devote himself exclusively to *his* Totenkopf Division, created in October 1939, which Alexander will join as a significant part of the contingent of the SS-TV.

In May 1939 Alexander is named Adjutant, the equivalent of aide-de-camp. He is then assigned to the commander of the 2nd Battalion, the SS-Sturmbannführer Hermann Schleifenbaum. From that point on, it is very likely that he was in Schleifenbaum's service full time and no longer participated in the camp guard duties. In fact, an Adjutant has the job of assisting and backing up his superior officer in all administrative tasks. Correspondence, relations with subordinates, promotions, routine paper work, and so on. A kind of human resources director. An Adjutant must be a man who is not only competent, but in whom one's whole trust can be placed. Clearly, Hermann Schleifenbaum, who in his position as battalion commander with eight hundred men under his command, trusts Alexander. He will keep him at his side for a year and a half. Trust, admiration, respect. A durable connection is formed.

Paris. I'm back, my mind bubbling over. Natacha cannot believe the mass of information that I've collected, and especially the astonishing synchronicities that punctuated my voyage, such as the meeting with Andréa in Plauen. On Natacha's side she had embarked on some therapeutic work with the healer and medium Évelyne Joly located in Grenoble. She is just back from her third and final session with this surprising woman, and she relates a few highlights from her meeting. She has never spoken with Évelyne about my work. She only mentioned my existence in her life, but without giving any more detail and especially, not for one moment, did she refer to my research around Alexander.

When she was preparing to take her leave, Natacha said to Évelyne, in order to refer to the work that she was in the process of completing: "It's funny, Stéphane and I are going to free ourselves at the same time from our shadows."

Without a second thought, Évelyne replies: "Yes, but with Stéphane, the man who he will free himself from is a tough one . . . That German . . . He has no feelings . . . He doesn't know what feelings are . . . He's a terrible man; he doesn't think about what he's doing . . . It's like that, and that's it—end of story. And besides, sometimes, that comes back up in Stéphane, doesn't it? . . . And when that comes back up in him . . . the poor man. He can't do anything about it."

Natacha was speechless. She is absolutely certain that she had never spoken to Évelyne about Alexander or even about a German man. Where did these perceptions come from?

Évelyne went on, speaking about me: "When that comes up in him, it's brutal . . . not in what he does . . . It's the anger . . . Somehow he can't fight it—it's just in him. But now he is repairing, and the man is not at all the same man . . . But my goodness, all that was not very pretty."

When that comes up in him!

But now he is repairing.

Oh yes. I do want it to end!

Do I need to reinforce the evidence of this inheritance? Or of the strange soul link that unites us? I have a deep feeling that we are not the same individual entity, Alexander and I. This dissociation flew in my face at Dachau. But the two of us are part of the same *totality*. An identical breath moves through us. The lives are fragments of unique and individual existences, but they are animated by an eternal consciousness. Through this deeply upsetting experience, it has been given to me to experience the reality of reincarnation and to grasp its profound nature. Not the reality of "someone who comes back," but the reality of this immortal breath that passes through autonomous bodies, through mortal identities. Take nourishment from it, learn, heal.

What do I retain? What do I let fall away?

Am I guilty of what someone else *in me* did before?

No, I am not.

31

Mediums

When I discovered Alexander's photo in the marriage folder, I said to myself that it would be interesting to show it to mediums, as I had done with photos of my brother and my father for my earlier books.[1] Having spent years studying, inquiring into, and testing these individuals who claim to communicate with the dead, I have now arrived at the conclusion that it is actually possible to do just that. The dead are still living *somewhere*.

Mediumship is not a magic power, a medium is not infallible, and it is crucial to exercise discernment during a session; however, it is actually possible to communicate with the dead via the intermediary of a medium. I acquired a deep inner conviction about this following a rational journalistic inquiry spread over many long years.

During lectures that I gave or in letters that I received, a question often recurred, "If we can communicate with the dead, what does that have to do with reincarnation?" Indeed. If, for example, I have the ability to communicate with my brother who died many years ago, does that mean that he has not reincarnated?

Formulating the question this way is important; it touches my heart. However, more than anything else this question reveals the partial view we have of reality. Because the spiritual world is infinitely vaster than we imagine. Our deceased evolve in an immaterial reality that, in fact, is not subject to the flow of time such as we experience it on Earth.

Upon dying we leave the world of matter, and our essence makes its way to a plane of existence *located* beyond time and space.

On Earth, time flows from the past toward the future. And besides, when we are located in a place, we cannot be in another place *in the same moment*.

We are caught in time and space.

As counterintuitive as it may seem, these two parameters of time and space disappear after death. For example, those individuals who have lived through a near-death experience speak of the surprising possibility of being able to *change location* at the speed of thought. Other people say they see time as if they were outside it, observing the past and the future as if they were watching a film in which they could display any particular moment at will. Also, when I questioned them relentlessly about the spiritual world, mediums have mentioned other dimensions where physical laws do not apply.

I think that this reality is unreachable by our thinking mind.

What I discovered in writing *The Test* showed me that the spiritual world where my father and brother are is only partly comparable to our earthly world. It is impossible for us to conceive of its reality through the force of our thought alone. How could a blind man know what the light of the sun is?

Our dead evolve in a kind of eternity.

They are *outside* of time.

As inconceivable as that may seem, they are able to contemplate and act on what, for us, is located in a past come back, or in a future that has not yet happened.

As our successive lives unfold one after the other on Earth, an eternal part of us observes these existences *at the same time* from elsewhere.

And this part can access all times and all locations.

Both you and I, we are each only one manifestation of our soul. Only one, among the numerous facets that it has. Those close to us who have died live new lives on Earth, while one dimension of them is accessible still and eternally in the Beyond.

The love that we hold for them and that they experience for us is the narrow passageway that maintains the connection.

I don't want to redo a test that was as intense and long as the one I conducted with my father, but I'm curious to see what will happen when I hand Alexander's photo to one of the mediums that I know. I will record each of the experiments in order not to lose any detail. These mediums have no knowledge of my adventure with Alexander.

The first with whom I try the experiment is a friend of my mother-in-law. The meeting takes place during a party held for the fiftieth wedding anniversary of my in-laws. Laurie Fatovic is a woman who smiles and is full of life. She is both an energy worker and a medium. The idea of showing her the photo comes to me as the two of us are chatting a little apart from the party guests. It's the first time I have met her, but the party helps us relax.

"What do you say—a little experiment? I show you a photo, and you tell me what you feel . . . "

"Yes. Why not?" she replies, amused.

Seated under a tree at the end of the garden, I pull up the photo of Alexander on the screen of my phone and pass it to her.

"This isn't a trick, is it? It's someone you know?"

"Yes, don't worry . . . "

"It's hard . . . You don't have another photo?"

"No."

"Do you have his date of birth?"

"Yes, 1916 . . . "

"Is it someone who is familiar to you?"

"I'd like to know what you feel."

"What's bothering me is that when I look at this photo I have the impression that the person I'm seeing is you."

"Oh really?"

"It's even very disturbing . . . There is something . . . What comes to me is the impression of seeing you. This photo is very disturbing."

"What do you feel?"

"I have the impression it's you . . . And my heart tightens, and I want to cry . . . I have an 'r' . . . I see like a void and a sadness in you . . . but in him too, by the way. Do you have his first name?"

"Alexander."

"Alexander . . . You're familiar with his life?"

"Tell me what you feel . . . "

"I have something about a voyage . . . There's something to do with the army?"

"Yes."

"There is war . . . He's given something. A medal?"

Friends arrive and interrupt the session. The conditions are not really ideal, and we agree to stop there. I thank Laurie for having played the game, and I am very shaken up by her very first remark: "I have the impression that the person I'm seeing is you." And then the sadness, the war, the "r," the voyages . . . Not bad at all within scarcely a few minutes.

A few days later, the medium Florence Hubert and the energy worker Patrick Manreza come to our house for dinner. Once again I decide to take advantage of the situation. Florence was rather stunning during *The Test*, and Patrick, too, has abilities in perceiving. After the meal I suggest the same experiment as with Laurie. Florence and Patrick know nothing at all about Alexander and my waking dream. I go off to look for a copy of the photo printed on paper, place it on the table, and start my recorder. Florence grabs the photo.

FLORENCE: My head hurts . . . Is this family?

ME: No . . .

FLORENCE: My head really hurts, all of a sudden . . . Is he dead?

ME: Yes.

FLORENCE: Yes, violently, quickly . . . He didn't believe in much— that's what I feel. I get a lot of timidity, introversion . . . as if there was a fear, a fear of not being able to explain . . . It's odd . . . And my head hurts . . . I'm being told about a baby?

Patrick takes his turn with the photo and begins speaking.

PATRICK: He died at less than thirty?

ME: Yes.

FLORENCE: And the baby? I'm being told about a baby.

ME: I don't know about that.

PATRICK: Twenty-five, twenty-six?

ME: Twenty-five.

FLORENCE: He died brutally?

ME: Yes.

FLORENCE: That's how I feel him . . . I get someone who has trouble expressing himself.

PATRICK: It seems to me he did something with violence . . .

FLORENCE: Yes, he has trouble talking about that . . .

PATRICK: As if he had killed . . .

ME: Yes.

FLORENCE: . . . How long ago did he die?

PATRICK: My head hurts too . . .

ME: More than seventy years ago . . .

PATRICK: Yes, I think that he killed . . .

FLORENCE: He wasn't able to express himself. There are things that he would have liked to say . . .

PATRICK: However, it's terrible, the things that he did . . .

FLORENCE: He killed someone?

PATRICK: Yes . . . for me, yes . . . he killed!

ME: Yes, no doubt. He was a soldier.

FLORENCE: Do you know how he was killed?

ME: In the war.

FLORENCE: With a bullet to the head?

ME: No . . .

FLORENCE: But didn't he have a blow to the head? Why does my head hurt?

PATRICK: Yes, me too, my head hurts . . . He killed, and I think that it wasn't right at all . . . not at all . . .

FLORENCE: Was he German?

ME: Yes.

PATRICK: It didn't go as far as atrocities . . . but he participated in things that were terrible just the same . . .

FLORENCE: Did you know him? My shoulder hurts too . . .

ME: No, I didn't know him . . . That's why I'm collecting all this information . . .

FLORENCE: I think that his left side was shattered . . . And there's a baby . . .

PATRICK: I don't sense a baby but a young girl.

FLORENCE: Yes, but there's a baby . . .

PATRICK: I don't know . . . But I feel that the young girl is someone he loved.

FLORENCE: For me it's "baby" that I hear . . . And then a name in "Lu . . . " What's his first name?

ME: Alexander.

FLORENCE: I have a name with "Lu . . . "

ME: His wife was named Luise.

FLORENCE: Do you know if he had children?

PATRICK: I see a skirt with big stockings under it . . .

ME: For his wife?

PATRICK: Yes, you know, big skirts with thick stockings underneath . . . The woman I see is over twenty, a little chubby. She died young too. The woman he was with.

FLORENCE: Afterward, I get a psycho-rigidity . . . in his character. And things unspoken . . . or else he did things . . . Was he a spy?

ME: No. He was in the SS.

PATRICK: My noggin hurts like hell . . .

FLORENCE: Me too. He's coming to explain things, but it's hard for him.

PATRICK: I hear, "I'm coming back from far away." Yes, killings

... he participated in killings ... and not just one person ... there were deaths, many deaths. The blood ... it's intoxicating.

FLORENCE: "I have no choice." Perhaps he would like to ask forgiveness ...

How truly surprising, all the doors that open sitting around the corner of a table after a meal. As if Alexander's world was there—available—accessible to whoever has the ability to go there. Once again, many astonishing elements—information that apparently could not be deduced from just looking at a photo: timidity, introversion, fear of not being able to explain himself, a baby, a brutal death when young, violence, he killed, German, a name with "Lu," psycho-rigidity, unspoken things, he's coming to explain things, there were many deaths, perhaps he would like to ask forgiveness ...

Perhaps he would like to ask forgiveness?

And then this woman who died young ... So it's not Luise. And this baby?

The third medium that I see is Pierre Yonas. He also participated in *The Test*. He has a few minutes free, and I meet with him in his home. And, as usual with Pierre, things move very quickly. Recording.

PIERRE: I sense a person with many abilities ... someone connected to spiritual realms, divided between good and evil. His mind bothers me ...

ME: What do you mean by that?

PIERRE: Like a mind that is suffering ... but brilliant. However, I pick up on the life in him ...

ME: You pick up on life?

PIERRE: Yes ... someone who is alive.

ME: Meaning?

PIERRE: Not like dead ...

ME: He is dead, though.

PIERRE: Yes, but I see him alive. As if he was still around us ... I can assure you.

ME: It's not like that with all spirits?

PIERRE: No. It's as if he is representing something that is continuing to be kept alive . . . as if he didn't want to be forgotten. There's a lot of moving around, a lot of voyages . . .

ME: Yes.

PIERRE: I see him really moving . . . Secrets too. Many secrets also . . . He's family?

ME: My family? Not directly, no.

PIERRE: He's the brother or the cousin of a relative of yours, by marriage . . .

ME: Tell me what you're feeling.

PIERRE: I feel that he's from your family . . . Was he a resistance fighter, this boy?

ME: No . . .

PIERRE: There's a history of war . . . of military . . . because I see him in military attire . . .

ME: He was in the military.

PIERRE: A soldier?

ME: Yes . . .

PIERRE: There you go. I was not mistaken . . . because I see military attire . . . very straight, serious . . . I see intransigency in him. Like someone psycho-rigid . . . very hard! Why am I being told about countries to the east? Did he go there?

ME: Yes . . .

PIERRE: I'm being told countries to the east. I hear, "He straddles two eras." Was he really between two eras?

ME: What do you mean exactly?

PIERRE: I'm hearing, "He straddles two eras."

ME: Astonishing.

PIERRE: As if there were two different eras . . . and he straddles two eras. I'm telling you what I'm being told. "He straddles two eras." And it's a real message.

◆ ◆ ◆

Once again, the perceptions are quick and accurate: someone divided between good and evil, someone who is still living, voyages, family, military, upright, serious, intransigent, psycho-rigid (Florence also described him using this term), hard, countries to the east, and then what comes as an important message in Pierre's eyes: "He straddles two eras."

I still have the medium Henry Vignaud to see. But first what can I conclude from these three sessions? In fact, I don't really want to *conclude*. Is Alexander really my previous life? Am I his reincarnation? More and more that's what I feel deeply. However, I don't manage to see any contradictions in the fact that the mediums manage to communicate also with him.

A part of him is in the Beyond; another in me.

The way in which we view reincarnation seems more and more erroneous to me as step-by-step I discover the relationship between Alexander and me. The idea that an individual entity passes from body to body postulates the existence of an immutable soul. However, based on my experience, it's the very notion of individual that is eroding.

The more the relationship between Alexander and me becomes precise and clear, the less I want to think of it in intellectual terms. Instead of reflection and analysis, I prefer the exploration of my feelings, of my intuitions—the direct experience of the connection.

The thinking process seems to me to be too limiting to measure the ultimate nature of the relationship between us.

Engaging in reflection, coming up with words and hypotheses seems more and more pointless in relation to the intensity of what I am experiencing. Intellectual analysis distances me from the heart of my experience. I thought I was looking for "explanations," but everyone spends time defending their own explanation against other people's explanations. And what does that lead to? Nothing.

Everybody has an opinion on everything, books overflow with hypotheses, but after long years researching these topics, I feel that the truth is not reducible to such and such a theory. On the contrary, it goes beyond us. It is even dizzying, and our limited senses allow us to perceive only a few reflections of it. So spending one's time formulating and defending postulates, which are ephemeral by nature, isn't it kind of a waste of time? Being a journalist in my soul, I am beginning, however, to accept that many elements of reality escape me and will always escape my intellect.

The dizziness begins.

My dreams are transformed into a space for learning, and my subjective feelings become powerful tools for exploration.

In each one of us there exists a doorway, a direct access, intuitive, experiential, to reality.

I opened this door.

Since the shock of experiencing the discovery that Alexander died as I had seen in my dream, I saw with inner conviction that we are linked. And that there is a reason for our *encounter*.

The three mediums and Henry Vignaud, whom I will meet soon, confirm this link. But Alexander is also a whole other being who is not living only through me. This aspect of him the mediums also picked up on—as I myself had felt it in the streets of Bad Arolsen and Plauen and in the courtyard of Dachau. He's an individual, and this individual is perceptible. By the mediums and by me.

Alexander is at the same time a being *living* elsewhere and a part of me.

32

A Dramatic Twist

I proposed a real working session to Henry Vignaud. I should have perhaps done the same with the others, rather than attempting a connection on the fly, during a party or after a meal. I want to see just how far it is possible to go in the exploration of my relationship with Alexander using a mediumistic contact conducted in optimal conditions. I meet Henry in his office; as with the others, he doesn't know why.

Before leaving home, I discover I have an email in from Germany. Andréa has not slowed down. Following my departure from Plauen it hasn't taken her long to move things along significantly. She lets me know that she was able to access documents held in the Plauen archives and in which she discovered various important details about the family.

Otto, Alexander's father, died October 23, 1942. A year and three days after Alexander. This date was found in a town register. The archivist whom Andréa was in contact with was able to put her hands on it. But Otto did not die in Plauen. Andréa will try to find out more on this topic.

The most promising information concerns Alfred, Alexander's brother. He left his native town many years ago. This is why we were never able to find any Herrmann descendant in Plauen today. He left and settled in a little town situated not far from Berlin—Jüterbog—in 1959. He passed away the same year at the age of forty-eight. Andréa let me know that he and his wife Inge had four children. Two girls and twin boys. Alfred and Inge left Plauen with the boys, Bertram and Alwin. The girls, one married and the other studying pharmacy, stayed in Plauen.

The older daughter is named Marlene. It was only in 1967 that she left her hometown for a little hamlet not far from Wismar on the Baltic Sea. She left with her husband and has not used the name Herrmann for many years.

Marlene. She is the one mentioned in the file of her uncle Alexander with the symbol for "female." She was born in 1938. She was barely three when Alexander died.

An intense new emotion takes hold of me. Marlene: this is the little girl in the dream! I have very little time, but I begin immediately some Google searches. Marlene Herrmann produces no result, but I find a Dr. Bertram Herrmann in Jüterbog, the town where Dr. Alfred Herrmann settled.

This cannot be by chance.

My head is spinning. It can't be a coincidence! Once more I have the impression of having the right cards in my hand. Thanks to Andréa. But once again this dilemma: I don't know what to do. The problem of the language, afraid to take a long shot blindly . . .

Should I call this Bertram?

Of course, he needs to be called, but right now I have no time. I'm torn, but Henry is waiting for me.

The medium receives me in a dark little apartment that I'm beginning to know quite well. On opening his door and noticing my state, Henry suspects that I'm coming to submit him to another one of my tests. With patience and some amusement, he has me take a seat at his little session table and lights a cigarette. We chat about one thing and another, but he must be picking up on my impatience because he invites me with a big smile to present the photo that I said I was bringing. When I hand him the black-and-white document from Alexander's military folder, he knows strictly nothing about it. And nothing about my dream.

"I see someone who has died older than in the photo. He did not die very old, but older than in the photo. I have images of geographic maps—a notion of countries, travel. He's a traveling man . . . He died a long time ago."

"Yes."

"A good forty or fifty years ago. Easily."

"Yes."

A truck goes by on the street and honks. Henry remains silent for a few moments, as if having to reconnect.

"It's odd, but when the vehicle went by, it hit me as a shock, and I saw old images. From the 1930s and 1940s with old-time vehicles, you know . . . I have the impressions that foreign lands are important to him . . . I don't know. Or he's a man who traveled a lot . . . I don't have his spirit. I have to find a wavelength to reach him . . . "

"What does it mean that you don't have his spirit?"

"I have access to his spiritual aura in the Beyond, but I don't feel him coming down toward me. I'm obliged to go up toward him, in fact, because he left a long time ago. I'm receiving fragments of him. It's not as if his spirit came down beside me and I felt his personality . . . Ah, now I'm on his wavelength, like a link that he's trying to get going. Not easy . . . "

"Yes . . . Don't hesitate to give me all the images that come to you."

"It's twice now that I see that . . . I'm not saying he died from that, but there's a reason for it: I was opposite the barrel of a rifle or pistol. Not too sure. Opposite the tube. And now again. I see a hand on the trigger. But without pressing the trigger. I didn't see death, but does he have a firearm? I don't know . . .

"I see people. Masses of people. Finally one person in particular. Elevated . . . You might say he had a reward, a medal . . . I see a jacket lapel . . . "

Up to this point, Henry seems to be onto the right person. Weapons, medal: Alexander received several military decorations, and then "masses of people" is suggestive of extensive military maneuvers . . . However, I give him minimal confirmation.

"Yes . . . "

"Were his eyes blue gray or gray green? You don't know. Sort of light colored?"

His military folder mentions that he had blue eyes. This is totally indiscernible in the poor quality black-and-white photo.

"Yes, he had blue eyes."

" . . . I feel he was intellectually quite quick, this boy. Not someone run-of-the-mill, ordinary in the day to day. Not just anybody, you might say. I understand that he could be confused in his way of seeing things or in his way of acting . . . There's the impression that, through personal conviction or through obligation perhaps, through temperament, he's someone who is trying to flee from reality, from this family . . . in order to exist, to experience things. Distancing himself to experience things, a need for adventure. There's a feeling that he was part of an elite. People who are not content with everybody's everyday round. Do you understand?"

"Yes, completely."

Yes, I understand. An "elite," which is how the SS described themselves.

"I think he must have loved traveling, this man . . . For a moment or two now I'm feeling that—adventures in foreign lands, you see?"

"Yes."

"Need for adventure, for a quest, for delving into things—it's very clear. I think he must have participated in an adventure of exploration, you see? Taking off somewhere with several others."

"Hmm. Hmm."

It's odd. It's as if Alexander is remaining distant, vague. I feel that. He's keeping a subtle distance. Yes, he traveled, participated in an "adventure of exploration with several others." The invasion of Czechoslovakia, Poland, France, and then the USSR!

"I feel the loss of someone dear to him that completely shattered him before he left this world. Do you know anything about that?"

"No, I don't."

"Once again I sense this need to experience things not like everyone else . . . "

"Yes . . . "

"You know—like those kinds of people who are driven by a need to experience things at any price, to have challenges . . . Does that speak to you?"

"Yes, that speaks to me."

"I think that he had a way of seeing things that was a little special. Just as much as he could be loved for his cultural richness, to the same extent he could be disturbing too—sometimes."

"Meaning?"

"Perhaps his ideas? This is someone who must have had a kind of sensitivity."

It's obvious. His way of seeing things, his "ideas" . . .

"Can you see how he died?"

"I have the impression that he was not free of himself before leaving."

"Before dying, you mean?"

"Yes, that's the impression I have . . . "

"Not free of himself in what sense?"

"As if he's someone who is blocked from acting. Loss of the notion of freedom . . . "

"Loss of the notion of freedom," yes, embarking on one of the most gigantic wars of extermination that humanity has ever known. This is also connected to what Marie-Pierre Dillenseger said. Surprising.

"In fact, I'm trying to understand the connection that I have with this person . . . "

"Really? Wait . . . I . . . I don't know what connection you could have with him, but I have the impression that there is a vibration . . . As if you were the continuation of his personality. His personality but in a different way . . . as if you had fragments of his mind but in a different way . . . Yes, there's something . . . He is not easily accessible. I feel fragments of him. He lost his mother young?"

"No. That is not the case."

"Oh, really? Who is this silhouette of a woman that I see lying in bed? Her face is not very old, more than twenty-five, less than fifty, perhaps . . . "

Once again I can't prevent myself from being upset by this information. Such as the mention a little earlier of the upsetting loss of someone dear. Henry is the third person to mention the existence of a loved one who played an important role in Alexand,er's life and whose departure or death was dramatic. It can't be Luise, who died at fifty-seven from cancer. Patrick spoke of a woman whom Alexander loved and who departed young. Marie-Pierre Dillenseger said Alexander had an intense and secret love affair.

What a mystery.

What a disconcerting enigma.

How could I find some trace of this love affair that three different people detected, without any collaboration among them?

Who is this secret love?

It obviously will have left a trace in me, a memory, a wound; perhaps . . .

Oblivious to the emotion he has just stirred up in me, Henry continues.

"It may appear strange to you, my question, but for some time now haven't you had little things that bring you back to him? Haven't you noticed that? Glimpses of his personality, his experience, his life. As if there were points of convergence, similarities? I sense the fluid of spirit on you, and for me that means there is a connection between the two of you, the spirit that follows you . . ."

"Yes, I do. But perhaps you could be more precise about what you're feeling."

"There is something I feel in common between the two of you.

Convergences. As if you were the continuation of the mind energy of this person . . . "

I am impressed by all that has come through to this point, and I am very intrigued by this expression of Henry's saying that I would be the "continuation of the mind energy" of Alexander. I decide to recount my whole experience in detail, starting with my waking dream and including all the confirmations obtained afterward. Then I ask him abruptly if he thinks that Alexander is my previous life.

"No."

He did not hesitate. I'm having trouble following him.

"But what is the difference between being the continuation of the mind energy of a person and being the reincarnation of that person?"

"It's very difficult to find words for what I'm feeling . . . But I perceived that I should not be identifying you with him as if it were your previous life. I understand your process. That's why I was made to understand that it wasn't you. There are points of convergence, similarities, something that connects you, but it's not you in a previous life . . . "

Interesting. Incarnating the mind energy of a person without being the reincarnation of that person. I'm not too clear about what that means, but the fact is that it resembles the contradictory perceptions I have been experiencing for some time. In fact, as I've said, I feel at one and the same time that Alexander is part of me and is an entity external to me. When he is guiding me, when he places things on my path, when I speak to him, I have the impression that it's an external being that I'm addressing. However, when I am inspired in Plauen to go behind his house, when I perceive with pride the great oak trees on the Grosse Allee in Bad Arolsen, I feel that he is in me. And if Henry was perceiving only a part of reality? And if the truth was a little of both?

One of the keys in this quite enigmatic story is to be found perhaps in the office of this Dr. Bertram Herrmann, in Jüterbog.

33
Doors Wide Open

Everything is speeding up. Is it because October is approaching with, as a goal, the anniversary date of Alexander's death and my trip to Russia? I still have trouble imagining that in three weeks I will be in the heart of the Valdai region, where Alexander spent the last days of his life. It seems so far away, so unreal. As it must have been for him when he left the tranquility of the area near Bordeaux in May 1941.

Given my hesitation, Andréa suggests she will be the one to call Dr. Bertram Herrmann, the probable son of Alfred (Alexander's brother). This man lives in Jüterbog, where Alfred moved in 1959 with his wife and the twins—one of whom was called Bertram. I prefer that Andréa handle this first contact. She will certainly know better how to proceed than I do. She will call explaining that she is a genealogist from the Vogtland region and that she was contacted by someone who wants to know more about Alexander Herrmann. She seems confident, and I am clear about her talents as a diplomat.

The aim is to establish contact, and if, as we both think is reasonable, Bertram is really Alexander's nephew, then I will immediately plan a second trip to Germany before going to Russia, and when I meet him I will give him the full version of my story. But sitting down in front of him, eye to eye. And he will be able perhaps to let me know what has become of his elder sister Marlene.

Because she is the one who is most important.

Marlene, the one who I am now convinced is the little girl from my dream.

A strange end-of-September day in Paris, where nothing is in hand and nothing holds me back. The city has resumed its full activity after the summer holidays. August's heat still hangs over the capital, and there is not a breath of wind sweeping through the choked expressways. A pollution gauge hangs at gray yellow over the whole Paris Basin. Warning peaks come one after the other. And the sun pursues its course.

I leave Paris for the country, which I get to at the end of the afternoon. Blue sky, welcoming century-old oaks. Calm, silence. In front of the gate, a lime tree with a massive trunk is one of the guardians of the house.

A little before 8:00 p.m., I receive the following laconic email from Andréa: "The doors are wide, wide open . . . " What does she mean? Why no more details? Immediately, with a certain feverishness, I write, "What a mysterious email. Is it good news?"

Her reply comes only an hour later. An account whose incredible content instantly sweeps away all my impatience. Andréa gives me the details of the conversation she has just had with Bertram—a long discussion of twenty-five minutes, and the even longer conversation that followed with . . . Marlene.

I am stunned.

They are definitely Alfred's descendants, she confirms. Her email ends with these words, which transport me, "Both of them are totally surprised, excited, touched, and everything else that you can imagine . . . Call me."

"Hello, Andréa?"

"Yes, Stéphane . . . I don't know where to begin."

"You called Bertram then?"

"Yes. I called him saying that I was calling from Plauen, the town of his birth, and that I wanted to know more about his family."

"How did he react? He really is Alfred's son?"

"Yes, he is. He was very friendly and open. Besides, it's funny, he confided in me that they had a family reunion in Plauen last May."

"Oh, really?"

"He confirmed for me that everything we found in the phone books is correct."

"That means that Alfred, his father, moved with his mother, himself, and his twin, and that his sisters stay in Plauen . . . "

"Yes. And besides, he very quickly suggested that I call his elder sister, Marlene."

"I don't believe it."

"He assured me it would be better because he is youngest of the family. He added that she is the one who is interested in the history of the family. And do you know what? He gave me her phone number and address."

"You are incredible."

"No, I've been practicing genealogical research for more than forty years, and my local accent puts people at ease. Luck—nothing more."

"But still . . . "

"Bertram specified that his sister has already done a lot of research on Alexander."

I am taken by an enormous surge of emotion. Everything is so fluid, obvious, easy. I don't believe it. Andréa is also quite stirred up, although she shows it less. She continues:

"So I called her. I called Marlene and we spoke for more than an hour."

"Tell me about it."

"She was married before, but her first husband died many years ago. It was with him that she left Plauen in 1967. She is living today in Wismar with her second husband Joachim. They are both totally excited about you appearing, and they are eager to meet you. But the conversation could be difficult because Marlene does not speak anything but German and her husband has only a little English."

"Why don't you come with me? We can meet up in the closest town to us both? Or I'll just come and get you."

"It's tempting, but it's impossible for me to leave Plauen right now."

"I will go as soon as possible. Do you think I need to write to her? How should I proceed?"

"Wait a moment. Marlene confided so many details about the life of her father, about her childhood, and about the research that she conducted on Alexander, as well as on other members of her family who died in the Second World War. I have to relate all this to you first . . . I'm a little emotional; I'll try not to forget anything."

"Fine, go ahead . . . "

"So among the most important things for you, first of all about Alexander's brother Alfred. He also fought in Russia. Like Alexander. But he was a soldier in the army, inducted in his role as a doctor. And he was taken prisoner during the war and remained in custody in Russia until 1948."

"I don't even dare imagine under what conditions . . . "

"Marlene said he never spoke about this period. He never spoke about his brother Alexander either."

"Ah, no?"

"No. And she doesn't know if she ever saw her uncle. She doesn't remember him, but anyway she was too young. However, she told me she has a photo of the two brothers."

"She must be the niece mentioned in Alexander's folder."

"Yes, most certainly. She was born December 24, 1938."

"1938. That's her."

"She told me that she had recently done a great deal of research on Alexander."

"Why? Why did she feel the need to do research on an uncle of whom she had so little memory, or no memory at all?"

"That's what's astonishing. And besides—the timing."

"Meaning?"

"Marlene has a daughter from her first marriage, and this daughter recently undertook some research on her own uncle, the brother of Marlene's first husband, who disappeared during the war. This is what gave Marlene the idea of also doing research on her own uncle, Alexander. This was a few months ago."

"No doubt at the time when I myself was beginning my own inquiry work?"

"Astonishing synchronicity, right? In any case, Marlene explained to me that she felt that someone ought to take that on. This mysterious uncle whom her father never spoke to her about. She contacted the research service of the Red Cross and the WASt . . . "

"The what?"

"The WASt in Berlin, the Deutsche Dienststelle, which is the information service of the Wehrmacht for those who died or were prisoners of war."

"OK."

"She obtained some information concerning him, as well as some dates, but no doubt less than you did. Besides, I have promised to send her your documents. I hope that's OK with you."

"Absolutely."

"Just for your information, while I think of it, I really told her a strict minimum about you, to the effect that I felt there was a connection. To which Marlene replied, 'Alexander must have known someone from his family,' referring to you."

"How is she going to react?"

"Why would she react badly? You will see. Let me finish: I received from her side more details about the circumstances of Alexander's father, Otto. He died totally unexpectedly from a heart attack in a hotel in Eger on October 23, 1942. It's a town that today is called Cheb, in the Czech Republic, but at the time it was Germany. Otto was there as a business representative for the company in Plauen he was working for."

"A heart attack?"

"Yes. He was fifty-eight. He was born in 1883. And she also

clarified for me about the apartment at Martin Mutschmannstrasse 48; you know, the one you went to first in Plauen."

"Yes, the one that was bombed."

"Exactly. In 1945 when it was destroyed, Hedwig, Alexander's mother, was still living there alone, since she had been a widow for two years. After the war, she left to live in a little village north of Plauen; then she ended up moving to the West and died in her ninety-first year near Frankfurt, where she had settled with her younger brother. Marlene confided in me that she never really recovered from her favorite son Alexander's death or from the death of her husband."

"Alexander was her favorite son?"

"Yes."

I am once again moved by the irruption of this image of a suffering mother. Whatever a son might do, he is still a son for a mother. Her favorite son . . . Alex.

"Thank you, Andréa . . . I don't know if you believe in spirits, but I can tell you the spirits believe in you."

I hear her hearty laughter at the other end of the line.

"You know, Stéphane, your story is not the strangest that has ever happened to me. That doesn't mean that I don't believe in your dream, even though it's difficult to believe. Besides, I would no doubt not have been able to believe it if I hadn't had a similar experience."

"Really?"

"Not as intense and not with verifiable elements, but much more real than a simple dream. I don't want to go into too much detail, but just know that I 'died' for the first time at the age of eight or nine. Since then I know that death doesn't hurt. You simply leave your body and observe things from above. It seems to be something very brilliant and loving, and there's no reason to be sad about it."

This is really incredible. Not only did I happen upon the most gifted genealogist in Saxony, but in addition she has had a near-death experience. In a cheerful voice she continues:

"But if I want to remain rational, there is another reason I believe you: I am a little deaf. In a concert, I can see the musicians playing without being able to hear them when the notes are too low. My husband André doesn't see colors. He is unable to make out forms that I can see easily. So why would I doubt that you have receptors, antennae that other people don't have? That's why I am impatient to know the next stage of your adventure with the Herrmann brothers. I know simply that nothing and no one is ever lost and that everything is connected. Also I really wonder what you're going to discover."

"So do I, Andréa. And I owe you so much. I will tell you all about it, for sure . . . "

"I hope so. Good. There we are, Stéphane. I've given you the most important facts from my discussion with Marlene. She is expecting your email to arrange a rendezvous. But I'm going to share one final confidence from her: in a certain way, I have the impression that she was expecting you."

We hang up, and the calm of the night carries me away.

I'm up at dawn. In front of the house, before the sun has yet appeared, a young roebuck deer is exploring the garden. I go out into the cool air, he looks at me for a moment, we both remain motionless, then he takes off, bounding away strongly, making raucous cries.

I depart on roads leading north. Banks of fog are still stuck to the earth, tangled in the trees and valleys. The sun appears timidly and turns to pink the bands of clouds that are mixed with mist. I am really moved as the mist refreshes my face. Moved especially by the last thing Andréa said: "In a certain way, I have the impression that she was expecting you." I can't believe it.

Back in my Paris office, now that the sun is high, it's up to me to handle the next stage. As agreed between her and Andréa, I write to Marlene directly in English. I receive an answer a short time later. She proposes that we meet on October 2 in Wismar, if the date suits me.

October 2 is my father's birthday. The synchronicities are not letting up. October 2 is perfect. Five days from now.

Wismar is located all the way north in Germany on the coast of the Baltic Sea.

I have quite a bit of driving to do.

34

Einsatzgruppen

Suddenly, I have in front of me the information that I feared I would discover. It looms up in front of me right from the first pages of a book I've had for some weeks, but which up to now I had put off reading since there were other more urgent books to read. It's a book by the historian Charles W. Sydnor, Jr. entitled *Soldiers of Destruction: The SS Death's Head Division, 1933-1945*, published by Princeton University Press. No doubt the most complete historical study on the Totenkopf Division.

The first two chapters go into the creation of the division in autumn of 1939 from sections of the SS-Totenkopfverbände. Details are also given on the campaign in Poland that preceded it.

At this stage in my research, I have a fairly clear idea of the course of Alexander's life. In parallel, the history of the rise of Nazism and of the Third Reich is beginning to be familiar to me. My knowledge about certain periods is still certainly incomplete, but these gaps concern relatively few periods. For example, what did Alexander do in Poland? This question concerns a lapse of time of a few weeks between September and October 1939. The lack of clarity about the Division's activities puzzled me, without my being able to make it any clearer. I didn't realize that the discovery of a clarification would have such consequences. The worst deeds were committed in this country.

September 1, 1939, Germany invades Poland. Fifteen days later, the Soviet Union also attacks from the east. Within a few weeks, Stalin and Hitler divide up the conquered territory. From that point on, terror comes crashing down. Six million Polish citizens will die in the war years, nearly 20 percent of the population. The Soviets and the Germans did not coordinate their policies but they targeted the same categories of the population. Mass deportations and executions begin.

On September 7, the three regiments of the SS-Totenkopfverbände are deployed in the territory. The Führer delegates to them complete authority to conduct, behind the German lines, police and security measures. This involved removing direct control from the army and assigning to these regiments the Reich's supreme police authority in the provinces of Poznań, Łódź, and Warsaw.

Alexander is at this time Adjutant (aide-de-camp) to the commander of the 3rd Battalion of the SS-TV Brandenburg, a battalion that has under surveillance a large area around Poznań and the whole west-central part of the country. It is in this region that his regiment is involved in extensive massacres of civilians. These killings were assigned by the SS officers themselves—notably by the SS-Standartenführer Paul Nostitz, who commanded the Brandenburg Regiment—in activity reports on the implementation of "cleansing and security measures." These reports were sent regularly to Theodor Eicke, commander of the division.

And they have come down to us. Sydnor goes into detail about them in his book: "SS 'Brandenburg' was commanded by Standartenführer Paul Nostitz, a trusted Eicke subordinate who carried out his orders thoroughly and fanatically. During the three weeks it remained on active duty in Poland, SS 'Brandenburg' gave the villages and towns through which it passed a fitting introduction to the character of German rule. In his report summarizing the actions of SS 'Brandenburg' in Poland, Nostitz described how his SS-TV had conducted house searches, secured villages from 'insurgents,' and had arrested and shot large numbers of 'suspicious elements, plunderers, insurgents, Jews, and Poles,' many of whom were killed 'while trying to escape.' In the perverse clerical jargon of the SS, this report referred to the savage measures SS 'Brandenburg' took against the inhabitants of the cities of Włocławek (German: Leslau) and Bydgoszcz (German: Bromberg). SS 'Brandenburg' arrived in Włocławek, some seventy miles northwest of Warsaw on the Vistula, on September 22, and began a four-day 'Jewish action' (Judenaktion) that involved plundering Jewish shops, dynamiting and burning the city's synagogues, and arresting and executing en masse many leading members of the local Jewish community."[1]

While the horror was taking place in Włocławek, Nostitz receives the order to deploy two battalions of the Brandenburg Regiment to Bydgoszcz in order to conduct what is termed an "intelligentsia action." In fact, another massacre. During two whole days, September 24 and 25, the SS arrested and executed approximately eight hundred Polish citizens whose names had been recorded on lists of intellectuals and potential resistance leaders.

Alexander participated in these actions. I am in shock.

In his role as Adjutant, he is charged with supervising administrative efficiency and seeing that the 3rd Battalion commander's orders are carried out. And during four days, the SS brings terror to these villages. Adjutant Alexander Herrmann has the lists in his hands. Lists of persons to be looked for in their homes, to be taken away, and to be executed. He must be sure that the ordered "Jewish action" is properly conducted. Designating the victims to his men.

It is no longer possible for me to not know what he did.

I search for other information, details about these days at Włocławek and Bydgoszcz, and I quickly come across some photos. One in particular. A faded image, in black and white, that gives rise to a surge of nausea while at the same time engulfs me in immense shame.

In this poor-quality photo, several soldiers, laughing hilariously, surround a man on the ground. The caption explains, "German soldiers kicking a Jew, Włocławek, occupied Poland, 1939." The Germans are wearing the black SS uniform of the Totenkopfverbände. This photo was taken when Alexander was at Włocławek. In front of the man on the ground, an SS soldier in boots moves forward to kick him. The SS man is laughing. He and the other SS soldiers in the photo are making fun of this person, who is hesitating to get up, and their amusement speaks to the total horror that is going to follow.

The SS soldier who is kicking could be Alexander or one of his men. He is tall, well built, muscular. He is young.

He thinks what he's doing is right.

The contemplation of this image transports me *elsewhere,* and I then see Alexander laughing like the others. I cannot know his feelings, but, knowing what his path has been up to this point, why would he react differently from the men in black in this photo? The historian Laurence Rees provides a clear description of the state of mind present in the men who made up this ideological army. "The vision of Hitler's world: a dark universe where any pity is banished, and where life comes down to a Darwinian struggle in which the weak deserve to suffer—because such is their fate."[2] In the space of an instant, I understand, I feel that Alexander was behind what he did in those autumn days in occupied Poland. Michel Onfray reminds us, "Even those who do evil, do it thinking they are doing good."[3] This is what is most terrifying because how could that ever come to an end? Yes, Alexander was essentially a combatant, but if fate pushed him into another assignment, such as in these Einsatzgruppen that caused hundreds of thousands of deaths in the East, or in the concentration camps, why wouldn't he have done *his duty* unquestioningly? This photo throws in my face the whole sickening reality of what Alexander was engaged in. He would have done what he was told. No matter what it was.

Even if it means haunting eternity with nightmares.

My discomfort is deep.

No attenuating circumstances.

The discovery of this overview of Alexander's story awakens a thousand doubts in me. Suddenly, I'm questioning myself about the relevance of this book. Why write? Why recount this inquiry into the confines of the darkness of the soul? To heal myself? Yes, of course, that I will follow through on, but share this process in a book?

And then this book's necessity finally looms large. It has to be told—this story—because this horror—we all carry it in us.

The smile and the brutal kick of this SS soldier in the photo etches into my heart. It is Alexander that I see in the image. It is *I* that I see hitting a poor man on the ground.

There comes back into my memory, petrified, this dream I had months before in which I entered armed into a farm building where there were assembled several women wearing shawls and men dressed in rough clothing. Old people, young people, and children too. I am standing facing them; then I aim, I fire, and I take down everyone, one by one. No one resists, no one fights back. Just a mother who holds her infant up so I can take better aim and finish it off on the first shot. Then I finish off the woman. So I execute most of those present . . .

A dream, a memory. The horror.

The conduct of the SS-Totenkopfverbände units in the Poland campaign provokes a shocked reaction, disgust, and unease among high-ranking officers of the German Army. But this brutality is the Führer's intent, received directly. Generals who oppose too vigorously these "cleansing" operations will be denounced. Thus, General Johannes Blaskowicz, revolted by the atrocities committed by the SS, delivered to Commander-in-Chief Walther von Brauchitsch two detailed memoranda about what he did not hesitate to call "war crimes." Hitler, furious at what he called the "naive" attitude of the general, relieved him of his command. The veil that was still hiding the reality of the regime from a good number of Germans, as well as from many military personnel, is beginning to lift and reveal the dark Nazi designs: destroy Poland. Make a clean slate, and turn it into virgin territory, ready for colonization. Darwinism in its most extreme vision applied to the human species. All that happens less than eighty years ago. Here, at home. In Europe.

The reading of Charles Sydnor's book imposes a more precise, more disconcerting and terrible picture of Alexander. The reading clarifies SS behavior and attitudes. It highlights clearly how the SS, and even more so the Death's Head Division under the direction of Theodor Eicke, constituted an astounding brainwashing machine. A structure capable of grinding down the conscience of each individual—its victims, it goes without saying, but also its own members.

There is a name that is mentioned several times in the Polish section of *Soldiers of Destruction*: SS-Standartenführer Paul Nostitz, who commanded the Brandenburg Regiment. This name is not unfamiliar to me. I noticed his signature in several documents in Alexander's military folder, and notably under an evaluation (Beurteilung) dated June 1939. Alexander was in close daily contact with this man. He was his superior. It is SS-Standartenführer Nostitz about whom Sydnor writes that he carried out orders "thoroughly and fanatically."

A friend with whom I shared this story writes to me: "No freedom without forgiveness and no forgiveness without memory."

I am carrying the guilt of too many killed. Those killed in my nights, those killed in my memories, and those killed in my dreams. An unconscious guilt.

Too many killed.

Too much pain inside me.

This guilt has taken on another face. It is what I experienced after the death of my brother. And I am in tears as I write these words. The emotion is intense . . . and I feel suddenly that my brother is present, wrapping my shoulders with his warmth. Enclosing me in his love. I haven't done him any wrong. But my cells carry a pain. I did not kill my brother. I didn't kill anybody. Then I suddenly understand, with devastating lucidity, that this is the reason I have wanted so badly to communicate with the dead for so many years now: so that they will forgive me. Thomas, but also the others.

Where are you, you who were killed by my innumerable hands?

Will you forgive me?

35
Guilt

The date of October 2 is approaching. To say that I'm impatient is a euphemism. I can't sit still. And then I begin to feel the need for all this to end. The need for this inquiry to finally let go of me. There is something incongruous, heavy, in my present activities, and time has worn away the initial curiosity. A melancholy is with me. It disappears when I am in the company of other people, but in moments of solitude it is present, making me feel that I want to just curl up in a corner.

For years now I have been interested in life after death. I have no doubt about life after death anymore, but I now need to think about life after death for a criminal, a murderer. If Alexander has come back *in me*, what justice is there in that? Shouldn't he pay? Can he commit evil, kill, and *come back* to live a happy life? Is there no judgment? He died in 1941, meaning that, for more than seventy-five years, a part of him is turning in circles in his prison of remorse and dragging me into his nightmares. Is that justice? Living in a whirlwind of pain, projections of his inner torments?

In questioning myself in this way, am I not in the process of mixing justice and vengeance? What is just? Isn't it that every criminal finds inner peace, in the same way as do those who suffered through their fault? But then, even SS soldiers? Well, yes, perhaps.

Is our desire that those who have done wrong suffer through natural consequences the same as our need to see a punishment applied? But is punishment justice? On the level of men, justice has the role of surveillance and punishment, to take Michel Foucault's formulation. But is that *just*? And in the Beyond? Beyond life and death, are there rules of a universal justice? One thing is certain, death does not deliver us from torment. On certain nights Alexander still wakes up screaming, because Alexander's dreams are sometimes my dreams . . .

The ascension of this man toward the light is being done through me.

His redemption is passing through my cells, through my body. I no longer have any desire, from now on, to slow this process down. The therapeutic interest of my inquiry, for him and for me, is not in doubt, but I want to be done with it. My role is not to pay for him but to repair.

And then I have a life to lead.

I was able to have a few succinct exchanges with Marlene. I write short phrases in English that she translates in Google, and in return I do the same. She has found an interpreter for our October 2 rendezvous. I really hope that it's someone competent because I feel a certain distrust peeking through in Marlene's emails—Who is this man? What connection does he really have with Alexander? And the explanations that I'm going to supply her with will need to be very faithfully translated so she perceives my sincerity and my honesty. Once again I am apprehensive about the moment when I'm going to have to recount the circumstances of my dream. How will this be taken by this woman who accords so much importance to her uncle Alexander? If a person showed up in my life telling me they had met one of my ancestors in a dream, what kind of welcome would I give them?

Photo Journal

Grand scale reporting, a passion that has always been with me.
Here, at age 27, in northern Afghanistan.

November 1989, in India. My obsession with questioning violence and war leads to conversations with personalities such as the Dalai Lama.

Investigations in the Pamir region, Central Asia.

In the Amazonian forest. It is here that the encounter happened.

Verlustmeldung d. SS- ...

Gemäss Mitteilung ⚡⚡-FHA.A[

Der SS- Ostuf, H e r r m a n n

vom   2./⚡⚡-T.-Inf.Rgt.1

bei   Kirillowtschina

am   Brust-u.Halsschuß(I.G.)

Ergänzt laut namentlicher Verlus

Berichtszeitraum: ....

Grablage: Orstausgang Mirochny,[

Heimatanschrift: ....

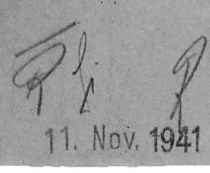

11. Nov. 1941

1187

T.-Division. o o o o o o o o o o o o o o o o

a/Tgb.Nr.4673/41 geh.v.1.11.41.

lexander, ... geb. . 21.8.16,

ist am .20.10.41.

fallen. xxxxxxxxxxxxxxxxxxxxxxxxxxxxxxx

ldung Nr. .264(Ostfront)SS-T.I.R.1

Nr. 50

30. Apr. 1942

Copy of Alexander Herrmann's death certificate in the military folder received from the American archives.

D.R.

The fuzzy and mysterious photo that I discovered at the beginning of my inquiry. This is the photo I showed to mediums.

The same portrait, this time crisp and full of information, supplied by the national German archives. I discovered it after I had finished writing this book.

The building at Neundorfer Straße 47, in Plauen, Germany.

The fourth floor that the Herrmann family occupied.

Behind the building located at Neundorfer Straße 47, the backyard that attracted me so irresistibly . . .

. . . and that I later discover was the playground of Alexander and his brother.

The photo with which Marlene tested me.

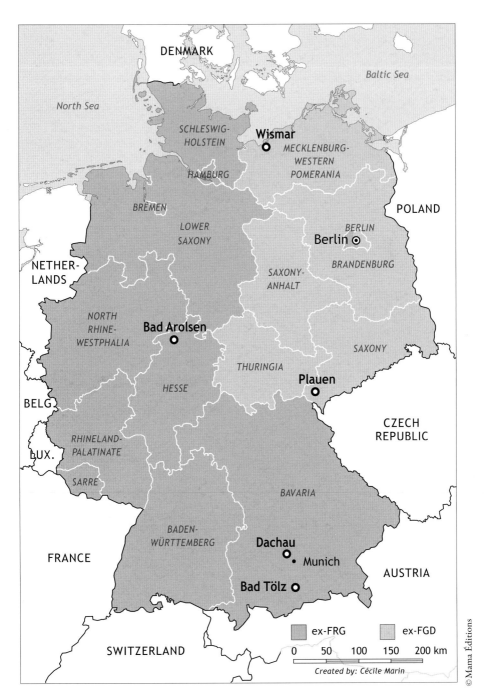

Key towns of my inquiry in Germany.

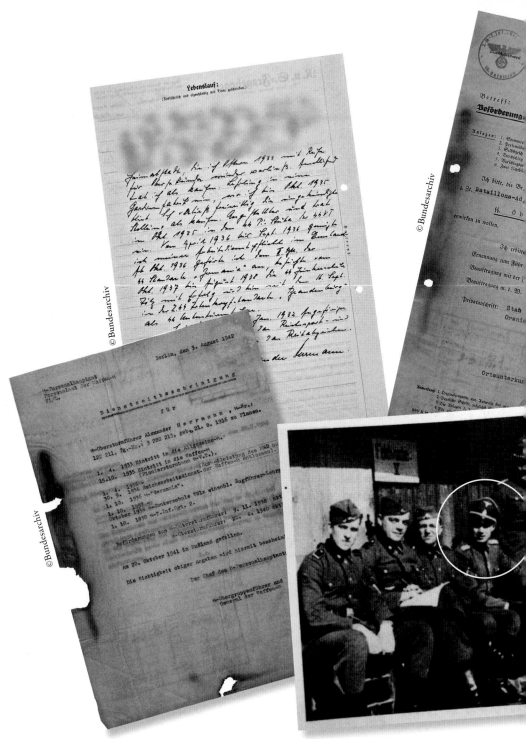

During months of inquiry and research, I accumulated archival documents.
Photo taken at a forward surveillance post on the demarcation line, at Bazas,
to the south of Bordeaux, in February 1941.

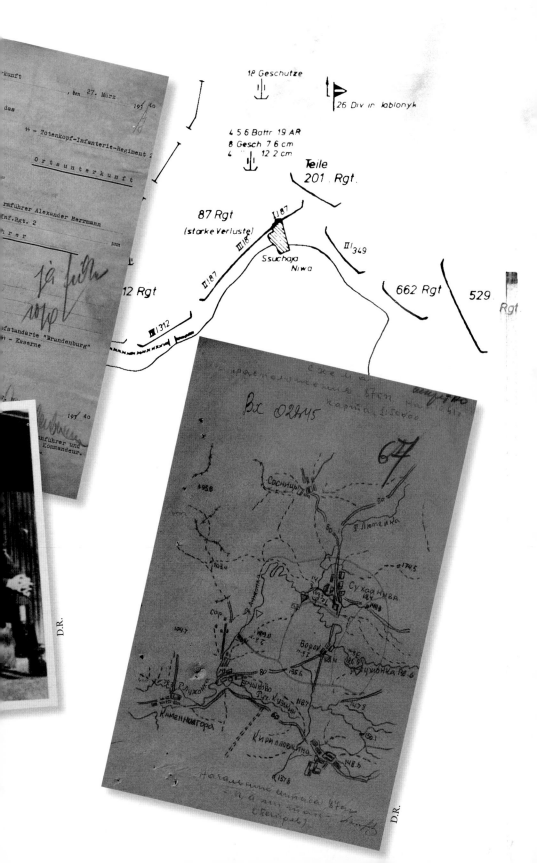

Dachau, the shock.

In Russia. From left to right, beginning on the top row: Tania's house in Mirochny; interior of the house where we slept in Mirochny; at a defensive position south of Sukhaya Niva; to the east of Sukhaya Niva, the denouement approaches; very close to the spot I had looked for so hard; the little door that allows you to enter under Tania's house.

"Our metamorphosis has begun."

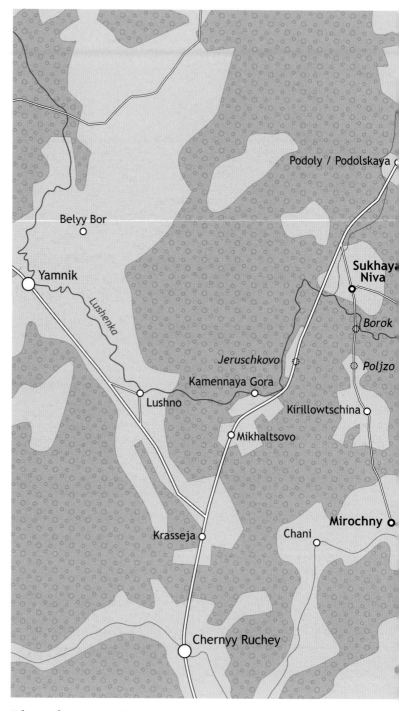

The combat zone in Russia

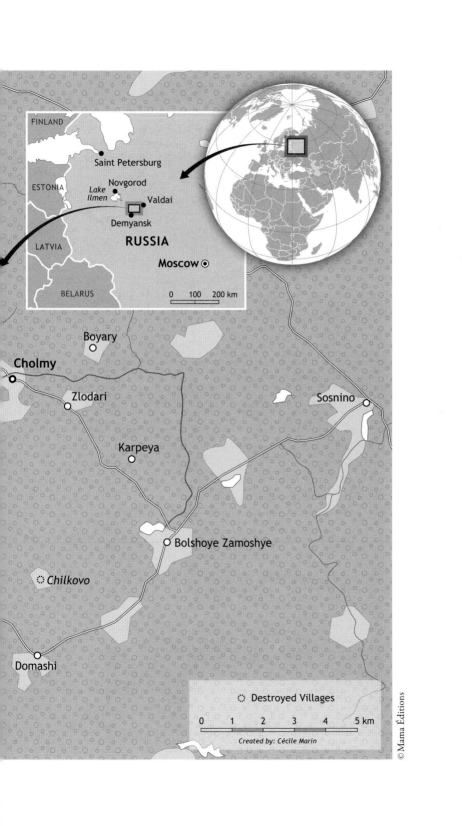

FINLAND

Saint Petersburg

ESTONIA

Novgorod

Lake Ilmen

Valdai

Demyansk

RUSSIA

LATVIA

Moscow ⊙

BELARUS

0   100   200 km

Boyary

Cholmy

Zlodari

Sosnino

Karpeya

Bolshoye Zamoshye

Chilkovo

Domashi

⟡ Destroyed Villages

0   1   2   3   4   5 km

Created by: Cécile Marin

©Mama Éditions

Top: in Plauen, working with the archives in the company of genealogist Andréa Harnisch and former French professor André Harnisch. Center: in Plauen with Andréa Harnisch. Bottom: in the village of Mirochny at the home of Valentina and her daughter, Macha, with Nicolas Fréal, my guide in Russia.

36

Baltic

It is 6:30 a.m. when I leave Paris on October 1. Destination Wismar, in the north of Germany, for an improbable meeting with the niece of a man who has been dead for decades and was encountered in a waking dream. Alexander Herrmann.

Like me, I foresee that Marlene is expecting a lot from this meeting. But she is thousands of leagues away from imagining what I'm going to reveal to her. I'm afraid of her reaction. I'm afraid of her amazement, of her anger, and I'm afraid that this single living doorway to Alexander may close.

I sweep through more than a thousand kilometers in one shot. Ten hours of driving. And here I am on the shores of the Baltic Sea in the middle of the afternoon. The center of Wismar is charming. The city, which was located in East Germany during the time of the GDR, was Swedish until the beginning of the twentieth century. But once outside the historic heart of the city, you find the colors of ex-Eastern Bloc countries: bricks, bad cement, and sadness. Several arms of the sea form a kind of port that doesn't look like anything special. A few centuries ago the Swedish had made the spot into one of the largest maritime fortresses in Europe, but today the city reeks of abandonment. All the port buildings are in a sinister red brick. Windows with broken panes allow the escape of those ghosts who prefer to flee. A cold wind coming off the open sea chases away the clouds. Along the quays, sturdy wooden ships are moored. Some of them operate as snack bars. Music, running children, punks sipping their beer, young women with pale faces. The East. Rostock is a little farther along the coast.

As I stroll through the streets, I am struck by the telescoping of the current with what was happening in Germany in the 1930s. For example, the arrival for several years now of hundreds of thousands of migrants in Western Europe brings us face-to-face with our fears and with our humanity, as it was with the political and social circumstances right here after the First World War. What attitude do we have toward those who *bother us*? Those who disturb our comfort? Those that "the authorities" (political, social, media based, etc.) designate as being a *problem*?

The unfurling of such distress at our front door touches each one of us in the depths of our being. These current events (refugees, terrorism, etc.), just like the rise of Nazism in its time, brings into question our ability to hear—or not—the voice of our conscience and our ability to not let ourselves be invaded by fears whose roots are self-serving. For yes, current events touch us, make us nervous; and that's very normal. But as in former times, the legitimate disturbance is amplified by the political forces currently at work in Europe and that take hold of the debate in order to profit from it. Accordingly these forces no longer speak about the reality but are content, for their own short-term interests, to add fuel to the fire of our apprehensions and our worries. Thus, once again, a disturbing debate is spread and makes itself heard, stigmatizing certain categories of persons.

Feeding fear and guilt.

Was it so different during successive elections that, at the end of the 1920s, in Germany, saw the Nazi and Communist parties confront each other? How to choose in good conscience what kind of citizen we want to be when the political debate is simplified, distorted, and quite naturally handed over to extremists? When Alexander joined the Nazi Party, he was *sincerely* convinced that his choice was the best one, the most just, as did millions of other Germans. Between two devils, which one is the lesser of two evils? But no, our choice does not come down to that.

Our era is so strange that, as the American writer Joyce Carol Oates says, we spend our time picking apart little phrases of the politicians, TV hosts, or other people, looking for something to be *shocked* about, while what is really important for our society we are indifferent about. Fear can drag nations into horror, but it can also wake us up to the light. Freedom is a risk.

The restaurant is half full. Quick dinner. Sleep calls, and soon I am back in room 508 of the Steigenberger Hotel.

The next day, October 2, at the moment of awakening, I regain consciousness, eyes half closed, still in the energy and the atmosphere of a dream that is fading; then I open my eyes. I see the drawn curtains, a thin band of light coming past the window frame, and suddenly there I am in the *real* world. Instantly, a familiar and diffuse sensation of melancholy spreads through me.

The memory of my dream is still present: I am with other men in a war scene. In a city, a big city in ruins, preparing for a major attack. The enemy artillery starts up, and bits of burning shrapnel whistle around us, incandescent. I have not really taken cover, waiting in the middle of a group of combatants. I have several rifle bullets in my hand. Five or six long rifle cartridges in my dirty hand. I study them. Once again, a possible correspondence with Alexander's life disturbs me.

He advanced into French territory with the Totenkopf Division on May 19, 1940. A violent advance. This first real experience of exchange of fire for these SS soldiers doesn't go as well as they had hoped. The men leave a wake of blood behind them. On May 28 and 29, the Totenkopf Division heads back in a northerly direction to participate in the pincer movement against Allied troops at Dunkirk, and they get ready to take Bailleul. My discovery several weeks before of the name of this little town in the north of France, and the fighting that the Totenkopf men engaged in there, evoked enormous distress in me.

Bailleul.

A name that I had thought I *heard* during my dream in Peru. I had even written about it the same day in my journal: "Once again, a ruined town or village and the feeling that it's named Bagneux or Bayeux—actually neither of those two names but a name like that." It wasn't either Bagneux or Bayeux, but a name like that.

Bailleul.

Why this agitation? What happened there? This morning I have the intuition that the place was important to Alexander. Before capturing the town, the fighting is very hard and, especially on the morning of May 29, the division comes under an enormous English artillery barrage that has everyone running for shelter, even Eicke, who accompanies his men on the front lines that day. At 4:00 p.m. Bailleul falls into the hands of Alexander's regiment. He leads the advance accompanied by the men of his battalion. Is this perhaps the first violent combat in which he participated? Did he lose a friend at Bailleul? It's still a mystery among others that punctuate this inquiry.

The morning passes. I stay stretched out on the bed, not moving, breathing slowly. This is one of the most important days in my inquiry. It's also the day my father was born, who is no longer in *this* world. I know that he sees me and stands close to me, but I would have liked to speak with him face-to-face about Alexander, feel his astonished look, and have him support me with his encyclopedic historical knowledge.

I am dreading the moment of meeting Marlene, while at the same time I'm boiling with impatience. I am not in Wismar by chance. That's for sure. It is not my imagination that has drawn me to the shores of the Baltic today.

Marlene knew Alexander.

Alexander guided me right to her.

She is the living connection between us.

37

The Little Girl

Only a few seconds left. She must already be down in the hotel lobby. Outside a veil of misty clouds holds back the sun's heat. Early winter is coming in from the north.

I think of my mother, all alone in her big house in the forest. She lived there with my father these last forty years. Today, only the wind of spirits whistles through the pines and bamboo. The day is sad. It ought to be an anniversary day, a day of birth, of joy, and it's a day of hurt and silence. Solitude and cold. I feel tired; my skull is heavy. How to describe my state? Sad, yes. I would rather be elsewhere, even though I'm supposed to experience so strong a moment today.

Do I blame myself? Is it my father's melancholy that is brushing up lightly against me? Am I too apprehensive? Is it because unconsciously I'm afraid I'll be disappointed that I downgrade the importance of the day? It's some of all these things, but also I'm afraid I'll be thought badly of. Other people's opinions have such importance for me. Having anyone doubt my sincerity or my honesty wounds me more deeply than anything else.

I reread for the thousandth time the pages of my journal from Peru. As if I still didn't believe it, as if a part of me wanted still to hang on to the idea that this whole story is due to chance. The vision of my dream, however, is so present in me: "I see a playful little girl—blonde, smiling, joyful. She must be between two and three years old. He is with her. Is she his daughter? And then once again death, screaming faces, and suddenly he is near a lake in the countryside, and it is summer. He has his shirt off and another man is lying on his stomach beside him—a man a little older whose face I can make out quite clearly. There is a strong connection between them."

There it is.

A few moments more. I don't dare move, waiting for the last moment. 3:58 p.m. . . . 3:59 p.m. It's time. I grab my folders, leave, and lock the door. My footsteps echo in the long corridor. The entranceway stairs appear, and I walk down to the ground floor. The lobby. Not many people. One group is talking animatedly.

An elderly woman walks away from the group. Slim and elegant, she looks at me.

It's Marlene.

She emanates a noble presence. A fine figure of a woman, soon to be eighty years old. Her clear eyes stare at me with a mixture of timidity and force. She has short hair, square cut, strawberry blonde, obviously dyed. I move forward to meet her, oblivious now of anything else. I dive into her, fascinated. Marlene. By looking into her eyes, it is certain, there will appear in the space of one second all the answers to questions that have been burning in me for so many months. Behind these pupils the keys to the secret are obviously hiding. I scrutinize her, looking fixedly, magnetized by her. I await the emergence of an emotion, an intuition that will spring up in my mind. I'm attentive to the slightest sensation. Some deep feeling will provide a hook, a way in. *Something* is going to happen. This is the little girl that Alexander has led me to.

I have found her—outside of time.

And . . . nothing. Nothing happens. My belly is tense, I am emotional, I'm short of breath, but the sky doesn't open to allow through a cohort of angels carrying THE revelation. No thunder rolls, no cavalcade of cymbals or heavenly drums. Nothing special takes place.

Just a distinguished lady observing me with curiosity.

What did I expect?

The flow of time regains its normal course. The fire in my eyes decreases in intensity. A veil covers them, and I *come back*. My hand lets go of her hand.

Marlene introduces me to the rest of her family. A tall bald man with a beard and a pleasant smile says hello enthusiastically. Then another man comes up to me. He has a sportsman air about him and is wearing a casual shirt: her brother Dr. Bertram Herrmann, one of the twins. Marlene's daughter has come as well; we must be, give or take a tad, the same age. The last of the group, in the back: the translator recruited by Marlene. Our precious bridge.

We make our way to the private room in the hotel that Marlene has reserved. A bright room where we take our places around a big table.

Immediately, Marlene takes hold of the reins.

"We are very curious to know why you are interested in the Herrmann family."

It's true that they must be impatient to learn about "the French branch of their family." What else could they be expecting? I have to be the product of Alexander's illicit love affairs in France. His grandson or grandnephew. Andréa and I must have seemed so mysterious. I prepare myself to *really* surprise them. I'm as nervous as if I were preparing to speak in front of hundreds of people.

"A big question, a big question mark," insists Marlene.

I take a big breath.

"It is also a big question for me. Perhaps you have looked me up on Google?"

"Yes, we have discovered things about you."

Well, that will reinforce what I'm going to say. I begin by describing the general outlines of my professional career. I speak about my craft of investigative journalism, my books, the television shows that I hosted. Right from the beginning I mean to not leave any doubt in their minds that they are dealing with a serious person who is recognized as such. I'm neither a crackpot nor a visionary, and my career bears witness to that. Given what I'm about to announce to them, I can't stress this point enough. My sentences are short and precise using simple words. The translator has to be comfortable, and her translation has to flow. After a few minutes, when I have the full attention of the whole family, I come to my trip to Peru. I unburden myself of the whole thing with hope, sincerity, and transparency. Was I raised like that? I am convinced that complete honesty is the best guarantee of being believed. Only it must be accepted that my account is no doubt, in spite of everything, somewhat altered in the translation. And it is above all very unexpected. A waking dream? A spiritual kind of encounter? A surname, a forename, a war scene, the face of a man, a little girl, and so on. As I'm finishing, I see clearly that Marlene, like the others, doesn't look like she quite understands that I'm really serious. A silence follows the end of my tale. I ask the translator to reclarify several details, among other things that I was not asleep when that happened to me.

"He was not dreaming. He was lying down, was conscious, and saw all of that in front of him," she tells the dumbfounded listeners.

After a few seconds of embarrassment, Marlene is the first to react.

"Indeed . . . It's incredible. Knowing the name like that . . . "

Of the four, her husband Joachim seems to be the most captivated. As for Bertram, he looks at his sister with embarrassment. Marlene's daughter is wide-eyed. The translator fidgets in her chair. This wasn't what they were expecting. It flies in their face. There is mistrust, but I perceive nevertheless that my story has awakened their curiosity. These are intelligent people, and I can imagine the conflict that is unfolding in this very moment in their minds.

Marlene begins speaking again in order to share her astonishment with nevertheless a great deal of tact and respect. Yes, they had guessed that I was going to reveal to them that Alexander had had an affair in France and that I was the result. They have trouble understanding the story of the waking dream. In fact, they find that really hard. But my seriousness, my professional history keeps them from getting up and walking out on me. I'm not someone who is off his rocker, even if what they just heard is preposterous. Then, after a brief moment of feeling suspended, we continue the meeting as if in the end everything was moving along just fine. I take out Alexander's military folder that Andréa had already forwarded to Marlene. And we begin to talk about the uncle who disappeared. As if there was nothing more natural in the world. I calm down.

"Why do you think your uncle joined the SS?"

I've felt for a long time that Alexander's decision was not to his family's taste. It must not have pleased his parents or his brother. Marlene perhaps has information about this, obtained either from her father or from her grandmother Hedwig (Alexander's mother), with whom she lived for a time.

"I don't know," she replies.

"We don't know any more about it than you do," adds her husband Joachim.

"For my grandmother, right up to her death she could not understand it. What was the particular reason that this son joined that unit? Right up to her death this remained a mystery."

"You didn't talk about it with your father?"

"We never exchanged a word on this subject with my father. I found out about the existence of my uncle Alexander from my grandmother."

"Oh, really! Why didn't you speak with him?"

"My father lived as a prisoner in Russia until 1948, following his capture by the Russians in Romania in 1944. He came back from that very affected . . . "

"And then, in the GDR, you couldn't in any case talk about it," added Joachim.

"It was forbidden," Marlene confirms. "In the GDR Nazis were hunted down intensively. So probably this is the reason that the subject was taboo at home. We were children, and if they had confided in us that our uncle was an SS member, we could have made a gaffe in class or elsewhere. It was too risky. It remained a secret. My father never spoke to me about his brother."

"But what do you think yourself?"

"Just what you must already know yourself. Alexander had the typical profile: tall and blond. He was lured in—that is obvious. He was the ideal model for the SS. But he was the ideal model *on the outside,* because he was very young. According to my grandmother, he was actually a gentle person . . . "

"Your father was a prisoner in Russia?"

"Yes. A very hard period for him."

Joachim interjects:

"He was captured when Romania changed camps. This country was allied with the Germans; then in 1944 they capitulated."

"My father never said a word about his captivity. Not a single word."

I've just put my finger on an open wound. Alfred, the father of Marlene and Bertram, was captured at the moment of the defeat of the Axis powers in Romania. He was then transferred to Russia, as were innumerable soldiers of the Wehrmacht. Marlene informs me that he was a military doctor during the war and that he did facial surgery. Four years in captivity. Four years of unimaginable hell. And then, without warning, one day in December 1948, Inge, Marlene's mother, receives a phone call and learns that her husband, who disappeared so many years before, will be coming home in a few days. Marlene was about to be ten. Being the eldest, she was helping her mother look after her little sister, born in 1940, and the twins, born in 1943. Hard to believe that Bertram, sitting opposite me, was more than seventy. His brother died five years ago. I feel that Marlene and Bertram are touched by mention of their father's return from captivity. Marlene explains.

"He was a man destroyed. I have the memory of him seated, shut up in his room, plunged in darkness, the curtains drawn. Every time that we entered his room by accident, he was there with his head in his hands. My mother got us out of there quickly. She told us our father was thinking about his friends who had not returned."

"I have trouble imagining what he must have endured," I say.

"He never recovered from it. We never saw him in any other state.

Broken. He died of a heart attack eleven years after his return, in May 1959. He was forty-eight."

"He was a broken man," Bertram adds, with great feeling.

"He never spoke to his children. He never said anything to us, not about the war, not about his captivity, not about his brother. Nothing. He was traumatized, and in photos taken after the war, you see that clearly. He seemed to have aged so much . . . "

After what the Nazis put the Soviets through, I can't imagine how the German prisoners could have survived the frightful conditions of their internment after the fall of the Reich. A silence of death and darkness engulfed what was left of the Herrmann family and what was left of Europe. Silence and amnesia. Immense suffering once again. Bertram and his twin both became doctors, like their father, who spoke to them so little. What suffering for these children. A father destroyed and mute in whom they observed so great a hurt without knowing what they could do about it. In this whirlwind of unspoken things, only Hedwig, Alexander's mother, kept open a thin slice of memory. She was the one who kept the inheritance of memory. What did she transmit to Marlene, her granddaughter?

"What else did your grandmother tell you?"

"She kept touch with Luise, Alexander's wife."

"Oh, really?"

"Yes, they saw each other every year. She also told me that my grandfather Otto, Alexander's father, never got over the death of his youngest son. He developed a heart condition and was found dead in a hotel room not long afterward."

A father who does not get over the death of his son. Once again the intimate side of information. These few words, "Otto never got over the death of his younger son," touch me. This feeling is heightened by what took place in my own family after the accidental death of my brother in Afghanistan. The pain made Otto heartsick, and the next year he had an attack that he died from. My father was destroyed by Thomas's death, and he also developed cardiac problems following this drama.

He was hospitalized in the months following his son's death, and we thought we would lose him, but he had the good luck to recover his health and to live twelve more years. The parallel hits me hard.

Suddenly, I wonder. What have I come to do in this family? With them, feelings are padlocked. However, I sense a lot of contained emotion that is only asking for release.

"Do you want to see a photo? We have one," Marlene suggests suddenly as if to cut short too much emotion.

I had forgotten about that photo. Andréa had told me that Marlene had confided in her that she owned a portrait of the two brothers together, Alexander and Alfred, but since the beginning of our meeting I hadn't thought about it. However, it's been days that I've been dreaming of seeing it—this shot. A new photo of Alexander. Marlene removes a cardboard folder from her bag and holds it enclosed in her hands, like a treasure.

"We're going to show you the photo, but we'd like to conduct a little test: will you recognize which of the two is Alexander?"

Joy sweeps through me. From the point of view of discovering once again an image of Alexander, of course, but also because, after having related my dream in detail, if they decide to show me this photo, it's because I have touched them. Perhaps they don't believe me completely, but they judge that my relationship with their uncle is *legitimate*. And this form of recognition touches me sincerely. What an immense pleasure. We've progressed to a new level.

Marlene opens her envelope with solemnity and places the sepia photo before me.

Two young men. A beautiful studio photo with well-designed lighting. They look out, each with a beautiful steady look—one of them looking at the photographer and the other to the left. What expressions!

And then, surprise. I recognize him instantly.

But not Alexander, his brother! The man looking at the camera.

A violent emotion assails me. Once again my gut is clenched and tears, like a wave coming from the center of my body, threaten to sweep everything away. His brother is *the other man* that I saw in my dream. The man stretched out on the grass, while I saw Alexander standing to his right. "A man a little older whose face I can make out quite clearly." I have trouble controlling my dizziness, but I manage to hold back my tears in front of this family who are observing me. These few seconds of amazement are intense.

"This one is Alfred, and so here is Alexander," I say, pointing my finger finally at the man on the right in the photo.

The whole family looks at each other, dumbfounded. I have correctly picked out Alexander.

"My first sensation was to recognize them both. Both are familiar to me. But I really recognized the one on the left, Alfred, because I saw him also in my vision."

"Did you not recognize Alexander? You seem to hesitate . . . " Marlene asks me.

"His face is familiar to me, obviously, but it is honestly difficult for me to affirm that I recognize him. For so many months I have been remembering his face in my dream. I have thought about him too much, and my initial memory has to have been altered with all of my successive remembering. But in contrast, with the other man it was spontaneous because it was completely unexpected. I saw Alexander's brother in my vision. I saw your father . . . "

I am very, very moved. My sensations are powerful. I recognized Alfred. Therefore the little girl in my dream is definitely Marlene. The face of Alexander's big brother matched immediately with my memory, before my analytical mind could pollute the scene. I recognized the man in my vision.

38
Life's Traces

Alexander was loved. This memory, this truth is carried all the way to me by Marlene. The little girl in my dream delivers this detail to me—a detail so innocent and yet so full of meaning. Alexander was a son who was loved by his mother, and whose death shattered his father to the point of having him die of grief. Alexander was a cherished son. A pampered younger son at the heart of a little family where goodwill and respect seemed to reign. Before the disaster of the Second World War sweeps away their fate and that of tens of millions of others. That makes even more mysterious his leaving so young to join the SS. The wave of anger and darkness over Germany must have been awfully powerful.

In the photo that I hold in my hands, I see his look for the first time. His eyes are clear, and he must be seventeen or eighteen. He and his brother are elegant—suit jackets and silk ties. Paisley motif for Alexander. He's wearing on his lapel a discreet little emblem that I don't notice right away. Round and black with a double *sig*, that you would take for a double S, whereas it's a runic symbol. He belongs then already to the SS when this photo was taken. The two brothers have their hair combed carefully straight back. Flattened and smoothed with hair cream. Foreheads bare. Alfred also has very clear eyes, but his are curious, inquisitive, soft, while those of Alexander hide a little something that is tougher, more determined. The skin on Alexander's face is smooth, his lips thick and firmly delineated. There is something a little feminine in him. Perhaps his youth? The fineness of his face as he leaves adolescence behind? In any case there emanates from his personage an energy that is unwavering. Yes, he is sure of himself in this photo. He already knows where he is going. He is already in the arms of the shadow. It's in the process of happening. It's obvious when looking at the picture.

Marlene suggests I keep the photo. She had a copy made for me. Her gesture touches me. After all these emotions I try to pick up the thread of my questions.

"Have you saved any documents, his letters, after he was killed?"

"Yes, my mother received a message."

"No, I meant personal letters, documents that had belonged to him . . . "

"No. When the apartment where Hedwig was living was bombarded by the Allies in 1945, she had only time to grab a single suitcase before fleeing to shelter. This photo was in the suitcase, as well as a few others, but all the rest, everything she owned, disappeared in the rubble and the flames. Souvenirs, letters, documents, clothing. All that remained of her life was a single suitcase."

"And you, what do you know about Alexander?"

"I know about him what my grandmother told me about him. She recounted that Alexander was a very sensitive being. Very sensitive, as she was herself. She described him as someone good, very obliging, willing to help."

"Do you have any memory of him?"

"Me? No, I was born in 1938."

"But you might have seen him? He, in any case, has to have been acquainted with you."

Marlene was born in December 1938. It's obvious they must have met. She is the living link between Alexander and me. That she retains no conscious memory of course makes sense. She was so young. The last time when Alexander would have been able to return to Plauen was at the latest the springtime of 1941—if he had actually been able to obtain permission. Marlene at that time was barely a little more than two years old.

"That could have been possible. But I don't know about it. We have several photos of the family, and he isn't in any of them."

"Really? Do you know why?"

"I don't know."

Marlene again leans over her handbag and takes out several old photo albums. To my great amazement they contain numerous photos of Alfred and Alexander as children.

"These are the few photos that were able to be saved from the bombardment."

I see the brothers in their early years. Alexander has a round mug and laughing eyes. Improbable haircut with bangs across his forehead that are no doubt "homemade." He looks cheeky but kind. He's not smiling in two portraits posed in a sailor outfit, but in all the others he emanates a childhood joy. A little rascal. On several taken outside I recognize the back of their building in Plauen on Neundorfer Strasse. In one in particular where the two boys are bursting with laughter, I recognize very clearly the inner garden and the brick wall of the back of the building. This is the spot that I didn't manage to leave because I found it so *familiar.* The brick wall, the weeds along the fence, the same drainpipe, the same landing . . . The tranquil life of two carefree little boys. What was it that swung the head of the younger one?

Here's all that remains of a life.

A few images, bursts of laughter frozen onto paper.

Everything else disappeared in a bombing, and whatever ended up in the possession of Luise, Alexander's wife, has gone missing, it would seem. The meager traces of a life on Earth.

I can't but be aware in this moment of so many families exterminated by the Nazis who left behind absolutely nothing. No photo, no letter, no trace, not even a memory in those still alive. As Samuel Pisar said, our memory is their only tomb.

◆ ◆ ◆

I contemplate these images taken on the spot in a life that was still peaceful, at a time when not for a second could the growing cataclysm have been imagined. Marlene turns the pages of the albums. She's going too fast. I discover the debonair face of Otto, Alexander's father, and the face of Hedwig, the gentle and devoted mother. The family at Christmastime 1927. Alexander is dressed in a sailor's outfit, standing, straight as an arrow beside the fir tree. Hands crossed. He's eleven. Alfred, behind his parents, is sixteen and is gallantly wearing a tie. Otto, in a three-piece suit, is sitting in a good chair, while the armchair is reserved for Hedwig. A little wisp of a woman. Slender and dressed simply. The resemblance with Alexander is striking here. The same fine eyes, the same general shape of the face. She's holding a little dog, I think, but the animal is moving and the image is fuzzy.

The pages turn. Suddenly, Marlene exclaims.

"Ah, you see. This one is of my father's marriage. Alexander is not in the photo . . . "

"When did that take place?"

"The civil marriage took place in November 1937 in Berlin. Alexander was married in Arolsen, his mother told me, but for my father it was in Berlin. For both of them there was a civil marriage and a religious marriage."

"In November 1937, Alexander was at the SS-Junkerschule in Bad Tölz in Bavaria. Perhaps he didn't receive permission to leave the school? Besides, it's a hell of a long way to Berlin," I say.

"Perhaps . . . "

"Do you think that Alexander didn't have a good relationship with his brother?" I asked.

"No, I don't think that was the case. They were five years apart, but I think that they got along well . . . otherwise the photo of the two of them would never have been taken."

"The two brothers must have been very different in their education and their opinions, though."

"I think that's definitely true. In reality, Alexander is not present in virtually any family photo."

"If he was in uniform, perhaps those photos were destroyed after the war. You told me that Nazis were hunted down in the GDR. It would have been unwise to have kept such damning images!"

"Yes, you're right . . ." Marlene says to me. She seems to have come to this realization at the same time I did.

"I suppose you don't know where Alexander met Luise?"

"That's right. I don't know. At Arolsen, probably. My grandmother stayed in contact with Luise right to the end. Luise treated her as her mother-in-law. She went to visit her every year. But I know little more than that."

Why did I come here? Why did Alexander lead me to his niece? We have finished looking at the albums. Marlene allows me to take photos of the images that interested me. The translator is beginning to get tired. She has been making ceaseless efforts for hours. And I become aware that, of all those present, it is I who know Alexander the best. This is both reassuring and disconcerting. I come looking for answers, and it's I who is giving them. I realize that I will learn very little more. With much tolerance, openness, and kindness, Marlene and her family have shared with me the small amount of memory they have of this sad era. Suddenly the thought comes to me that my trip to Wismar was perhaps important *for them*.

Perhaps Alexander had me come here to heal a wound in the disaster of this family? Suddenly, the point of view changes. Yes, no doubt it is I who can do something for Marlene, her brother, and their descendants. Even especially since the final stage of my crazy adventure is approaching. I am leaving for Russia in less than two weeks.

"As I told you by email, I will soon be going to Russia to the place where Alexander died."

"To his grave?"

"Yes, and to where he spent his last weeks. I know where he is buried. Is there something I can do for you there?"

"Yes, I would like that, but what? I think you will not find much. When are you leaving? October 11?"

"The fifteenth. I want to be on site at the location where he was killed on the anniversary of his death, October 20. In eighteen days."

"I don't know . . . Perhaps with this trip you will be able to bring this topic to a close in yourself, so that it stops weighing you down."

I am surprised by her remark. She is kindly, and not for an instant do I detect any reproach. I look at her conspiratorially.

"You don't think I'm a little crazy?"

"No, no. I wouldn't say that. But we are not familiar with these kinds of spiritual things. We are . . . I'm looking for the word . . . yes, *bodenständig,* we are down to earth."

Joachim tactfully adds:

"I would not allow myself to make a judgment about what you're saying."

And Marlene clarifies further:

"We cannot completely understand this sensitivity, this parapsychology, or whatever you might call it . . . because it doesn't correspond to our nature. You know, we grew up in the GDR, in a materialist world."

I am all the more grateful to them for having granted me their trust. Marlene seems to be thinking out loud.

"There is perhaps something you could do in the cemetery . . . "

Once again she goes looking for something among her folders. She brings out several sheets.

"Here we are. The Volksbund Deutsche Kriegsgräberfürsorge* wrote to us to tell us that Alexander was buried in their military cemetery . . . "

"The what?"

"The Volksbund Deutsche Kriegsgräberfürsorge. I thought that you would have been in touch with them. It's an organization that is

---

*German War Graves Commission —Trans.

concerned with the bodies of German soldiers who have died throughout the world. We wrote to them a few months ago, and they sent us this."

Marlene hands me an official document on the organization's letterhead.

"They are saying that Alexander's body is located in the military cemetery in Korpowo. In block 20."

The translator reads me the text. A cemetery for German soldiers was constructed at Korpowo, a location situated not far from Demyansk. I think that it must be about fifty kilometers from there that Alexander died and was buried. Fifty thousand soldiers killed in the Second World War and who fell in this region of Russia were exhumed from makeshift graves scattered here and there where they had been buried, sometimes in the heat of combat, and moved to a commemorative location.

"Are they sure that Alexander was transferred to this location?" I asked.

"They say that he was originally buried in Mirochny, grave number 50."

"Yes, that's how it is indicated in the military document that I have in his folder," I say.

" . . . and they say that he was exhumed and taken to Korpowo. You see, it is noted here that one day all the German soldiers will be buried there."

"I am going there. I will take a look at the spot."

"I believe that he was transferred without having been identified. They did not find his military badge."

"But then how can they be sure?" I ask, surprised.

"They explain that graves dating from the time of the war were pillaged and that identifying elements disappeared. You can keep these papers if you like. They presume that Alexander is in the grave that they must have dug up, but without having been able to identify him either from his tag or from anything else. If you are going, perhaps you will find something? His name on a commemorative stele in block number 20 in the Korpowo cemetery, for example."

"I will go and see."

"There must be the remains of so many unknown soldiers. Try to find the name Alexander Herrmann. I would be curious to know if what the Kriegsgräberfürsorge is saying is right."

"I promise."

"What are you going to do afterward with all this information? Have we helped you?"

"Yes, enormously. I am very touched by these photos. As for what's next, I would like in the end to understand why I had this dream."

"You know more about this than we have ever known. I don't know if Alexander had something in particular, I don't think so. I know so few details about my uncle, or even about my father. I only know that Alex's mother was an adorable woman."

Night has fallen when we finally part. I am exhausted, but I want to get back to my room quickly to get down a maximum of details about this incredible afternoon before they fade away. Bertram, whom I see as being the most distant, on his own initiative, takes me in his arms for a fraternal farewell. Marlene does the same and holds me against her for lengthy seconds. Then it's Joachim's turn, who begins by looking at me tenderly before hugging me close to him. I can't explain it, but I feel a great affection for this man. If they don't manage to believe me, they are paradoxically convinced of my sincerity. They find themselves in this space of strange and unsettling uncertainty, which is sometimes the prelude to other upsets.

Once more, what a great distance between the violence and the brutality of the personage observed from afar and the man portrayed this evening. Alexander, who was a child born in a cultivated and loving family. Why did he so quickly become this *other man*?

One part of the answer is perhaps in the words of the Führer, untiringly repeated to his troops before he sends them off to Russia at the beginning of the summer of 1941: "You must resist the temptation to be human."[1]

39

Saint Petersburg

The Air France flight heads toward the north of Russia. I doze, my head against the little window. I feel tension mounting. I am fragile. Uncomfortable. Nervous fatigue has been accumulating for weeks. My night was short, very short. Couldn't fall asleep last night. For days, in fact, my sleep has been disturbed. I am now alone facing Alexander. He has remained *at a distance* with everyone, except me. The times are blending, our minds mix and intermingle to the point sometimes of being confused. Approaching so close to the day of his death is awakening extreme emotions. I want to be done with it. It's October 15, afternoon. He dies in five days. Reality is a fragile and fleeting décor in which my mind is dreaming.

I take out the photo of Alexander and his brother while the plane is skimming through the clouds. I still can't believe that I obtained this image. I dive into his strange look.

When, returning from Wismar, I showed the portrait of the two brothers to Natacha, she spontaneously thought that Alexander was the man on the left. When I told her that it was the reverse, she was very surprised.

"It's crazy. I was visualizing Alexander as a warrior."

"And you find that the man on the left is more of a warrior? It's Alfred, his older brother. He was a doctor . . . "

"Yes, I was sure it was him. The other man looks to me to be more self-effacing, more sensitive, almost feminine. For me, it's impossible that this is the SS soldier that you have spoken to me about."

"Feminine . . . that's funny. This is also a feeling I have about Alexander."

I make a few notes, then open the book of the historian Timothy Snyder, *Terres de sang* (*Bloodlands*), that I slipped into my bag. Born in 1969, Timothy Snyder holds a doctorate from Oxford University and teaches the history of central and western Europe at Yale. By "Bloodlands" he is designating the territory that extends from central Poland to western Russia, passing through the Ukraine, Belorussia, and the Baltic countries. A region that has known death and desolation like few other places. The Second World War was the deadliest conflict in history, he explains, and close to half the soldiers who fell, out of all the battlefields throughout the world, died on these lands of blood.

We're speaking about millions of people. It involved soldiers but also men, women, and children, most of whom were not bearing arms.

Since I began studying in detail the progress of the war in the East, I'm realizing the extent of the horror inflicted on the peoples of the Soviet Union during the same period that Nazi madness reigned in Europe. By analyzing in parallel the evolution of the Nazi and Soviet regimes, Snyder demonstrates how Hitler's abominable crimes eclipsed in a way the atrocities of unbelievable proportions perpetrated by Stalin. "The Soviet Union triumphed over Nazi Germany on the eastern front in the course of the Second World War, which earned Stalin the gratitude of millions of people, and also played a crucial role in the establishment of European order after the war. The record of Stalin's massacres was almost as extensive as Hitler's. In truth, in times of peace it was even worse. With the excuse of defending and modernizing the Soviet Union, Stalin presided over the death by hunger of millions of people and, in the 1930s, the execution of 750,000. Stalin killed his own citizens just as efficiently as Hitler killed those of other countries. Of the fourteen million individuals deliberately killed in the bloodlands between 1933 and 1945, one third are due to the Soviets."[1] When the unthinkable absurdity of the communist dialectic transforms millions of victims of famine in the Ukraine into enemies of the revolution, that is, persons to execute following quotas drawn up by regional political cells, we are not far from the thinking that cast a people into gas chambers. Mass purges, deportation, and so on. The account of the Yale historian is unsettling. It reminds me once again that just yesterday we were a humanity gripped by madness.

The horror of the one must not mask the horror of the other; otherwise we are abandoning thought, and it will happen again.

The humanity in which my mother and father were born was demented.

Let us be vigilant so that our humanity of today escapes these diabolical temptations. We can.

Fatigue wins out. I close the book and drift into a half-sleep until the landing at the international airport of Pulkovo. The flight was quick. Passport control, taxi, sun on the city, and I arrive in room 5069 of the Oktiabrskaya Hotel on Ligovsky Prospect, right in front of the station where tomorrow morning I'm taking the Moscow-bound train.

I came here once before more than thirty years ago, in June 1985. Saint Petersburg was called Leningrad then. A school trip organized by our Russian teacher. So many years ago, and I recognize nothing. Memories of my current life, such as the previous trip to the USSR, or even other memories about my early childhood, have completely disappeared. How could it be surprising then that reminiscences of a *previous life* would be totally inaccessible? During the previous stay in the Soviet Union we took the night train from Leningrad to Moscow. The rail line passes a few tens of kilometers from the place where Alexander was killed. How could I have even suspected that, cradled as I was by my youth and by my carefree attitude?

The Oktiabrskaya Hotel has a restaurant. Too tired to go out, but also because, curiously, I don't feel completely comfortable, I take a seat alone, in an isolated corner. I've just gotten off the phone with Nicolas, a former French military man who today advises foreign enterprises about entering the Russian market. Nicolas has been living in Moscow for years. His contact info was given to me by the photographer Thomas Goisque, who came to Russia numerous times, notably with the writer Sylvain Tesson. For this trip, I needed what we call in the jargon of journalism a "fixer"—someone able to accompany me, having a car available and knowing the terrain, and able to speak Russian fluently. Thomas let me know that Nicolas would be the ideal person. And in fact, during our email exchanges, Nicolas seemed enthusiastic. Besides, he is passionate about the Second World War and knows a lot about it. It's agreed that he leaves Moscow by car tomorrow morning. I will meet him by taking the train from Saint Petersburg. Our *gathering point,* as he puts it, is the little town of Bologoye, situated halfway between us. Four hundred kilometers southeast of Saint Petersburg. I'll get there at 4:30 p.m.

Night falls. I am the only customer in the restaurant. I can't stop thinking about the city of Saint Petersburg during the blockade that it was subjected to during the war. Encircled by the German army, its population put up a heroic resistance. How to imagine the extent of the suffering of its inhabitants? How to describe what happened here starting in the summer of 1941? Where does the pain hide once the events that caused it belong to the past? Does the pain fade away? Does it remain, stuck to the earth, to the houses? Is the pain a ghost? A ghost that wanders around, haunting hearts.

I still have a little strength left before crawling into bed in an over-heated bedroom, so I prepare the documents that are going to be useful tomorrow. The first place I want to visit is the German military cemetery that Marlene spoke to me about. Korpowo is located about forty kilometers southeast of Staraya Russa on the road to Demyansk. It's a

military burial place constructed for the burial of German soldiers who
fell in the region of Demyansk. The land covers about three hectares.
The process of locating the graves and transferring the bodies began
in 1997. By the end of the year 2013, 33,643 bodies had already been
interred. In the letter addressed to Marlene by the office in charge of
this memorial site, the information is not very clear. They speak of the
village of Mirochny, where Alexander was buried in October 1941, but
they don't say clearly that they had identified him. I had an accurate
translation made: "In Mirochny, one hundred and ninety-one German
soldiers were exhumed from partially pillaged graves that had become
invisible on the surface. They were transferred to the military cemetery
at Korpowo by our Commission. Not all the bodies registered for this
location were able to be found. Unfortunately, none of the exhumed
bodies bore the identity tag of your loved one. Other indications did
not allow identification either. However, it is very likely that he was
among the German soldiers who are at rest in block 20 of the German
Military Cemetery at Korpowo."

Further on, there is mention made of granite steles that were erected
on each block engraved with the names of the men buried below it.
"The identity of your loved one has not been engraved yet. As soon as
the engraving has been done, you will be informed on an individual
basis. If you are interested in a group visit to the cemetery, we suggest
that you make contact with our travel service."

Why was his identity tag not found with his supposed corpse?

How could they affirm having exhumed Alexander's body if they
didn't conduct a formal identification? It's one of two things: either
his grave is still there where he was buried in 1941 or it was pillaged
and objects such as his tag disappeared. But then why maintain that an
unidentified body is his?

Nevertheless, this official letter is very precise, and all the information that it contains is exact, notably the fact that his grave was number
50 and that it was located in Mirochny. His surname, forename, rank,
allocation, and registration number are all accurate. So is it possible that

he is one of the German soldiers at rest in block 20 at Korpowo? Isn't wanting to find traces of one body out of millions of dead men a crazy endeavor?

Am I going to be able to discover where Alexander lies? Am I not in the process of comforting myself with illusions?

40

Operation Barbarossa

On June 14, 1941, Alexander learns from the mouth of his battalion commander that the war against the Soviet Union will begin in a few days. There you have it, the news is finally official. It had been circulating for weeks after the Totenkopf Division received the order to leave France for East Prussia.

Since Poland, Alexander has been in all the battles of the Totenkopf Division. He was with the occupation troops in France. Almost a year was spent mainly in the southwest, with, no doubt, one or several excursions to Paris. In mid-June, now in the confines of Prussia, he has just left behind a pleasant and familiar world.

On June 19, after nightfall, the division initiates its movement toward attack positions and continues taking up positions the following night. During the day, the columns of vehicles are hidden in the woodlands or under camouflage nets. The evening of June 20 all units of the Totenkopf have reached their predetermined positions in the shadow of forests.

During the day on June 21 all is calm.

Alexander has finally obtained a command position. Proud officer at the age of twenty-four, he has been placed at the head of the 2nd Company of the 1st Battalion of the 1st Infantry regiment of SS-Totenkopf. He has 180 men under his command. His battalion, commanded by SS-Sturmbannführer Hellmuth Becker, has about eight hundred men.

Like millions of his compatriots, Alexander doesn't know that he's setting out on a voyage to hell. A voyage of no return. An inhuman war, far from civilization.

Just after 3:00 a.m. on June 22, 1941, a deluge of fire and iron comes swooping down on the Soviet Union from the Baltic Sea to the shores of the Black Sea. And more than 3.5 million men invade the Soviet Union. This is the largest military operation in the history of humanity. Baptized Barbarossa by Hitler after the nickname of Emperor Frederick I, it will cause the downfall of the Third Reich through the overreach of the means it deployed.

Three groups of armies attack together. Three units of autonomous command. One group moves toward the south of the Soviet Union—Ukraine, notably. The one in the center has Moscow as its goal. And the third, Army Group North (Heeresgrupe Nord) targets Leningrad. Starting from East Prussia, they will go up through Lithuania and Latvia in order to attempt to take the former capital of the czars. The Totenkopf Division is part of Army Group North.

Why did Hitler throw himself into such a project? Why did he make Stalin, who had been his fortuitous ally since 1939, into his sworn enemy? The about-face is so unexpected that Stalin himself is totally stupefied on the morning of June 22 and cannot manage to accept the idea that Hitler has actually thrown his army against him.

However, the East has always been a goal of Nazi Germany. Repeating the desire since his accession to power that the Reich imperatively needed to increase its "living space," Hitler never hid his ambitions for colonization. And where should this living space be conquered except toward the immense and rich lands to the east? This conquest was justified based on the Nazi idea that since the German people were "racially superior," it is lawfully correct to take what brute force gives them access to. Three weeks after the invasion of the Soviet Union,

Heinrich Himmler addressed the men of the Waffen-SS in these terms: "This is a battle between two philosophies, a battle between races. In this battle, there is on one side National Socialism, a philosophy supported by the values of our Germanic, Nordic blood; on this one side then a world as we conceive of it: beautiful, correct, socially just, [...] culturally rich, in short, the world that resembles our Germany. On the other side, a people of one hundred and eighty million individuals, a mix of races and populations with un-pronounceable names and whose appearance is such that we can do nothing but fire on the masses of them without mercy or pity."[1]

This thinking, unfortunately, is shared not only by a handful of SS fanatics but extends to a very large part of the German Army and the German people. This is a veritable war of extermination that is being embarked on, and everyone will take part in it. Hitler specifically ordered the generals of the Wehrmacht as well—not only the Einsatzgruppen SS—to liquidate all Bolshevik commissars and Communist intelligentsia who fell into their hands.

The Totenkopf Division does not participate in the first day's engagement. It is placed in reserve, and it is only on June 24, a little before 8:00 p.m., that it receives its deployment order. As soon as the border is crossed, another world begins, very different from the France that Alexander and his men were familiar with during the previous year. An SS soldier writes in his journal, "Beyond the border, the first impression of the country is unforgettable. The contrast between East Prussia with its carefully tended roads, towns, and villages and Lithuania with its impenetrable trails and miserable thatched roof cottages, announce to us that here begins another world."[2] He doesn't know how right he is.

On June 26 the first skirmishes take place between sections of the Totenkopf and groups of isolated Russian soldiers. First victims. During these days of rapid advance, the division faces only sporadic resistance. The forests are still overflowing with combat units, but the German steamroller is much too powerful, too imposing to be troubled by Russian troops that are not prepared for such an unfurling of force.

However, very quickly the Soviet soldiers ("Ivan," as they are designated pejoratively by the Germans) recover from their astonishment and from June 30 onward they bring a lively resistance to bear. From then on rarely does a day go by without engagement. The Totenkopf crosses Lithuania and then enters Latvia at the beginning of the month of July. The division has orders to march as quickly as possible to the "Stalin Line," which marks the real entry onto Russian soil. It is imperative for them to reach this sector before the Soviets regroup. In fact, the Soviets retreat, leaving behind only a few rearguard units whose job is to slow down the German advance.

The terrain turns out to be infernal, and harassment is constant. Losses accumulate. For Alexander and his men, the war takes on an unexpected aspect. The Soviet soldiers prefer to be killed on the spot rather than surrendering. "The men of the division therefore gradually adopted the habit of not taking too many prisoners except during mass surrenders. Facing them, the Soviets adopted a similar attitude: woe to those soldiers who fell into their hands!"[3]

Merciless fighting, sandy roads, swampy areas, deep forests in which isolated snipers are lurking; finally, at the beginning of July the Totenkopf men reach the Stalin Line, a fortified zone several kilometers wide.

On July 6 the division's artillery relentlessly hammers the Russian positions before moving to attack. In the afternoon the Soviet lines are broken through. The attack proceeds. With each position taken, Alexander and his division dig in, fearing Soviet counterattacks. They do happen, they are suicidal, and it takes all the fanatical determination of the SS not to retreat under enemy pressure. Holding out until the last man. This fighting is costly. It's fierce, and losses are high; the hand-to-hand fighting is grueling, physically as well as psychologically.

It takes five days to definitively break through the Stalin Line. Alexander's battalion is very harshly put to the test in this fighting. The few days of respite that follow will be the last for the young lieutenant. In fact, after July 18 he and his soldiers will be engaged on a daily basis until death offers deliverance from this man-made hell.

August arrives. The Totenkopf advances painfully at the cost of continual losses. The terrain is hostile. Fatigue begins sometimes to engender short seconds of doubt in Alexander's mind. He loses weight, he is exhausted, and fear is now a constant companion.

On August 21 he *celebrates* his twenty-fifth birthday. At the end of the month of August, rain transforms the dirt roads into a quagmire. September begins. The Totenkopf continues its offensive, but Soviet counterattacks are constant, making it clear that their resources are inexhaustible. The fact of tens of thousands of dead in their ranks seems never to alter their ability to continually send new troops, fresh and determined, into the assault.

At the beginning of September, the division is located south of Lake Ilmen, facing the Pola River. While Army Group North pursues its difficult advance, the Totenkopf finds itself with a new objective: in the region of Valdai, to cut the road that links Leningrad and Moscow. The division then moves due east, on a broadening front in the direction of the city of Demyansk. When the first assault companies of the division reach the banks of the Pola, they are greeted by Russian artillery. They ford the river as best they can with water up to the chest and clean out the trenches dug by the Soviets on the opposite bank. The enemy doesn't relinquish one thing. After more than two months of fighting, it becomes clear that the price to be paid will be colossal for the German Army. The Totenkopf, constantly engaged, is severely put to the test. As it makes its way through a strategic point in the locality of Starye Gorki, the particularly audacious engagement of Alexander at the head of one of these assault groups is mentioned in his battalion's report. This account makes its way to me, and I find it upsetting to read. "An attack group led by SS-Ostuf Herrmann was assigned to clean out a zone of the river in the shape of a U near Wasiljewschtschina. The Russians constructed extensive defense fortifications there. Being well camouflaged, the combat group managed to infiltrate the Russian positions and attack from behind. Under the intelligent command and the personal engagement of the head of this attack group, the fighting unit succeeded in eliminating the enemy positions without significant losses and with the capture of sixty prisoners."[4]

Their fate was hardly enviable.

What did Alexander do with the sixty prisoners?

No Geneva conventions in this territory. One more reality that I don't know the extent of. The statistics chill the spine. "According to conservative estimates the Germans slaughtered half a million prisoners in the Soviet war. Through hunger and mistreatment during transport, they killed close to two million six hundred thousand more. In total, it is perhaps three million one hundred thousand Soviet war prisoners that were killed. Far from bringing down the Soviet regime, the brutality seems to have reinforced the Soviet morale. [. . .] In fact, the policy of starvation and mistreatment strengthened the Red Army's resistance. Knowing that they would be condemned to die of hunger in the hands of the Germans, the soldiers could do nothing but put more energy into fighting. Knowing that they would be killed, Communists, Jews, and political officers had no reason to give up. As knowledge about the German policy spread, citizens began to wonder if the Soviet power wasn't perhaps preferable."[5]

This error of Hitler's is hard to understand. Because of the behavior that he demanded of his troops, he alienated a population that had suffered so much from Stalinist domination and that he would have been able to win over. But he wanted to crush Russia and lost all notions of strategy, such as common sense.

On September 6 the Totenkopf Division crosses the Pola with most of its infantry and a part of its artillery. Unarguably the most difficult part seems to have been accomplished. Actually, on September 7 the Soviets conduct a general retreat. But it's a trap. Which is what was done to Napoleon's armies: draw the enemy even deeper into the heart of the country, getting them to move into this limitless land, stretching their supply and support lines beyond anything reasonable. Until they're exhausted. Then strike and harass without respite.

By mid-September Demyansk is reached and moved past.

However, the positions freeze and become fixed a few tens of kilometers to the east.

Not one German will go farther. In the whole war. The Leningrad-Moscow route will never be cut. The region where Alexander is going to die, starting in the winter of 1942, will become even a Stalingrad for the Totenkopf: the division will find itself encircled in what history will remember as the "Demyansk Pocket."

Defensive positions begin to be constructed on both sides. A sign that the lines are stabilizing and the combatants are digging in. Winter is far away, but it will yet surprise the men here. Under artillery fire, and being a target for Soviet planes and continual insane attacks, the SS try, as best they can, to control a front line that is very stretched and susceptible to infiltration. The division has reached the zone of Lushno. Sukhaya Niva is on the front line.

On September 24, for the first time, there is frost in the course of the night.

Between the end of September and the beginning of October, week after week, *tens of thousands of men* lose their lives in an area of a few square kilometers. The Soviets multiply their suicidal assaults and suffer frightful losses without that seeming to affect their offensive intent. In this period the 1st Regiment of the Totenkopf Division, in which Alexander is serving, is attempting to hold on to eleven kilometers of front line facing three Soviet divisions. Alexander and his men are trying to fend off constant attacks. The Russian positions are visible, at only a few tens of meters from trenches dug by his men. In three months of campaign, Totenkopf losses rise to 6,610 killed, wounded, or missing.

On October 10 it snows.

Everyone in the general headquarters and Hitler first of all foresaw a victory in September. At the end of autumn, German losses approach one million, while victory seems more and more uncertain.

On October 15, 1941, the division prepares to launch a new assault.

Alexander's battalion is located east of the village of Mirochny, occupying lines in the forest, dug in.

An SS soldier writes in his journal: "The operating conditions of the Division are really bad. From the heavy rainfall that is almost incessant and is mixed with snow, the roads have lost their stability and have become impassible. The fog and poor visibility do not allow any airborne support to approach. After having painfully gained this position which shelters us from the miserable weather, both the commander and the troops are not delighted with this new mission. Moreover, we know the strength of the Russian positions. But what's the use of complaining? An order is an order."[6]

41

Valdai

This morning Saint Petersburg is under overcast skies. Rain taps on my windowsill. Rain and cold, like this same October 16, 1941. I get up and turn in circles in the room. I have coffee and bread sent up. Outside the street is wide and sad. Opposite, zinc roofs. Antennas and balconies. Traffic has bathed my sleep with the sounds of engines and horns. I don't want to go out. In fact, I'm afraid. I am invaded by an imprint of fear and fright, which is there, deep inside me. *Something* that pushes me to stop moving, to not go out, to remain hiding in the shelter of this room. Like in a hole. In four days Alexander will be dead. Dead, in violence and stupor. Is it this next perspective that is distilling in me and leaving this burning trail? I'm snug here, but I have to go out. I must catch my train. In fact, this country is sinister.

In the great station concourse, I decipher on the screens the track number for my train. And I watch people walking without smiles, slowly, like ghosts that are waiting. What is the value of a man's life? So, so many have been crushed. Waves and waves of men swallowed by the earth, and all without a grave. Where are their names? Do they even know that they are dead? The violence was such, the indifference so great, that the death of an individual must have been forgotten by his brothers-in-arms after just a week. How to keep track of so, so many *fallen ones*? Faced with so many victims, how can the individuality of each one still be perceived?

There remains an hour before my train departs. As always, I've arrived early. I make my way to a cafeteria that is a little old-fashioned to get something to eat. The place reminds me of the snack bar at Charles de Gaulle airport where my parents, my brothers, and I had a drink together before my brothers, Thomas and Simon, and I embarked on a flight to Afghanistan in February 2001. A flight from which Thomas wasn't ever going to return alive. We took a photo that day. Was it I who took it? Dad and Mom were with us and were joking with Thomas for the last time in their lives. Mom was emotional, as on each one of our departures. A family of travelers—that's hard for a mother. But how could they have imagined what was going to happen? What sadness. I think of the photo, I think of that day, I reexperience the emotion, and I'm so sad. Our parents wanted to savor that moment, slow down time, and we only wanted to hurry, get to the boarding lounge, the plane, adventure.

And our parents returned to their house encircled by pines.

And we left.

And a few weeks later I called at dawn. I woke them from sleep and told them that their son was dead.

Then I brought back my brother's body to this house encircled by pines.

Life—so fragile, so illegible sometimes.

Once again the pain, touching me to the quick, in this station in Saint Petersburg.

I look up. Before my eyes there is an aquarium. The fish that are in it will never leave it. They will die in this little rectangular space without ever knowing anything else. And yet they are living. What is the size of the aquarium in which we are in the process of living?

It seems to me that Alexander is afraid. I'm bringing him back to a moment and a place that brings together too much suffering for him.

He is there, but silent, not moving, and prostrate. Prostrate is a bit strong as a word. Atonic, rather. Detached, distant, reserved.

In the station concourse, a tall officer is accompanied by two soldiers. I don't know what army unit they belong to. The officer is handsome, fine, no doubt a figure like Alexander's. He's wearing a cap and is speaking with calm authority to the two others. They are observing the concourse.

Things are tumbling around in my head. All sorts of disorganized thoughts are stirred up in me, impossible to return to calm. It's more or less as if what happened during my first evening in Bad Arolsen is happening over again: all the faces of the Russians around me take on the mask of another time. An era appearing transparently. Like a filter, a veil added onto our reality. A woman in a shawl, these square-jawed soldiers, these faces of men and women with Slavic features. Red-cheeked faces, clear looks, and the voices; Russian words, rough and inflected.

The enemy.

This world is the world of the enemy. It is not mine. I don't feel the shadow of threat, no, but Alexander *in me* is surrounded, and he is afraid. These Russians, these Ivans observed through binoculars, touched, banged against in terrifying hand-to-hand combat. They are here. All around. These faces that he saw opposite him were the faces of death. Their death, which he inflicted, and then his own, in a few days.

I bathe in death.

In blood and snow.

Seated in the cafeteria, I watch people who come and go, people who live life, who move about, exist, and are at peace. However, as for me, once again, I am in another *location*. Somewhere in my body there is a temporal doorway.

A doorway that opens onto madness.

To terror, to cold, and to shadow. To mistrust. The vigilance of bygone times has metamorphosed into pure paranoia. The threat, everywhere. The danger, permanent. The faces of my friends are a fuzzy memory that struggles to appear. How many have disappeared into darkness in the course of these last weeks? As for those of the enemy, screaming, frightened, dead, disfigured. Hostile, dangerous, insanely tenacious, and fighting right to the end in a mixture of crazy courage and absolute hopelessness. These faces, these faces of a time gone by appear on all those whom I pass in this station, in the taxi yesterday, in the street, everywhere.

Why don't I become mad?

I would if I weren't *helped*.

How many are irretrievably tormented among those who perceive like me the echoes of the past? "Help! Don't leave me alone with them." Before getting on the train, I pull myself together and address the void before me. A *space* where I know that there are to be found my brother, my father, and other guides, other allied forces: "Help me! I'm going to need you there where I'm going. Watch over me. Protect me, please."

My train goes all the way to the Caucasus. The passengers in my compartment are settling into their bunks for a voyage of several days. As for me, I'm getting off at the first stop. Bologoye. There was also a first-class express shuttle service that would have dropped me at my destination much more quickly, but Nicolas reserved a one-way ticket for me on this particular train. Car five, bunk eighteen. The car fills up; bags, suitcases, and bundles dumped all over the place. Provisions for the South. Soon the loaded train pulls away. Wheels clack, jolt, the cars bang into each other, and once past the switching tracks in the suburbs, we're soon chugging along at a good clip and in a straight line.

Three women in my compartment. One elderly and a bit heavy and two my age. One of them is making up the bed for the elderly woman. Are they going to sleep? It's the middle of the day! They're all getting comfortable, and they ask me to kindly wait in the corridor for the time it takes them to change. When I come back the sturdy babushka has changed into a kind of plain cloth nightshirt and has brought out pickles, butter, cream, and other victuals that are making my mouth water.

The rain has stopped.

A text message from Nicolas lets me know that he's been en route since this morning. He will be on time.

From now on, the Russian forest dances in the windows. Birches reach up with their yellow and red foliage. Innumerable and immortal pines. Flat, wet country, lakes, marshes. Nature is not at war with man. Nature is not threatening. She is not the enemy. The train moves on at a good speed, swaying on its rails.

Nicolas is waiting for me in the parking lot of the station at Bologoye, sad town that it is. Country attire, beret, bright and sparkling eyes, mustache that he aligns with his thumb and forefinger. He stands straight, full of vigor and elan, beside a gray Audi A3 that looks as if it has made a circuit around the Earth several times. We're about the same age. He thinks he's meeting a journalist for a *normal* historical inquiry—in his case too I didn't want to reveal anything by email—the hour-long drive to Valdai will be time enough for me to give him all the details.

When we arrive at the hotel Valdaiskie Zori, he knows my story. He's surprised.

Nicolas served five years in the army. An experience that disappointed him. He retains a certain rectitude about it that is a little outdated.

The region is not ugly. The hotel is built facing an immense lake. The young receptionist asks for our passports authoritatively. As I hand her mine with a big smile, her face lightens up, requiring some effort for a smile to begin. Unaccustomed behavior.

In the entranceway there's a minimuseum that has assembled vestiges of the Second World War. Various objects, Russian as well as German, found in more or less official excavations. Nicolas had spoken to me about this, having been himself an adept on the former combat zones around Saint Petersburg. Searching combat sites from the "Great Patriotic War" is a weekend activity practiced by thousands of enthusiasts throughout Russia. The region of Valdai, and the Demyansk Pocket in particular, constitutes one of the most prized sites in the whole former Soviet Union. Obvious historic interest, but also financial. The relics get sold. Helmets, emblems, knives, weapons, boxes of cartridges, and so on.

Is that why Alexander's identity tag has not been found?

Nicolas has a metal detector in his trunk.

I really have gotten it into my head to *find* Alexander.

Looking for a body in a hell of gunfire.

At supper I summarize for Nicolas what I know about Alexander's last days: The Totenkopf Division has been fighting without interruption since June 26. It has suffered heavy losses. In October it is deployed in a sector that is somewhat secondary, since the principal thrust of Army Group North is happening farther north, against Leningrad. Because of the significant losses that it has suffered, it has inadequate manpower along a very extensive perimeter. A front that extends over about fifty kilometers, while some of the men must already be no longer fit for combat. At the same time, this is why the Totenkopf Division acquired the reputation of packing a huge punch: it was standing up to Soviet units that had vastly superior numbers of men available. It is a fact that beyond the courage, or even the fanaticism, of its fighters, the division is nevertheless very poorly managed. The offensive actions that are undertaken are of only limited scope and are more aimed at realigning the front than advancing it farther into the country. In discussions with Charles Trang I learned that, in the SS, the most significant losses concerned the officers. In fact, you had proportionally more risk of dying being an officer than being a simple soldier, because the SS officers had a tradition of being up front during attacks, in order to lead their men forward.

I bring out the maps that I have available and spread them out on the table in front of Nicolas, and his military eye begins to decode the situation as if he were reading a book. At Sukhaya Niva, Alexander has opposite him a whole battalion of the Red Army. The 1st Battalion of the 87th Regiment of the Soviet Fusiliers. In reserve, farther back, there is also another whole regiment. His company is preparing to attack units that are very superior in numbers. Nicolas, passionate about this period, plunges in with his remarks.

"In October 1941, the German Army still had munitions, and provisioning was good. Also it is likely that the attack would have been supported with an artillery group."

"But opposite them the Soviets had artillery too."

"Yes . . . "

"I know that, because of losses, Alexander's company, which in normal times mustered 180 men, could only count on 70 or perhaps 100 at the most. Do you have an idea of the number of Russians that he faced?"

"The Soviets had also undergone enormous losses. Your fellow and his company have perhaps two to three hundred men facing them. On the fronts in Russia, the enemy positions were very close together. Russians and Germans, in their defense trenches, were fifty or sixty meters away from each other."

"So close?"

"Yes, there was often hand-to-hand fighting. Fifty meters places you beyond the range of thrown grenades, but snipers on both sides must have picked off quite a few."

The discussion continues. The accumulation of these operational details enriches my vision of the situation. I want to understand, to go over each hour, each movement of Alexander's last days. The final months of his life must have been exhausting. I even have trouble imagining the state of fatigue and tension that accumulated, making him, perhaps in moments, prefer death to maintaining a waking state that was too taxing. I had run into that during my first voyage to Afghanistan, in 1988, when, completely empty of resources, after days and days of walking, I wanted nothing else but to stop, collapse, and sleep. Once or twice, I even told myself that death must be comforting if it puts an end to this ordeal. I almost wanted it. So too Alexander!

But he was in command of a company; he had to set an example. No way to call it quits. Hold on or die.

His death must have been a deliverance.

We go back to our rooms.

Rendezvous early tomorrow morning. Destination: the Korpowo Cemetery.

42

The Cholmy Offensive

F riday, October 17, 1941. As snow begins to fall again during the night, the 1st Regiment, which is to serve as the attack regiment, takes up its position for the offensive. Before dawn, in the most complete darkness, Alexander's 1st Battalion is located almost a kilometer northeast of Kirillowtschina, in the area of the village of Poljzo. A welcoming forest with airy undergrowth. A few hundred frozen men, camouflaged in their holes, hands blue, gripping their weapons. Fog adds to the apprehension. Then the glacial silence of the night is broken when the artillery explodes, directing fire grouped along the first line of Russian fortification. The offensive is launched. Muscles tense, adrenaline gushes, and the men of the attack company leave their trenches under the rain of metal that is supposed to protect them.

In the thunder of firing that suddenly lights up the night, Alexander and his men throw themselves into the offensive. They collide immediately with a particularly dense defensive network. The Soviets were expecting them. The losses are disproportionate to the territory gained.

Russia sucks up the German Army like blotting paper sucks up water.

The Totenkopf has been engaged for several weeks in this wooded and marshy region that is a real dead end. The Russian resistance is fierce. They don't give up, they don't retreat, and they fight right to the last man. Their artillery reacts to the German attack with more and more intense firing. The SS soldiers clear each bunker, each trench, but soon it is no longer possible to advance and Alexander's men discover a new, terrifying weapon: stationary flame-throwers hidden in front of the Russian bunkers shoot out on the German assailants immense bursts of flame from the ground up. Several soldiers burst into flame, screaming.

In the dawning light of day, and during the whole morning, the SS manage nevertheless to advance and move back toward the north. Gaps open in the enemy equipment, the artillery lengthens its protective cover of firing, which allows the 1st Battalion to take the area to the south of the village of Cholmy and a neighboring portion of the road toward Sukhaya Niva. Alexander and his company reach this locality exhausted. Cholmy is a little hamlet of low houses of poor brick situated on a height of land. It offers a strategic position overlooking the Russian lines to the north, which are below the village. In a westerly direction, the dirt road that winds through the forest leads to Sukhaya Niva, four kilometers away. Since dawn, Alexander and his men have been fighting, and certain soldiers have died, others are frightfully wounded. For the wounded a life of suffering begins that may be long or short.

The few tens of exhausted men of Alexander's 2nd Company have advanced several kilometers, like all those of the rest of the battalion. But what is the value of this victory? A few meters, a few parcels of land, and a village or two? At the moment that the 1st Battalion is settling into Cholmy, Russian tanks counterattack in the southwest at Kirillowtschina. Several tanks are destroyed. The line of the front is broken up over an immense distance.

Rapid nightfall prevents exploiting the tactical advance of the day. Besides, the fighters of the division are exhausted and are no longer numerous enough to hope they could conduct an effective new offensive. Reinforcements will not be available for several days. Also the division has received the order to immobilize the enemy in their current position and not to try to push through farther for the time being, or to try to gain more ground, which could only be done at the price of significant losses. For the 1st Battalion, an attack is planned the following day on Sukhaya Niva. From now until then, they hope, a few hours of respite, evacuation of the dead and wounded to the rear, re-provisioning, to the extent possible. Cold accompanies the returning darkness. The earth freezes. The men dig themselves into precarious shelters. Fear in the belly. The hundreds of dead from the day, like lost ghosts, wander in the forest, incredulous.

43

Contact

Valdai, October 17. Light sleep. Alexander passed this night in fog and glacial dampness, discomfort and danger. I, in a clean bed and a heated room.

I meet Nicolas outside, in the sharp cold and under a limpid sky. Far to the southwest, a wall of cloud gives warning of an approaching change in the weather soon.

First destination: the German War Cemetery of Korpowo, at 100 kilometers from Valdai. Is Alexander there? How will I find out? The military folders tell me that he was buried at the exit from the village of Mirochny, grave number 50, probably on the day of his death, October 20. The documents given to me by Marlene speak of 191 bodies exhumed in the village a few years ago, and of graves partially pillaged.

But no exhumed body bore Alexander's identity tag.

Could there be graves that were not found?

Nicolas drives fast. Shortly after driving out of Valdai, we leave the section of the Moscow–Saint Petersburg expressway and turn off onto secondary roads, without slowing down. The road isn't bad, but sometimes potholes have to be avoided. The terrain is hilly. Which breaks the monotony of the uniformly flat landscapes of Russia's interminable plains. Portions of the forests are dotted with lakes and marshy areas. We are virtually alone on the road.

Nature is moving into winter. The trees still have their foliage but are shading into yellow. We come to Demyansk but don't stop there. A medium-sized town whose name is loaded with history. Another forty kilometers in the direction of Staraya Russa, then, without anything announcing it, we end up coming across the cemetery: a gloomy esplanade set back a little on the left and virtually invisible from the road.

No one. Not one human for kilometers all around.

A large open piece of land, bordered in front by a stone wall. Mute solitude, under a sky covered with gray. An information panel, a reception booth, a planted cross, and tens of granite steles like lugubrious monoliths, engraved with tens of thousands of names.

We park the car, and I move into the enclosed space of the place.

Looking for block number 20.

On a stretch of grass I find a small stone plaque marked with the number 20. In crisscrossing the cemetery I understand better the organization of the place, and I see that certain blocks are not yet supplied with their commemorative stele. Such is the case with number 20. No monolith above the common grave holding the 191 bodies removed from Mirochny—and no doubt others. Nothing, just a square of green grass. And beneath the sod, under my feet, hundreds of men.

Already close to thirty-four thousand corpses have been brought to this place.

But Alexander *is not here*.

I feel it. He is not here.

I walk around the whole perimeter, very attentive to my perceptions. But nothing happens, the place is empty, without energy, without soul, without anything. I'm wasting my time here. I'm almost amazed at how sure I am of myself. But for several months, almost two years now, I've been learning to trust my deep feeling. Alexander is not here. Alexander's body has never been buried at Korpowo. The sky is now dark gray. I suggest to Nicolas that we should leave without delay.

The gravel and dirt in the parking lot screech under the Audi's wheels. Then the tires reach the asphalt, and Nicolas steps on the gas, heading due east. The same road in the opposite direction. We go past Demyansk without stopping; then the road veers off to the north. After about thirty kilometers, we reach a hairpin turn crossroads. On a blue sign is written: "Sukhaya Niva 0,3," 0.3 kilometers.

The village where Alexander died.

Nicolas turns, indifferent to the emotion that suddenly fills me, and we proceed on a road in very bad condition. I would have liked to arrive from the south and begin my discovery of the area with the village of Mirochny, where Alexander was buried, but we didn't find any other way in.

And we come to the village of Sukhaya Niva; the road goes past a row of houses and fences. I don't want to stop here today. Keep this moment in reserve. Nicolas looks at me attentively, waiting for my instructions. He now knows the importance of this journey for me and remains silent, for which I am infinitely grateful.

"Let's go on right to Mirochny," I say to him.

He goes through the village. At the southern edge, we go over a bridge spanning a little river, the Lushenka, and I suddenly perceive that it's there, just a little to the west, a few hundred meters away, that Alexander fell. This river is so similar to the one I *saw* in Peru. It was at the beginning of my vision: the German soldiers are walking in the riverbed, and then Alexander dies. But today I prefer that Sukhaya Niva remains *distant*. I close myself off to anything that is not Mirochny. Don't go too quickly. I want to move into the location of his death at the right moment. On October 20.

We're driving into the sun. Some villages indicated on my 1941 map ought to be right before my eyes, but they're no longer there. Nothing but forest and fields. After the river, on the left there was Borok. The fighting was right there in every house, in every barn, in every stone. Everything is gone. Even the dust. One kilometer farther we should have been seeing Poljzo from the car windows. But no, here too, instead of a hamlet there are only trees. Everything has evaporated. Even the memory no longer remains. Two more kilometers and we come to an inhabited place: Kirillowtschina, which we drive through. Four kilometers more and we reach Mirochny.

Mirochny.

I have been waiting for this moment for months. So much effort, so much energy to make it to this place. What an improbable moment. For these few words typewritten in November 1941 by a regiment secretary on a death certificate: *"Orstausgang Mirochny, Grad Nr. 50."*

"Grave number 50 on the way out of the village of Mirochny."

A few tens of meters before reaching the first houses, I *really* feel that Alexander is buried here. In this village. Perhaps even on the edge of this road, just at this entrance where I am.

"Can you slow down?"

Silence. My eyes are open wide. What's going to happen? "Alexander, guide me. I need your help." I have to find where he was buried. "On the way out of the Mirochny," the military document specifies; I *am* at one of the exits. The car moves slowly into the burg through the northern entrance. All my senses are on the alert. The village can't have more than about forty inhabitants, and we are immediately at the center. The road forks to the east. Another road leads off to the west. I indicate to Nicolas to go east. We're driving at walking speed past several houses; then, as we're going by the last one, I receive a jolt. Like a nervous reflex. I feel a discharge. *Something* in my belly.

A hand of energy that crashes down onto my chest.

Powerful, unquestionable, *physical.*

It is so unexpected that, for the space of a few seconds, I don't know what to do, what to say. And yet, at the same instant, a voice resounds— or is it a thought?—in my head: "It's here!"

"Stop the car!"

Nicolas is aware of my emotion. He brakes and turns off the engine. "It's here! . . . He is here," I say, opening the car door.

Nicolas looks at me tactfully. For twenty-four hours now, the irruption of a strange world in his life has him expecting anything. I can't believe the strength of my sensation. A surge, a shock, a flash through my whole body in one-tenth of a second. So fast, so precise. And so unsettling. We are at the east exit from Mirochny. In front of me: a field.

I get out of the car. I breathe. OK, very good . . . what now? Opposite me, to the south, fields. To my right, the way out of the village and the last house before the exit. And in front of my feet . . . the cadaver of a *raccoon dog*. Twenty centimeters from my shoe. Recently dead, on the side of the road, right here.

Right at the spot where I asked Nicolas to stop.

It looks like a mixture of a big polecat and a fox. Its thick fur is reddish beige, the tips are black. Eye half-closed. Lifeless. What do I need to understand as I enter the world of signs? This infinite space where the invisible uses all the forces available to it to send messages? What a stunning conjunction: this inner physical alert and the presence of this raccoon dog dead in the night. This is the first time that I've seen this animal, originally from the Far East. The raccoon dog is the *tanuki* in Japanese myth. He incarnates a *yōkai*—a forest spirit who has magical powers. Notably the ability to change form at will, because he is a master of disguise.

Change form at will.

Dead in the night.

The one who changes form at will is dead in the night.

I'm in the right spot! It's here. It's here that I am to liberate myself. In this place where the final phase of my healing begins. Alexander is here. He who *has changed form and is dead.*

His body is here.

My amazement now over, my analytical brain gets back to work.

"Turn back, I'd like to see the third exit, to the west."

Nicolas maneuvers our vehicle on the narrow road, and we go back into Mirochny. After five houses, the center, he goes down a path in a westerly direction and drives one hundred meters before having to halt in front of a rut full of water. Once again I get out and walk a few steps, looking at the surroundings. Logically, it's more likely that the cemetery would be here. The north exit that we were coming from and the east exit, where we came upon the dead tanuki, both must have been closer to the front and more exposed to enemy artillery. Common sense would dictate that the cemetery would be installed here. The more I think about it, the more convinced I am. However, I continue to want to return to the eastern exit. The one where the yōkai was waiting for me.

"Lets try to find some villagers."

Nicolas agrees and takes the car back to the center of the village.

We move away on foot, going door to door in search of the mayor. An old lady shows us where his house is: less than fifty meters away. We go there, and Nicolas approaches the woman who is digging in the nearby vegetable garden. He addresses her in a friendly and confident way in fluent Russian. We don't beat around the bush: we're looking for a man, a German who died here during the war. Nicolas presents me as a Frenchman coming from Paris especially for this.

The country woman, a beautiful blonde, no longer young, straightens up. Her eyes are clear blue, and she looks us up and down, both Nicolas and me. She suggests that she'll go and look for her husband and indicates we should wait in the yard. A burly, heavily muscled Russian, his hands and boots full of blood as if he was in the process of bleeding a large animal, comes out from behind the house. He comes toward us, wiping off the black blood which has seeped under his fingernails. Here he is—the mayor of Mirochny. He looks at us the same way his wife did: a mixture of friendly and mistrustful. He replies to Nicolas without asking the slightest question about our reason for being in Mirochny. If we are looking for the remains of a dead German, that's our business. We must have a good reason.

The man is a precious source of information: a German field hospital was located on the road going back up toward Kirillowtschina and a cemetery had been constructed in front of it. This is at the northern exit from the village, where we had initially entered it. Foreigners had come to make excavations in this cemetery in 2001, and they stayed a long time. The date corresponds; it was certainly the German organization in charge of Korpowo. The bodies that were exhumed and moved very certainly come from there. The man adds that these same people came back five or six years ago, to excavate in another property in the village at the exit . . . to the east.

When Nicolas, who is translating for me as the man goes along, tells me that, he has a strange expression on his face. He has in mind the memory of my reaction—so strong and yet inexplicable—at this same eastern exit, less than an hour earlier. As for me, I am upset and moved, but the man doesn't know much more. We take our leave, and I ask Nicolas to take us to this house.

The house is about thirty meters before the place where we stopped, where the dead raccoon dog is still lying. At the eastern exit from Mirochny.

A house of wooden construction.

An aggressive black dog, chained under a lean-to built opposite the single-story house, is barking nonstop. A fence encloses a fairly large property. The building is a bit shabby, but it is inhabited. The dirt yard is a veritable dumping ground. Garbage of all kinds, planks, buckets, unidentifiable objects, bottles; an infernal jumble litters the place. A boy plays alone in the enclosure. Nicolas and I approach the gate. A woman about sixty responds to our calls. Very mistrustful, she comes toward us reluctantly. Nicolas puts a diplomatic tone into his voice.

Unlike the mayor, this woman wrings out her information drop by drop. I leave it entirely up to Nicolas to negotiate this one. When he gives me a summary of his exchanges, I have difficulty hiding my excitement. The lady confirms that foreigners came and made a contract with her to be able to do exploratory excavations and remove numerous buried bodies, with their identity tags and their equipment. She makes clear that the foreigners had maps and seemed to have available an exact survey of the graves. They conducted soundings with metal rods and removed bodies buried at a depth of a meter and a half.

"How many bodies?" Nicolas asks.

"They brought out about thirty bodies, all the ones buried here," replies the lady with the same worried look.

"Where did they dig?"

"In front of the house, here," she says, indicating the part of her garden bordering the road.

"Only here, not elsewhere?'

"Yes, there were also some in the back, in the chicken coop . . . They took away all the bodies that were on our property."

We're in the heart of the Russian countryside. Some of the village houses, like the one we're standing in front of, are made with thick beams in the walls, on a solid foundation. Others are built with brick and covered with cob and lime. The lady tells us that opposite on the other side of the road, there was a substantial building of solid construction that housed the German command center. Nothing remains except parts of the frame in ruins. And two tall trees on one side and the other.

We thank the lady and move away a few steps. Nicolas looks at me.

"It's interesting; she mentioned that the people who came to remove bodies had precise maps showing the placement of the graves."

"Do you think that they could be wartime military documents?"

"Definitely. Especially at the beginning of the war. Things were well organized. What I get from this is that these people knew precisely where to search."

"Therefore, they must know where grave number 50 was if it's located here. Alexander's military tag was never found."

"He was perhaps buried at the other cemetery, the one at the north entrance."

"Yes, perhaps . . . "

"Don't you have any way of getting the survey that these men from the German service had?"

Suddenly I think of Andréa. I need to tell her what we've found and ask her about it.

"Someone in Germany may be able to help me. I'll send an email as soon as we get to the hotel."

A couple are working in the garden of the house next door. Nicolas and I approach. All smiles, a chubby old codger seated back a bit and a babushka all bundled up and smelling of smoke from an open fire graciously reply to our questions. After a cursory introduction, Nicolas asks them if excavations were undertaken on their land.

"No, there's nobody on our land!" replies this very old lady, her eyes all crinkly.

"And next door, did you see people digging?" he asks, pointing at the house we just came from.

"Yes, foreigners came to recuperate bodies. But there are still some there . . . "

"Still some there?!"

"They took away thirty bodies. They were well organized, but they only looked in the garden, and there are more under the house."

"How do you know that?"

"I was a little girl during the war. I saw them being buried. There were so many of them . . . "

"You were here during the war?"

"Yes . . . Before children were evacuated. The Germans took over all the houses, and we, the inhabitants, we were living in the cellars . . . About the bodies, the woman next door is not up to date. It's her brother that spoke with the foreigners. He didn't want them to destroy the house in order to get the bodies out, so he refused and gave them a permit to dig up only those in the garden. He told his sister that there weren't any more bodies on her property."

The old lady gets a kick out of the unintentional good joke on the part of the brother. Nicolas is flabbergasted.

And as for me, I'm in a pretty strange state.

286 • ◆ Contact

German bodies are still here. Perhaps a few tens of them.

Alexander is still here. I feel it. A few meters away from me.

But how to be sure? How to know? We spend the rest of the afternoon in the village without learning much more.

Back at the hotel in Valdai before dusk, I immediately send off a long email to Andréa. I explain the day's discoveries in detail and ask if she or Marlene could try to get hold of the map of Mirochny graves from the Kriegsgräberfürsorge, the German service that came to do excavations in the village. I know that it's very unlikely that she will succeed, but knowing her tenacity, she will throw herself into it, and if a solution is within her grasp, she won't give up. I conclude my message with a realistic comment: "It would be a real miracle, but miracles are happening these days."

After our supper in an almost empty restaurant, back in my room I can't sit still. How can I verify my perceptions? If it were possible, I would take a shovel, charge into the night in Mirochny, and start digging myself. Do I *really* want to dig up a dead man?

In the village a little earlier, several times standing in front of the house, I said to myself that I would have really liked to have a pendulum available. I don't use one, but I know to what an extent the pendulum can be a formidable tool in asking questions. Finding water, missing persons, and so on. My wife's grandfather was a healer and worked with a pendulum. Natacha also knows how to use one . . . Natacha. But of course! She has perceptions too. I call her. She's in the midst of having supper with our friend . . . the healer Robert Martin. Nice. I'm going to double my chances. Before sharing with her what has happened in my day, I proceed with a little test.

"I'm going to have the two of you help me out."

"Oh, really? OK . . . How?"

"As soon as you are ready, I'll ask a question in my head. A question that can be replied to with either yes or no."

"Fine."

My wife and I often do this kind of thing together. Sometimes I ask my question out loud, sometimes I just think about it, and Natacha speaks about the first sensation that comes to her. It's stunning. And often right on. It's a means where the rapidity allows you to circumvent the thinking process. But I can only ask a single question because with the second one it will be the thinking that replies. Still holding the phone, I open a map on the table and put my finger on the village of Mirochny.

"Ready?"

"OK, go ahead," Natacha replies.

Then I think very hard, *"Is Alexander still buried in Mirochny?"*

"Yes . . . Yes." Wow. I have shivers because it's so accurate. "The response from Robert is also yes," says the voice of my wife.

Both of them, at the same time, had a clear yes.

With my mind now at ease from what constitutes in my eyes an element of confirmation, I go back to bed and turn out the light.

But I can't manage to close my eyes. I am so impatient to discover what Andréa is going to respond with. And also I am in such a hurry for tomorrow to come so I can return to the site. Why didn't I bring a pendulum? I need to ask a pendulum. I *have* to do that. I never use a pendulum, but in this case it's stronger than me: *something* orders me to do it.

I'll rig one up.

I get up, turn on the lights again, and find sewing thread in my travel kit. I take off my wedding ring and tie it onto one end of a thread. I cut off a good length so that the ring hangs at about fifteen centimeters. And now I have my pendulum. Another trick from my wife. Next I just have to establish a *convention* with the pendulum. I lower my hand holding the pendulum, the ring touches the table and becomes stationary.

"Now tell me yes."

I lift my hand vertically; the ring is in the air and begins to swing from front to back. The swing increases, perpendicular to me. OK, this movement back and forth will be yes. I lower my hand again and rest the ring on the table.

"Now, give me no."

When I raise the ring again a new movement appears. Even though

the movement of my hand is exactly the same, this time the ring begins
turning lightly in a counterclockwise direction. Very good, this movement will be no.

My convention is established in exactly the same way as is done by
dowsers looking for water, who have been practicing this way since the
dawn of time.

On my map of the region, I write a big red letter on each of the exits
from Mirochny. An "A" for the north exit, a "B" for the west exit, and
a "C" for the east exit. I lower the ring again until it's stationary, and I
concentrate. I make myself as empty inside as possible and ask for help
with all my soul.

"Is Alexander now in Mirochny?"

Yes.

"Is he here?" My finger points to the north exit, "A."

No.

"Is he here?" West exit, the "B."

No.

"I stop the ring. Point to the east exit, the "C."

"Is he here?"

Yes.

In another state, both profoundly concentrated and at the same
time very relaxed, in the present moment, I continue.

"Is he on the property of the lady with the black dog?"

Yes.

"Under the house?"

Yes.

"Is he easily accessible?"

No clear answer. The ring almost doesn't move. It's impossible to
tell if it's swinging or turning. I begin again. Once, twice . . . no answer.
Natacha warned me that you can't insist in the case of an evasive
response. It means either that the question is not well formulated or that
it's not the right moment to get a response. So I stop. And give thanks.

Do I still have any right to doubt?

44

The Order to Withdraw

Saturday, October 18, 1941. Alexander, like the other soldiers, is hunched up in his hole. The biting cold is terrible, but less so than the incessant barrage of artillery and mortars of the Russian infantry. Since nightfall, the enemy has been showering with heavy fire, almost incessantly, the rear of the positions conquered by the SS during the previous day. Impossible to shut one's eyes; or if one manages it, it's only for a few minutes. Barely do the men fall asleep when suddenly a deafening uproar drags them from their dreams as the blast of explosions and clumps of earth shake their numb bodies. Suddenly once again it's real. The enemy is bombarding them. The world is brutal, hopeless. And once again there is fear. And cold.

As the end of October approaches, the nights are icy. Mud congeals, ponds freeze, and the darkness becomes an interminable hell. The cold penetrates the thick soles of the boots, insinuates through layers of felt in the clothing, saws away at the face and hands, and reaches down into even the bones. During the winter of 1941–1942, which is beginning, 60 percent of the German losses are due to sickness and the cold. The fighting will decrease in intensity, consisting only of maintaining the positions that have been won.

In the light from the explosions, Alexander looks at his men.

Each one is dug in as best he can. Burrowing into the frozen earth is barely possible it is so hard. And the digging has to be done in a hurry, after an exhausting offensive, all this while remaining too exposed in spite of the conquest of the hamlet of Cholmy and the road toward Sukhaya Niva.

In two days, it's the new moon. Only the Soviet shells fleetingly illuminate the area, then the most opaque black redescends, plunging the men once again into their thoughts. Impossible to warm oneself with a fire. Smoking a cigarette is sure to invite skillful shots from the snipers. Ivan is pretty good at that game.

Alexander and his men have been sharing this hell for months. "Friendship counts for a lot during war. This is somewhat strange. In a period of generalized hatred, men of the same camp are often bonded in strong friendship, whereas in times of peace doors close on the mediocrity of each one."[1]

Mediocrity.

Is it because he thought he could flee from mediocrity that he finds himself here?

Snow swirls over Cholmy and the tops of the trees. Wind whistles through the trunks. The night is too short, and yet it's never ending. Waiting without managing to regain a little strength.

Around 3:45 a.m., still well before dawn, Alexander and the other leaders of companies of the 1st Battalion that had invaded Cholmy receive the order to withdraw. They are too far ahead of their lines, and their flanks are exposed. The objective is to prevent a part of the division from being cut off from the rest of the troops, or even encircled by the Soviets.

As the order passes from man to man, the SS artillery launches covering fire to help the evacuation.

When day breaks and during the first hours of the morning, the implementation of the withdrawal proceeds so as to avoid certain pockets being encircled. But the day has awakened an aggressivity, and the Soviets throw themselves into an assault on all SS positions. Once again significant losses to deplore. However, certain positions on the heights were able to be held on to, allowing the heavy armaments to continue firing on the breach opened by the enemy to the east of Kirillowtschina. In return, a battery of Russian missiles opens fire on the area. The infantry can do little more than dig themselves in because, given the slightest movement, they attract heavy fire from the Russians. The elite Soviet sharpshooters make themselves felt in a particularly disagreeable way.

In the middle of the day, groups of scouts realize that the Russians are reinforcing positions that they have just regained, notably in Cholmy and south of the Cholmy–Sukhaya Niva road. Toward 4:30 p.m., the command post of the division informs its units on the ground that the offensive must be continued in spite of the difficulties.

At 8:40 p.m. the division receives from the army high command its mission order for the next day, Sunday, October 19, 1941. "The SS-Totenkopf Division is to hold the line already won and proceed to regroup in preparation for the offensive of October 20, 1941."[2]

A few hours of respite.

45

The Forest of Souls

Cholmy, the locality conquered for a few hours by Alexander and his men October 17, 1941. Today, with fewer than ten houses standing, it's a tiny little forgotten burg with tumbledown metal roofs. Having left Valdai at dawn, we arrive early. Gray, low sky. Three men are busy around a stiff, dead pig. The good-sized animal is lying on a plank in front of a wooden house, a thick gash in its neck. Purple blood on the grass. The men are meticulously burning every centimeter of its skin with various gas blowtorches. Burning off vermin to preserve the meat. The youngest throws us a fierce, sideways look. He is fat, wears a military jacket, and has long, greasy hair, pasted down over his forehead. Beside him a burly adult is scraping off the singed rind with a knife. The third, the oldest, moves toward us and says hello. Nicolas engages him in conversation and tells him we are looking for a man who fell here during the war. His dentures rattling but his mind clear, the old man responds to our questions with good grace.

"I was twelve years old at the time," he responds with great pride.

Indeed, he doesn't look his age.

"Are you from Cholmy?" Nicolas asks.

"Me? No. We were living in the village of Poljzo. But it was completely destroyed. Did you come down the road between Kirillowtschina and Sukhaya Niva?"

"Yes."

"Poljzo was there, between these two villages. Everything was destroyed like Borok or Jeruschkovo . . . "

"And so your family came to live in Cholmy?"

"After the war."

"Do you remember the war?"

"Not really. At the beginning, when the Germans arrived, we were very quickly deported to Latvia with the other children from here."

"For the whole duration of the war?"

"Yes, I came back in 1946. And since then I've been living here in Cholmy."

"Is this your house?" Nicolas asks, pointing at the semidetached building behind us.

"Yes," says the old man.

"What was it like before you were deported?"

"This village wasn't occupied by the Germans, but it was caught between them and our forces. Things were completely leveled here . . . There was so much destruction . . . When I came back I didn't recognize anything. Villages destroyed, trees destroyed, even the roads had changed."

And then, in a tone in which you could hear a certain melancholy for former times, when, in spite of the harshness of life, the world was nevertheless simpler:

"There was less forest at the time and many more people. The region was inhabited."

As we are silently contemplating with him the abandoned village, a couple comes out of the house opposite. The old man continues his monologue:

"These neighbors only live here in the summer. They're leaving today for Saint Petersburg to spend the winter. The winter is hard here."

It's true that the spot is deserted and a little sad. But I don't want to depart too quickly either. Savor these minutes; breathe fresh, pure air. In front of the house belonging to the couple from Saint Petersburg, the garden has been put in order for the intense cold. Plantings that have been cut back are covered with fir branches to protect the roots and the bulbs from frost. Hives have been brought into the shelter of a little barn, with their bees, for hibernation. Curtains are drawn. We wave at them as they make the rounds before leaving the hamlet. Half the houses are unoccupied and are falling down.

Cholmy is clearly on a height of land. To the south, the forest; to the north, a long perspective, all wild. The position is clearly untenable, much too exposed.

"Poljzo, Borok, I'd like us to go to the area of these two villages, to see if we could discover something."

"Sure. We're off," Nicolas replies, waving at the three men in front of their blackened pig.

We go back through Sukhaya Niva, again without stopping there. We veer south and cross the bridge over the Lushenka. After five hundred meters, Nicolas parks the car on the side of the road.

"Borok should be around here," he tells me, turning off the engine.

Hilly fields, waist-high grass, groves of birch and ash; no sign at all, however, of any kind of dwelling place. Nicolas and I push through the vegetation, taking big strides. Dew seeps into our pants and gets our shoes wet. We climb the hillside to the left of the road. A height that must have served as a line of defense in front of Borok. Nicolas reads the terrain with the eyes of an ex-military man.

"Borok must be down there, toward the river, and the Russian defenses, near here."

He points out a ridgeline one hundred meters above the road and toward which we are moving. I open my bag to pull out accounts of the fighting and find what I was looking for: the attack of the Russian bunkers where the Soviets greeted the SS with a new weapon shooting out a band of flames several meters high and thirty meters long. "The flames shot out abruptly at the approach of the German infantrymen. Caught in the fire, several SS men burst into flame like torches."

It was here precisely, facing Borok.

The discovery of the use of these giant flamethrowers stirs something in me. When, months earlier in Paris, the healer Agnès Stevenin did a healing for me in which she and I both had some kind of vision, she spoke to me about picking up images of destruction as she was working on my belly. More precisely she spoke of "a volcano, an upside-down cone moving up from the ground. Explosions that shoot up. Colossal destruction, smoke." Was this a *memory* from Russia, hooked to my gut?

Nicolas pulls me out of my reverie. He's just come across a trench. We discover another, ten meters farther, then a third, all in a row. Deep holes hidden by the grass. I go down into the first one. As I scrape away at the earth, rusty cartridge cases appear. The remains of a fight to the death. Right here. And suddenly the situation clarifies. I see that the Russian defense was a little more scattered than I would have imagined. Turning toward the south I study the grassy slope along which the Totenkopf men attacked. My eyes search for them. In thin air. Their attack followed a long preparation with artillery, but in spite of all that, there were still defenders alive who controlled the fire from hell. But that was not going to save them. Because I understand also how this height of land could be encircled. All the Russians, terrified, defended themselves to the last man in desperate hand-to-hand fighting.

There was extreme violence everywhere, but especially here, downstream from Borok.

In going back downhill toward the north, where the village should be, Nicolas comes upon an encampment of amateur excavators on the banks of the Lushenka. The men have spent several days here, going over the wooded land with their metal detectors and digging in the sandy soil when they get a reading. Horse skulls, pieces of artillery shells, cases of mortar shells, live cartridges are strewn around the abandoned bivouac. We explore the banks and discover traces of other Soviet positions. The forest is studded with them. Brush and sometimes trees are partially covering them, but Nicolas reads the landscape for me. Here a line of trenches, there a machine gun station.

"Oriented this way, they are protecting themselves from an attack coming from the east. Two men man the machine gun. No doubt there would be a third man with them taking cover . . . "

Nicolas decodes the slightest unevenness in the soil. A clump of earth, a hollow in the dirt are like so many indicators allowing him, with precision and detail, to understand the fighting that took place right here. It's impressive. At the same time that we're wandering together in this forest, he is teaching me to see another invisible world. The world of the war that was. The world of men fighting, a memory that has left these innumerable gashes on the land of Valdai. Marks so easily decoded by him. After a bit less than an hour of exploration, I understand the land better. Its volumes begin to speak to me, awakening me to their deep suffering. This is going to be useful for me in the morning the day after tomorrow, when I will enter alone into Alexander's footsteps in the forest southwest of Cholmy.

Silence spreads through the forest. Broken only by the discrete lapping of the Lushenka's water flowing below. Noon approaches.

"I'm getting hungry, aren't you?"

Nicolas agrees.

"Let's go down to Mirochny; maybe we can find something to eat there."

"I'm not sure we'll find anything wonderful . . . " Nicolas observes.

"In that case, too bad, we'll eat tonight. But nevertheless I'd like to go and see that old lady the mayor spoke to us about yesterday . . . and then I would like to try entering the house that Alexander is lying under."

"Exactly, let's go to see the Mayor."

It only takes us a few minutes to get to Mirochny. Several all-terrain vehicles and a group of armed men dressed in military attire with camouflage patterning are standing in the middle of the village. Lunch break for a group of hunters who look more like Spetsnaz commandos, Russian special forces, than retired Frenchmen tracking deer. All of them tall and fierce, they are equipped with weapons of war. Bear and wolves are to be found in the Valdai forests.

Nicolas starts a conversation. One of the hunters tells us that the house we're standing in front of is a grocery. To buy something you have to call the owner whose phone number is written on a scrap of cardboard stuck behind the glass. We're hungry, so Nicolas takes out his cell phone. At the other end of the line he's told someone is coming. While we're waiting, the hunters offer us a drink. A kind of red berry juice with alcohol.

From the end of the street going east there arrives a good lady walking along tranquilly: the occupant of the cemetery house, the house with the black dog.

With the keys to the house, she's the grocer!

She's smiling more than yesterday, but uncomfortable just the same. Later I will understand why. We buy some sausages and bread, chat for a few minutes with her, then walk out and eat our meal off the hood of the Audi as the hunters are leaving. In the last Lada to leave, a giant Armenian places his sniper rifle between his legs and gives us a big smile. The grocer closes her shop, says goodbye, and walks off toward her house.

Fortified by several slices of good bread, we head for the mayor's house. A heavy rain starts falling as we're knocking on his door. His wife sticks her head out and invites us in. Nicolas and I move into a big vestibule that serves as an airlock between the cold of the Russian winter and the home itself, where a delicious temperature reigns. After the airlock we enter into the kitchen, where a fire crackles away in a big brick stove. Built above the hearth, a metal reservoir keeps water really hot all the time. The mayor, his wife, their daughter, and her little boy are waiting for us. A baby is sleeping in the adjoining bedroom. In no time the table is laden with coffee, tea, sausage, cake, bread, crème fraîche, a box of chocolates opened especially for us, and other food that we are firmly urged to enjoy. And the two of us, like two idiots, have just gobbled down a half loaf of bread and a whole sausage, standing out in the cold. The mother is called Valentina and her husband, the mayor, is called Michael. Their daughter with mischievous eyes, a young mother with two toddlers, is called Macha. Iaroslav, her son of two and a half, is very excited by these two foreigners who dropped in out of nowhere. Valentina lets us know that she saw her grandmother—the old lady whom we were speaking with yesterday—and that she confirmed the information conveyed the day before.

"My grandmother has always lived in Mirochny. She is now eighty-nine years old."

"Was she present in 1941?"

"Yes . . . "

I do some quick arithmetic.

"She was . . . fifteen at the time?"

"Yes, about that . . . When I spoke to her about the figure that you had given me, she said that there were many more than 191 graves in Mirochny."

"That number represents the number of bodies exhumed in the village for transfer to the military cemetery of Korpowo, past Demyansk," I mention.

"She assured me that there were many more."

"Really?"

"There were those buried around the field hospital, on the right as you're leaving the village in the direction of Kirillowtschina; there were also some on the left and still others on the land where Tania's house is now."

"Tania?"

"The woman who runs the grocery. I believe you were there yesterday. The one with the big black dog tied up in front . . . "

"Ah yes, of course . . . we just ran into her . . . "

"My grandmother told me that a redheaded man, an SS soldier, was looking after the graves and that he came looking for flowers at our place when the soldiers were buried. He must have been the one in charge of the funerals."

"We went to speak with Tania yesterday, and she told us that foreigners had come looking for bodies at her place."

Valentina and Michael look at each other, smile, and raise their eyes to heaven.

"However, there are still lots of dead soldiers buried on her land! Tania only let them take one row. Everybody here knows this, except her! We were a little hesitant to tell you about it yesterday."

Now we have a second confirmation of the information given the day before by Tania's neighbor. I'm delighted. Michael continues:

"Her brother told her there were no more. I don't know if she really believed him or if she deliberately did not hear him, but there are many other rows of bodies, notably under the house. My wife's grandmother also told us that."

I turn toward Valentina.

"Your grandmother is sure about that?"

"Yes. Tania's house was built after the war by her mother, who by the way is still living there today. During the war, this piece of land situated between two other properties was empty. That's why the Germans made it into a cemetery. The bodies are only on her property, and not under other houses."

Nicolas and I are beginning to have a clearer idea of what has happened in the village. The field hospital cemetery as well as the one opposite were entirely emptied by the men from funerary service for former German soldiers. These same men received permission five years ago to exhume the first row of bodies from the land where Tania's house is. But many more are still there. And Alexander's too, most certainly.

"Do you think we could go and see your grandmother?"

Valentina is a little embarrassed.

"She is very old and tires quickly . . . And also speaking about those times makes her nervous. She doesn't want to talk about the war. She is still traumatized by what she saw."

"It must have been terrible . . . "

"Yes. One thing scarred her more than anything else. A horrible event. A truck transporting Germans took a direct hit from a shell and exploded."

"But how did Tania's house end up on top of a cemetery?"

"It was built after the war. People knew what there was underneath, but Tania's mother had no other options, clearly. And the graves were not visible. All trace of them had disappeared. So . . . "

And it's true; houses here do not have foundations. They are built right on the ground, sometimes with a kind of basement that can be used as a cellar but that only goes down a few centimeters below ground level. Tania's house must be constructed on this model. She is living there, with a very old lady—her mother. The brother who authorized the exhuming is not there. No doubt Tania suspects something but would rather not know anything more about it. That's why our presence makes her uncomfortable.

Having finished with the subject of graves, I ask Nicolas to ask a somewhat strange question of Valentina and Michael. Does the area have ghost stories? Nicolas translates, and Valentina's face brightens up. There is curiosity but also fear in her response.

"There are no ghosts! Only those who go digging up graves and taking out the skeletons see ghosts."

"Are there a lot of people digging?"

"Yes, a lot, and they regularly find graves in the forest. But the graves must be left alone . . . There was this man and his son who came from Moscow. They had so many nightmares after having come across a dead man that they stopped everything."

Valentina is not joking, and her husband, who would have liked to laugh it off, ends up being uncomfortable. Another anecdote comes back to him.

"A year and a half ago, Macha's husband, who was out gathering mushrooms, found a dead soldier in the woods—a Russian. The guy had all his stuff with him, as if he had fallen there and hadn't moved since. My son-in-law brought the soldier's things home and left them in the barn. And that night I heard whisperings, laughter, and noises too."

"Really?"

"Oh yes! I didn't like that at all. The next day, I asked my son-in-law to give all those things to one of those excavators, which he did two or three days later. As soon as all that stuff was no longer here, the noises stopped. I heard someone laugh and make little knocking noises. I think he was happy to have been found."

"Why happy?"

"Because when we find soldiers, we rebury them and offer a religious service for them, a service for the dead . . . But I was not comfortable at all because 'he' was so present in the house. It wasn't threatening but good . . . I heard laughter . . . "

A happy ghost.

"Sometimes children say they see ghosts."

Now feeling comfortable because of our attentive listening, Valentina continues.

"A few years ago, this little boy . . . What was his name? Anyway, it doesn't matter. It was a village boy about five or six years old. He got lost in the woods, and he recounted that it was a soldier who showed him the way to come back to the village. Another time, another child had gotten lost in the swampy area to the west, and similarly, he said that a soldier guided him to the village. But we've never seen these soldiers . . . I don't think we ought to be digging them up . . . "

I see in Valentina's eyes that she is very serious. And the afternoon continues in a good-natured way over coffee.

Finally, we take our leave of Michael, Valentina, and the charming Macha in order to pursue our explorations. The magnificent news is that in asking if we could sleep somewhere in the village the next night, Valentina suggested that we stay in her aunt's house, in Mirochny itself. I hadn't dared dream that I could sleep here locally between October 19 and 20 in order to be closest to Alexander on his last night alive.

Before the night, which falls relatively early, requires our return to the hotel in Valdai, I want to go a few kilometers farther east to go through the forested area around the vanished village of Chilkovo, where I discovered that Alexander's battalion had been posted in a defensive position from September 13, 1941, on.

Like the village, the road leading to Chilkovo no longer exists. A few decades were enough for the forest to swallow it up. The only existing road goes off in a southeastern direction from the village of Domashi. We get there after five kilometers. What is special about the place is that before the war it was where the great basilica of the area was located. An imposing orthodox building that today is a gutted carcass with birch trees growing out of it. The edifice was bombarded ceaselessly by the Soviets since the Germans were using the bell tower as an observation post for their artillery installed a little farther south. The thick walls and a part of the vault remain. Apart from that, the rest is open to the sky. Inside the church, you need only raise your head to see either the sun or the stars, depending on the hour that you visit.

Alexander lived in this area more than five weeks between the moment when the positions became fixed toward mid-September 1941 and October 20. Mirochny, before becoming his grave, was no doubt a place of rest and relative *relaxation* when he left his men and the defense positions of his company in the forest. Valentina definitely told us that the Germans had requisitioned all the solidly built houses for their officers. He must have spent nights in the village. Perhaps even in the house where we are going to sleep tomorrow night . . .

Leaving the ruins of the basilica, we head back up toward the northeast and the big hamlet of Bolshoye Zamoshye. Midway between the two localities that are on our left we come across a dirt road leading to the frontline zones. Before long the state of the road requires we leave the car and continue on foot.

We enter under the vault of the trees, in the forest of souls.

The SS positions are visible everywhere. It's impressive.

Long trenches in zigzag patterns in order to avoid dangerous alignments, firing emplacements, hundreds of men of the Totenkopf were guarding this line. Among them Alexander at the head of his company.

We run into a Russian covered in mud, a rusty machine gun on his shoulder: the discovery of the day. We soon wind up in fact in an area where he and other excavators were working today. Beside the freshly dug holes are strewn things just dug up that are too ordinary to carry off: stick grenades, circular machine gun loaders, helmets, shoes, gas masks, pieces of mortar shells, etc. The area that has been dug up is located a few meters below the German lines. And suddenly I understand: we are in the attack zone of the Soviet troops, facing the SS defense positions. At the exact spot where, wave upon wave, the Russian soldiers fell, cut down by the German machine gun fire and the bullets. I *see* them, these poor buggers, having no choice but to obey and to engage in suicidal attacks. All around me, bullets whistle by, hell lets loose, men are torn to bits, collapse, and are buried in the crumbly earth. Their bodies are still here. Day after day the excavators discover them and honor them with commemorative burial sites improvised on the sides of the road.

All these holes.

And how many bodies are still buried here?

Night falls. I feel heavy. Throat dry. Head spinning.

We make our way back, find the car, and loop around to head back north. We get lost in Bolshoye Zamoshye, but a drunken villager gets us back on the right road. We pass through one hamlet after another, able to see only shadowy outlines as darkness falls. Karpeya, Zlodari, and then we're back at Cholmy continuing in a westerly direction.

Three hundred meters before getting to Sukhaya Niva, in a state that's more and more unsteady, I suddenly again feel *something* incomprehensible, and I say out loud, "He died here."

"You want me to stop?" asks Nicolas.

"Just for a minute."

As in Mirochny yesterday morning, I have just perceived a kind of physical evidence, a flash. We passed very near the spot where Alexander died. I feel it. No houses are visible yet, but the village is nearby. To the left and to the right there are fields. I really don't feel well. I will come back here. Tomorrow.

◆ ◆ ◆

It is now completely dark. Nicolas drives fast, and the road to Valdai bobs up and down in the headlights. I feel more and more unwell. As if I am drained of all my energy. I'm taken by nausea. I feel really weak. My face is drained of blood. We need to get to the hotel fast. I am really feverish.

In *danger*.

Some of the forest is still stuck to me. Mud, blood, a kind of opaque dark goo bogs me down, sucks me in. I want to throw up, but we absolutely mustn't stop the car. "Drive, Nicolas. Don't stop." I slump down and pray with all my strength that I can hold on until we get there.

Once in my little room, I ask all the forces of the invisible world, my allies and my guides, to help me cleanse myself and remove from me anything that doesn't belong.

The souls of the forest watched me walking through their dream. Certain of them have followed me, thinking I could do something for them. Deliver them from their torment? Relieve them at their post? They glom onto me, hopeful. Without understanding what's at play, tossed around by their fright. One thousand ghosts, ten thousand dire needs. Energies gone astray that I am too weak to guide. They can't stay in the forest, but alone I am not strong enough. So in my room, I pray, I implore that help be offered us to lead them toward the light, toward their dear ones who wait for them still and who love them.

There were Russians, adults barely past adolescence and already cut down before having felt the warmth of a woman's belly, others older but just as lost, and Germans too, and certain of these souls have *recognized* SS-Ostuf Herrmann.

These are the lines held by his battalion.

It is Alexander that certain ghosts saw suddenly rise up from the void, come back among the dead, among his men. These are the ones who followed their officer.

His men.

46

Hand-to-Hand Combat

S unday, October 19, 1941. Right from the first hours of the day scouting contingents are sent once again to observe the Soviet lines. Upon their return they report no changes in enemy positions, but they are out of breath from the close call of having come under sustained enemy fire.

Opposite the zone where Alexander and his men are located, other battalions of the Totenkopf engage in hard fighting, much of which turns into hand-to-hand combat in the middle of the forest. Several Soviet attacks are also countered with artillery cannon.

A young SS sublieutenant writes in his journal: "Today, the Russians are completely mad. Grenades follow one another without a break. From our dug-in positions and around the artillery guns, you see nothing but craters from the explosions. We are moving forward nevertheless, in order to find a firing position near hill 172,2. We don't walk—we run and then throw ourselves to the ground. On this stretch of land, one absolutely must not be visible even for a brief instant. The creek bed behind the little fir tree is already called 'death hollow.' The wounded come back in an uninterrupted line. There is not a meter of this land that is without risk."[1]

To the west of Alexander, north of Lushno, part of the division is advancing toward enemy positions through a swampy forest. They break through successfully but with numerous, regrettable losses. The

Russians counterattack, supported by their tanks. The sector where
Alexander is stationed is relatively spared, in spite of an attempted
Russian breakthrough between the 1st and 3rd Battalions. It is the
artillery once again that frees the infantry from the Russian pressure.
Well positioned, it is capable of spraying the Soviets from all sides. They
sustain heavy losses and withdraw, around 5:00 p.m., to their original
positions.

These successive attacks and counteroffensives have seriously
impacted certain parts of the Totenkopf resources. For example, the 6th
Company of the 2nd Battalion positioned on the right wing now has
only 22 men instead of 180!

When night falls, the enemy artillery continues firing at the
same rate.

On October 19 at 7:40 p.m. the division receives from headquarters
its marching orders for the next day, October 20: "The SS-Totenkopf
Division is to attack beyond the Lushenka to the east of Borok toward
the north, then veer toward the west and move forward in the direction
of Sukhaya Niva."[2]

Somewhere in the forest, between Kirillowtschina and Cholmy,
Alexander enters the last night of his life.

47

He Is Here

The spirits of lost soldiers have left. *Someone* came looking for them. The night delivered me from the grip of these lost men. And they no doubt have found again a little light. I am alone in my room this morning. I feel better, once again full of energy and life. The night was long and gentle.

The sky is low; the soil, soaked and cold. The air, sharp. It rained a lot last night.

Strange day beginning. From now on I'm not counting down the days, I'm counting the hours.

Nicolas is an ideal travel companion. He is aware, extremely efficient, foresightful, and very unobtrusive. Silence is a refuge that I miss very quickly. The best part of my life I have traveled alone, and this tranquility is indispensable to me. Nicolas instantly felt it. We're driving at a good clip toward our area of investigation. Valdai was the closest town where it was possible to find a hotel, but tonight we will spend the night in Mirochny.

Today, we stop at Sukhaya Niva. I want to see what the village looks like and identify the progression of the positions of the various protagonists in the course of the morning during which Alexander died. The road through the place is bordered by spaced-out wooden houses and little gardens. In the middle, forking off due east is the road to Cholmy. I want to get my bearings for tomorrow morning. Alexander came that way, from the east. He must have fallen somewhere between his departure point, situated in the forest several kilometers away and the edge of the village. Somewhere along a distance of three kilometers. Tomorrow at dawn I will retrace his advance.

We park the car four hundred meters outside the village, precisely at the spot where, the evening before, I cried out, "He died here!" Fields stretch out to the left and the right. To the north of the road, the area is flat and open, completely exposed. It would be suicidal to advance in that direction. That says to Nicolas that Alexander's battalion must have advanced farther down, south of the road. In that place, the field is at a different level between a wooded area and a "course" to be followed—that is, a route hidden from the enemy. A little gorge about thirty meters wide with a stream running through it.

We cross the fence and approach that area. We are a few hundred meters back southeast of Sukhaya Niva. Right where the Totenkopf attacked. We move ahead under the cover of trees and descend to the "course."

Immediately, Nicolas picks out Russian defense positions on the edges of the gorge. They are oriented for protection against what might come from the east: the Germans. I understand better the logic of the attack. At this spot the attacker is invisible from Sukhaya Niva and is sheltered from direct fire. It was the ideal route for Alexander and his men in order to take the village with minimal losses. We follow the stream in the direction of the village. Nicolas explains to me that Alexander's battalion must have had barely 250 men (as opposed to 800 in normal times), each company having been reduced to 70 men and a battalion being composed of four companies.

"They must have advanced in staggered lines, one man about every fifteen meters, and Alexander, in his capacity as company commander, would have been either in the middle or on one or the other side."

"According to my documents, the attack was definitely concentrated to the south of Sukhaya Niva."

"It's clear. Just look: at the level of the road they are too exposed.

In contrast, in the 'course' they advance no doubt with heavy losses, but the Russian artillery gunners don't see them and can only fire based on where they think their enemy is. This is where I would have conducted the attack if I were in their place," observes Nicolas.

"He was nevertheless killed that way, by an exploding shell."

"The Russians must have done their range-finding calculations ahead of time."

"Meaning?"

"They knew where their own lines were. Also, when these positions fall into the hands of the Germans, if they fire on them, they have a chance of hitting the SS. It's unreliable but dangerous. The proof is your Alexander was hit."

We move along the stream and end up at the road at the southern exit of Sukhaya Niva, just before the bridge. We move out of the undergrowth and walk toward the center of the village to reach the fork in the road toward the east and our car. We remain standing there in conversation beside the car while I continue looking at a 360-degree view of the landscape. Yet another spot I don't want to depart from. Nicolas lights his pipe, I walk a few steps on either side of the road, then suddenly my phone rings. It's Andréa calling from Plauen.

"Andréa, what a surprise. You'll never guess where I am."

"No, I can't . . . "

"At Sukhaya Niva, no doubt a few meters from where Alexander died."

"It's incredible . . . "

I feel that she is quite moved.

"Your email really touched me, Stéphane."

"I wanted to share with you all the emotions that I was experiencing here during these three days . . . as promised."

"That touched me. By the way, I found time to phone the Volksbund Deutsche Kriegsgräberfürsorge."

"The people who came to exhume bodies in Mirochny—you're terrific!"

"It wasn't easy, because they don't give out this kind of information to the public, but I insisted, and I believe you are right . . . "

"Meaning?"

"Not all the bodies that are documented have been exhumed from graves in Mirochny. They confirmed for me that one landowner was against them doing excavations in his house."

"That's Tania's house. We went there, and several villagers told us that many bodies must still be located underneath it. So that's really official now?"

"Yes. But the person I was dealing with told me it was not possible to send us the layout plan for the graves, and that only their service was authorized to proceed with additional exhuming of bodies in this village, if the property owners were agreeable."

"It's fantastic that you've been able to obtain this information. And since they have never been able to find his identity tag on the exhumed bodies, Alexander is very certainly still there."

"Stéphane, you were right . . . "

The connection is bad, but I gather nonetheless that Andréa is deeply moved by what she's about to convey to me.

"I tried to get the employee of the agency talking about the placement of grave number 50."

"Yes . . . And so, what did she say?"

"She confirmed for me, reading between the lines, that that particular grave has never been exhumed."

"Never exhumed? What does that mean? It's not on their plan?"

"No, no. Its position is very clearly identified on their plan. They have archival documents available from the Totenkopf Division dating from the war years, and the recorded data are very precise . . . "

"And so? . . . "

"So they were not able to gain access, and it's still int . . . "

"Hello? Andréa? I didn't hear the end of your sentence . . . "

"Can you hear me?" she asks.

"OK. Now it's better."

"Grave number 50 is still intact . . . It is located under the house!"

My breath is taken away.

"Under . . . Under the house?"

"Yes . . . And I understood from the silent pauses of the employee that I was speaking to that there are numerous other bodies under this house. And under the barn too. In fact, they're all over."

This moment is magical.

The moment when an intuition is validated by a rational investigation: Alexander is under the house! Now we have proof of it. And learning this when I am right here where he fell, the day before the anniversary of his death, is simply incredible. As soon as I hang up I bring Nicolas up to speed. For him, having been impressed by the lightning-like power of my feelings the first day in front of Tania's house, this official confirmation is more than just unsettling. However, I have the impression that his pragmatic nature allows him to more easily accept the facts, even if they go against his vision of the world. After three days with me he is spoiled.

Alexander is still in his grave under Tania's house.

He has not budged since his death.

I can't believe it. My sensations, my intuitions are not just the result of my imagination. I'm picking up things. This revelation unsettles me almost as much as knowing that Alexander's remains are so near. If I listen inwardly, I can have access to invisible information.

We quickly go back down toward Domashi, the village with the destroyed basilica. Valentina let us know yesterday that an old lady of ninety-four was still living there.

There are no longer very many people living in this hamlet, and we have no trouble finding her house. A little izba, well looked after, and full of charm. We knock, the curtains shiver, but the door does not open. We knock again and wait. We seem to hear some sounds from inside the house. Then, after a long pause, the door opens a little. And there appears a minuscule and very old lady wearing a shawl, a smock, and big socks. Darting her blue eyes, the color of salt, over us, she asks what we want. Nicolas's voice is very gentle as he explains to her that we're doing research on the war.

"I don't know anything about the war . . . "

Diplomatically, Nicolas tries another approach, less formal. He manages to get a few scraps of memories. We learn that Domashi also was evacuated, because the area had become a German artillery position. Finally, Nicolas confesses to her that we're looking for the body of a German.

"It's in Mirochny that they're buried—the Germans!"

"Yes, we know. We've spoken with Tania."

"That's right, it's at her place . . . There's a lot of them, a lot of Germans, buried at her place."

"Do you know how many?"

"Right up to the well at the bottom of the garden . . . "

"Did you see them?"

"Yes, of course . . . The burials went right up to there."

Very definitely, this cemetery, everyone in the area knows about it. Or at least the old people do. The Germans have lain there for a very long time and have blended into the landscape of the times. An occupying force.

Right up to the well at the end of the garden! As we are on our way back to Mirochny, making a rough estimate based on the available data on the rows of bodies, Nicolas and I estimate that there are between 150 and 200 soldiers buried on Tania's land . . . and only 30 have been removed.

Valentina, the mayor's wife, was not expecting us so early. Her daughter, Macha, takes us to the house where we're going to spend the night. She brings along a plate of blinis and a bowl of thick cream. The house has two big rooms, each one heated by a brick stove that serves as an oven, a fireplace, and a water heater. Macha has come to get the one started in the area where we're going to sleep. It's already at a very pleasant temperature. The ceiling is low, and the room we'll be occupying is divided into two areas separated by a curtain. One part is the kitchen with a little bed situated in the extension of the stove, and a living room part with a second bed. Luxurious. Macha lets us know that this house belongs to her aunt. It already existed during the war and had been requisitioned by the Germans. It was filled with men at the time. It's likely that Alexander passed through this house. To rest, to visit an officer friend, and perhaps even to sleep there a few nights, warm and dry. Alexander's stay in this area was more than a month long. Even though he stayed most often with his men at the front, a few kilometers east, toward Chilkovo, these requisitioned houses were occupied by officers of his division.

Alexander lived here. He impregnated this time and space.

The place is welcoming. I feel good here. So happy to be sleeping here. I take the bed against the stove. Macha leaves us to settle in and suggests we join them for supper when we would like to do so. Russian hospitality. Barely has she left when Nicolas and I enjoy a few blinis with cream. A delight. Then, while my acolyte goes off for a walk, I take notes on the events of the day.

And the sun goes down.

A feast awaits us. Mashed potatoes, ground meat, homemade sausages, marinated mushrooms, and cooked cabbage. The mayor isn't there. We're dining alone with Valentina, Macha, and the children.

Sweet evening, warm and cozy. I bask in the moment. It's all incredible, beyond my expectations. After the meal, an atmosphere of trust and confidence pervades the room, so Nicolas asks me if I would allow him to recount my story. What a great idea! So he launches into it. Valentina and Macha then learn that we came to Mirochny because of a dream. A dream that I had. I don't know if Nicolas manages to translate "waking dream," but while he is relating my experience, punctuating his tale with answers to precisions requested by our hosts, Valentina looks at me fixedly. Her look is that of a woman who is not surprised by very many things. The look of a young grandmother who must be about my age and who has endured a rough life. However, there is excitement and gentleness in her eyes. Kindness and strength. My story calls to her and awakens in her the memory that the world is mysterious and immense. Women can remember that because they know that life becomes more flavorful when you allow certitudes to waver.

"It's good that you're sleeping here tonight," she says suddenly.

"What do you mean?"

"In Mirochny, in this house. Do you know why you had this dream?"

Why does she say that? What is she perceiving? She's looking at me as if she has access to secrets.

"No . . ."

"You are not at peace because you have not yet found . . ."

Why am I suddenly invaded by such an emotion? Valentina is sensitive to what I'm experiencing. She sees the strength of it. She stares at me intently.

"Alexander lived several weeks here," she tells me. "He knew Mirochny, and since you came all the way here, no doubt he's going to show you things. Explain them to you one way or another."

After having left our hosts and returned to our home, lighting our way with a flashlight, I slip under the thick covers. And sleep takes me away, very far away. For a night that is long and warm.

When I open one eye, it's still dark outside. But it's time. Dawn approaches. It's October 20.

I get up.

Outside, everything is white.

48

Death

Monday, October 20, 1941. Everything is white. Covered with snow and frost made crackly with a temperature that has fallen below freezing. In the middle of the night, somewhere in the forest between Kirillowtschina and Cholmy, enemy firing lets loose. Shells are screaming over Alexander's head. The Russians are continuously bombarding the whole area held by his division. Mirochny, Kirillowtschina, where the command center of the 1st Regiment is located, as well as Poljzo and the region to the north, are especially affected. And as if that weren't enough . . . the lines where Alexander and his company are dug in are also under fire from Soviet mortars, a harassment that explodes tree trunks. For so many days they haven't slept, as they shelter themselves so precariously on the front lines.

When the firing stops for a few moments, darkness is total. We're the day before the new moon. In the middle of the night the 1st and 3rd Battalions receive reinforcements who have come on foot from Kirillowtschina. The positions are secured. In a state of alert, Alexander gives the order to his men to position themselves in reserve with the rest of the 1st Battalion, in order to be ready to attempt to conduct a breakthrough southwest of Cholmy, toward the valley of the Lushenka River.

And suddenly, all the artillery regiments of the SS-Totenkopf leap into action. A deluge of fire and metal crashes down on the Russian positions along the Lushenka between Borok and Cholmy.

The offensive is launched. Just before 6:00 a.m. the order to attack is given. Alexander and his men plunge toward the river.

For this day, which the general command considers critical, Alexander's battalion receives the exceptional support of assault cannons. The SS-Totenkopf brings in its mobile artillery armored vehicles to support the 1st Battalion's offensive on Sukhaya Niva. The infantrymen shelter behind these metal mastodons, moving forward beside them in concert.

The first phase of the attack proceeds as expected, but already the losses are heavy in the German ranks.

An inhuman fervor has given way to unbearable fear of the night.

Fury is awakening in each one, metamorphosing all these young men who throw themselves against each other into hardened killers, capable of anything. No holds barred. Moral limits are unhinged. Moving forward in noise and danger, shooting, killing, crushing the enemy provokes jolts of pure pleasure.

The river is reached.

Does he tell himself that all this is absurd, before once again falling into the trance of combat?

The 1st Battalion constitutes the division's point of attack.

Alexander and his men go back up the flanks, cleaning out bunker after bunker, reaching, in the first light of dawn, south of the road between Cholmy and Sukhaya Niva.

At this point, Alexander turns west and continues to meet strong resistance. His temples are burning hot.

On his left flank, to the northeast of Borok, the companies of the 3rd Battalion also advance toward Sukhaya Niva. They receive the reinforcement of a company of soldier-engineers equipped with flame-throwers who one by one take the enemy's defensive positions.

An hour after sunrise, Alexander is thirsty. His throat is dry, his head is buzzing with a deafening uproar of weapons. He is numb with fatigue. Sheltered behind the assault cannon, its treads tearing up the earth, he and his men come into sight of Sukhaya Niva. They must be eight hundred meters away from the place. Progress forward is happening south of the road, under significant Russian artillery fire that is trying, unsuccessfully, to slow down the German offensive. Shards of metal ricochet off the armored vehicle with a whistling sound. Sometimes, a hit lands with a dull thud in the body of a man who then falls, stunned.

The 1st Battalion now has less than two hundred able-bodied men. Several of its officers have been killed. Alexander looks at his company. Barely fifty men, overextended but fierce, advancing, bent over under their heavy coats. *Absurd.*

The exhaust smoke of the assault cannon bursts out like a clap of thunder at each acceleration. The motor screams. Its treads spinning on the frozen earth.

They approach.

Smoke rises from what remains of the first houses of Sukhaya Niva in the gray air.

More than five hundred meters.

They are moving forward from the southwest. Farther down from the road, so as not to offer easy targets to the Russian rifles. Alexander encourages his soldiers, many of whom are falling. They cannot all shelter behind the armored vehicle. It takes the full fury of all the division's forces to win each meter. His boots are heavy. Air entering his windpipe burns. He's short of breath. So much effort for so many hours. He steps aside to look in front of the tank.

Then Alexander feels something hit his neck. His legs give way, he is suddenly without strength, he collapses . . .

49

The Last Dawn

Everything is white. Covered with snow and frost made crackly with a temperature that has fallen below freezing. Somewhere in the forest between Kirillowtschina and Cholmy reigns the most complete silence.

I am in the woods since dawn. Alone. In the calm and biting cold.

Nicolas dropped me off about two kilometers east of Sukhaya Niva. As the car was leaving, I left the road behind and strode into the undergrowth to join the ghosts of a vanished army.

The last dawn, being with Alexander.

I set out in his footsteps. Just the two of us, and the forest.

The pale light of the sun slips between the branches of the trees. Above the canopy the sky is clear, but at ground level everything is still dark and bluish. As if the night has not yet managed to give up its dominion completely.

A thick frost covers everything with a white film. Grass, bushes, dead leaves, areas of marsh, everything is frozen. It all crackles under my feet. My shoes penetrate deeply into the sleeping vegetation. Sometimes boughs covered in moss hide puddles of muddy water. The thin layer of ice doesn't hold, and I sink in up to my ankles, swearing. I make a lot of noise as I move ahead clumsily. I would make a lousy scout.

Everything is white. Like in my dream.

Not one animal. Not one fluttering of birds, not one song, no trace of life.

My heart is beating madly. What if I get lost? After thirty minutes I veer off in a westerly direction, to where I think the road is. And quite soon I do come across it. I cross the ditch and stand for a few moments in the middle of the road, motionless, hesitant, looking toward the east.

A hot life flows in me.

The silence is oppressive. Nothing is moving, only the dead are walking in this forest.

I retrace my steps and engage once again with the woods, accompanied by a strange apprehension. My glance is mistrustful, and I watch for the slightest movement in my surroundings; however, everything is still.

I begin to experience a certain discomfort. My fear feeds itself and is increasing. I go ahead slowly, taking big breaths. I need to calm down, reason with myself. There is nobody in this forest. And who would want to hurt me? Abruptly I turn around, scrutinizing the bushes. Motionless trunks, air hanging. There's nothing. I'm not afraid of the dead, by the way. But afraid of what then? I halt and listen carefully. A thick silence gathers immediately. No rustling interrupts it. I would be able easily to hear anyone approaching, I am definitely alone. I start walking again, breathing. The fear that haunts this place scares me.

Calm down.

I continue to walk. In places, I come upon a tangle of brush that I have to go around, trying to hang on to my cap. I move forward, guessing at the direction, and soon come to a gorge with a little stream running through it. I've found it! It's the stream that Alexander and his men were following. I stay on its north flank, following the water's path, and I can see the bunkers that served as Russian defense positions. No solid buildings, just hollows, humps, holes that Nicolas taught me to identify. The farther I proceed the more numerous they become.

At each bunker, moving slowly, in danger and in the screaming, you had to kill the occupants, sometimes with blows from a shovel, trying not to get fired on by those in the next line of bunkers. On the pale screen of yellowed leaves, in the empty, silent air, there appear, surging up in my awareness, men who are invisible and driven insane. They are fighting hand to hand, their immaterial eyes full of panic. The vegetation was not as dense in 1941. I am now accompanying Alexander's men. They are moving forward around me, in difficulties that I'm not aware of. I sense that Alexander is not yet dead at this hour of the day. This course is a trap. The movement forward is very costly in terms of human lives, in spite of the uncertain shelter provided by the assault cannons that accompany the battalion, but he is still alive. Alexander is in command and advances among his soldiers.

It's the first image from my dream: a view from above, very high above, with men like little black dots, moving along a stream in the middle of two or three tanks. "I see an assault tank and men advancing, protected behind it. They are soldiers. They're German. It's war. They're advancing, sheltering behind the tank." The land where I am is similar in all respects. Historical elements coming from the battalion reports also correspond.

Everything matches so precisely! I am already very impressed to find myself today where Alexander was fighting in the final hours of his life. However, a new emotion hits me as the real and the memory from my vision are superimposed so precisely on each other.

What I dreamed really happened—right here!

The scene played out in this place. Day for day. The two hundred men of the four companies of the 1st Battalion advanced along this line, following the stream. The company commanded by Alexander was on the right of the course, between the stream and the road.

This morning, coming out into the darkness of the early day, the cold gripped me, and I was imagining my suffering as if I had been obliged to spend the night outside. How did they manage all those weeks in the icy, wet forest? Whereas with me, after two hours of walking following their path of advance, with daylight already present, the cold overcomes me each time I stop. In the feet, in the torso, even though I'm wearing good clothing. How not to desire with all one's being that this suffering finally end? Crawl into a warm bed, fall asleep in a calm, silent place. A deliverance so inaccessible to Alexander.

After a kilometer in the dense forest, I emerge into an area of more open undergrowth, at about five or six hundred meters from Sukhaya Niva. Now it's fields that border the stream on both sides. And still this apprehension that lives inside me. A diffuse, strange fear. Personal memories also arise. Childhood fears that came upon me in the forest, that paralyzing terror in the city of Ai-Khanoum, in Afghanistan, under fire from the Taliban—I didn't want to budge from my hole—and so many other scenes, too, that get mixed in, phobias that blend together and become one. A maelstrom with a familiar taste—the taste of death.

I look at my watch: 9:12 a.m. Alexander has not yet been hit. I know it. Yes, he is still alive.

The cold stiffens my fingers.

My lips become dry.

I am almost out in the open. At the height of the place where we parked yesterday, but lower down. I leave the gorge behind and move past the few trees that separate me from the field. To the west, I can make out the rooftops of the first houses of Sukhaya Niva.

Alexander's company made its way forward on its course, sheltered when following the stream, toward the area to the south of the village. I had it in mind to follow this itinerary, but something makes me hesitate.

A tree has fallen on the edge of the field, and I take a seat on it.

The sun is well up, but frost still covers the plain.

I make a few notes, take a mouthful of water, check my watch—9:20 a.m.—and remain seated a moment in silence. Then I stand up and move toward the road. Here I am in the middle of the field. My thinking tells me to go back down to the stream, to follow it west, but I don't budge. I take a few steps, then turn around, like an indecisive puppet. I push forward up to the road, cross the fence, then go back into the field and return to my seat on the fallen tree.

Where did he fall? My eyes scrutinize the outlines of the landscape
while my mind pulls together all the data that I've accumulated over
the months. But why am I focused so much on the exact spot where
he died? I've been in this village, in this area for days now. Why do I
always want something more? I turn the question around in all directions and begin to understand that I'm not going to be able to obtain
a more precise indication. Thanks to the details in the military documents that I've consulted, I've narrowed down the time frame and the
geographic area as much as possible. But no report is going to tell me
where he fell to the nearest meter.

So I stay put, cold mounting up my legs. The minutes tick away.

And something lets go.

I let myself be invaded by the dream, the story, the transparency of
the countryside.

I stop waiting.

Then I decide to go back to the village and look for Nicolas, who
must be waiting for me. But scarcely am I standing when once again I
find myself unable to move forward, gripped by hesitation. Which way
to go? Enter Sukhaya Niva from which direction? The confusion weighs
me down. Go along the stream, like the handful of surviving men of
the 2nd Company, or go along the road? Once again this strange confusion. I am attracted magnetically by this field. Stuck on this little open
space, sheltered from direct firing but not from the light artillery or
mortars. I'm at the height of the terrain where I said, on the second
evening, "It's here that he died!" when we were driving on the road.
I remain undecided on these few meters of land that my body cannot
resolve to leave. It is now 10:00 a.m. At this very moment, fighting in
the village was raging. The men of the division were taking the village
house by house. The various Soviet pockets were being reduced. In half
an hour, Sukhaya Niva will be entirely under German control. It was
an unbearable dinning noise, and yet here, now, I am surrounded by a
great silence . . . leaves are falling from the trees, carried by a light breeze
that has come up. What peace. The sun is warming me up, the sky is

cobalt blue, the frost is evaporating. Since I had stopped at the edge of the field, forty-five minutes have elapsed. For three-quarters of an hour I have been literally going around in circles on this little area. And suddenly I understand why: It's here that Alexander died!

At this very second, a powerful wave comes up from the ground and makes me vacillate. Once again, emotion bears down on me. And I am submerged by how obvious it is.

It is here, at this spot, that he fell. Under my feet.

That's why *something* held me here for nearly an hour.

As usual my head wants to stay in control, reflect, analyze, but as for my body it has known from the beginning where Alexander fell. And when I knew to let go, the accuracy of my perceptions took over forcibly. I look hard at the space in front of me hoping to see his silhouette appear. *His silhouette . . .*

But it is located in another dimension that my eyes cannot see.

I'm still not able to budge. We are at the anniversary date of his departure, at the very hour that it happened. I've been waiting for this moment for so many months. We had a rendezvous here. "You led me here."

A rumbling, at first imperceptible, suddenly fills the sky. I look up and see a strange black shape coming very slowly from the east. The sound increases, the object gets bigger, threatening, powerful. It comes right over me, at a very low altitude. A Sukhoi, a Russian fighter plane, alone, passes right over my head with a deafening roar. I notice distinctly its double tail fins and its long, pointed fuselage. It's the speed that surprises me—slow, as if suspended in the air. What an unreal apparition!

Exactly above Sukhaya Niva, it banks very calmly and makes a loop to head off in a northerly direction. Black emperor of the sky. Technological eagle. I'm speechless.

A warplane, alone and floating in the sky, limpid and blue, first sign of life on this day, at the exact moment of Alexander's death.

Like a salute, a farewell to arms.

It is 10:10 a.m.

50

Spirit

Monday, October 20, 1941, 10:00 a.m. The lifeless body is lying on the ground; his men continue their advance. His blood flows out on the grass that has been burned by freezing temperatures. Alexander is stretched out at his full length, his head turned to the side, his cheek flat against the wet earth. His eyes are dimming. He looks at the fineness of a blade of grass touching his nose, a few centimeters from his eyelids. Farther off, in the background, an indistinct landscape is wavering, black shadows, a mass of metal, sheaves of fire. And *at the same time*, he is standing, floating at a good height, taken by a whirlwind of light. He doesn't understand anything because suddenly these two worlds are straddling each other. In the one that is dissipating and being erased from his sight, there is furor, noise, violence, flames, and specks of frost spinning around. In the other, he's fine, he no longer has cramps, or thirst, no pain, as if wrapped in a gentle warmth. A strange silence reigns, and then this light draws him so far away . . . It's so disconcerting that he begins to be afraid. His fears increase and turn into veritable panic. His heart is beating too fast and too hard, each of his heartbeats resonating through the whole body, which becomes a gigantic drum. He's sweating, and at the same time he's icy. He is burning, and at the same time he is carried by the wind. He no longer feels his body. Terror has submerged it. It's atrocious—how is it that he no longer controls anything? He's going to be absorbed, buried in this terri-

fying panic attack. Crushed in a titanic press. No help is possible. He
wants to cry out, he screams for someone to help him but no sound
comes out. There's nothing around him now but the void. His heart is
going to explode, his body is torn apart. He is overcome with nausea.
He's not seeing his limbs any more. He would like to lose consciousness,
but that, too, seems impossible. He is in the process of dissolving. Of
disappearing. Could it be that he's dead? Has the moment come? The
moment when everything stops? No, he's just been wounded; someone
will take care of him . . . They're going to take care of him . . . He's
on the edge of a gulf. Obsessive thoughts invade him. Is his body ceas-
ing to live? But no, he's living because he's afraid. A gigantic and massive energy penetrates each one of his cells. An entire universe crashes
down on him and dislocates him . . . Words fade away, thought dies out.
Black, yes, black. The void. Alexander disappears, swallowed up.

And suddenly all is calm, and there is this light . . .

And once again he knows.

Sukhaya Niva is surrounded and declared taken at 10:30 a.m. The division losses were very heavy. All the officers of the 1st Battalion were
killed. The division has only 137 able-bodied men, and its four companies participate in the end of the offensive under the direction of subofficers, before being retired from the front lines.

The Soviets are still bitterly defending their positions on the hillside
to the southwest facing Borok. Attack is complicated there because of a
steep slope. They are crushed under the shelling, but a Russian defender
is not giving up. They finish off in fierce hand-to-hand combat.

In the middle of the day, the Soviets launch a counterattack on
Sukhaya Niva. It is repelled by a violent artillery barrage and the companies of the 3rd Battalion.

The conquered positions are cleaned out and secured. The wounded
begin to be evacuated. The dead, brought together and lined up on the
ground, will follow.

Alexander's corpse is thrown onto the metal floor of a truck. The engine starts, and the vehicle slides around in the mud, stabilizes, and then heads south toward Mirochny. The jolts from the broken-up road maul the abandoned body of the young lieutenant. The skin on his face is diaphanous, his eyes half-closed. Locks of blond hair plastered with blood. With each jolt, his head bumps around and rolls over ridges on the metal floor. The throat, open and bloodless, yawns with the movement. His contorted limbs, now lifeless, flail around.

Alexander watches the scene: a dead body bumping around and looking familiar to him, while above the crests of the forest, around him, there are floating innumerable great luminous forms to which he feels close.

51

The Grave

I'm distracted. Nicolas drives in silence. Toward the south, toward Mirochny. The bumpy road jostles me, and I *see* Alexander's lifeless body sliding around on the floor of the vehicle that is going down toward his grave.

I am the dead man, and I am the man who's alive.

The sun floods the sky and my eyes with a dazzling light.

Once in the village, Nicolas stops in front of the house with the black dog, the house under which there lies his grave. The gate is open. I have only one desire: get him out of there. It's a really absurd idea, but I've been obsessed with it for weeks. If his remains are actually there under the house, he is no longer there. I perceived the presence of his body; this property is full of cadavers, but life is no longer there.

Just nightmares.

Alexander is in an eternal time that I cannot reach. A space situated beyond visual materiality, paradoxically very close, but just the same inaccessible. And he is located in me as well.

So why do I want so badly to remove his earthly body?

Does Alexander want to be moved? No. Today he is so far from that October 1941 day. Returning to his body plunges him again into an unfortunate existence: suffering, anger, and war.

He doesn't want that now.

So why am I obsessed by this desire? I would like to bring into the light his bones, his skull, ruffle through his pockets, no doubt they are hiding a letter, a photo, a word, something *that is meant for me.* The dead soldiers were thrown into the ground with all their effects. What did he take with him to his grave?

Suddenly I notice that the car parked in the yard has German license plates. It's comical. A young woman comes out on the landing, comes toward us with a severe look on her face, and asks us what we want. Nicolas explains, and that breaks the ice. She lets us come in. Nicolas and I come through the gate. This is Tania's daughter. I let my acolyte begin the discussion, and I move toward the house, deeply moved by being able to approach it. When Nicolas brings up the excavations of the German funeral agency, the daughter looks at him questioningly.

"They excavated under the chicken coop. Do you want to see?" she asks us.

We follow her to the back, to see that traces of the excavated graves are still visible.

"There you are. You see—the bodies were there, under this part of the land."

She too seems not to realize that a great many of the graves still remain on the property and under the house.

"Actually, the emplacements are very precise. When was the house built?"

"In 1947 . . . Those who came for the dead soldiers opened three rows and removed seven bodies from each row in this location."

"Were you present?"

"No, it was my uncle who told me that. I live in Germany . . . "

"Is that your car out front?"

"Yes. Why?"

"No particular reason. It's just startling to see a German car in these parts."

"I come regularly with my son to visit my mother."

"Where do you live in Germany?"

"Near Berlin. My husband is German. We're planning to come here to live together soon."

What's happening? What energies are at play here? What is the part played by chance, by coincidence, or by invisible influences? It's so improbable: a German marries the granddaughter of a Russian woman living in a house built on a cemetery full of dead SS soldiers, and with her husband and their boy of fourteen they decide to come and live on this land. Is this move really a deliberate *choice*? Are these dead looking for a guardian? A way of getting out of there? Are they hanging on to life by this sort of proxy arrangement, without even realizing that they were dead? A shiver runs down my back.

I notice a low hatch that leads under the house, and I turn toward the young woman.

"Where does that go?"

"To the cellar."

"Can I take a look?"

She agrees after a brief moment of hesitation. I too am taken by ghosts. They've been sticking to me for months. I unhook the metal bar that's holding the little door shut, pull up, and discover that in fact rather than a cellar this door gives access to a space that is less than eighty centimeters high, running under the whole floor of the house. The building doesn't have any foundations; it is simply resting on the ground. The floor of the living area parts is raised, and that makes it possible to store of all sorts of foodstuffs in this confined space underneath. The dirt floor is at the same level as outside.

"Can I go in?"

"If you want."

On my hands and knees I make my way into the interior. The "cellar" is full of cases of vegetables, potatoes, pumpkins, and squash. Cabbages are hung up, attached to the beams that are holding up the floor. I have trouble maneuvering, but I manage to enter completely under the dwelling. Tania's house had been off-limits to us since our arrival in Mirochny, and today it opens to us, on the anniversary day of the death of the man whose grave was dug here in the welcoming earth. This is no small thing. The strange magic of existence is gripping at certain moments. Stretched out in the cool darkness, under the floor of an izba, I'm at my destination.

In a tomb.

Lying on Alexander's grave.

So close to the body that was *mine before.*

The black earth surface gives off a damp odor. I would like to attack it with my hands. Right here, now, dig, get my fingers into the fertile humus. Free up a channel, a tunnel, an access toward him, breaking my nails doing it.

Alexander is so close.

At this moment, less than a meter away from me.

The *impression* that all the answers are there but still inaccessible. I am torn apart. What to do? Are the secrets of our connection under the earth? There has to be a message for me; he carries it on him. I stay still, lying down, and undecided. I'm at the end of the road. I cannot resolve myself with the idea that the inquiry is going to end like this.

But finally, I come back out. Because what else is there to do? I stand up. I need calm, silence, and I need *to find myself.*

Nicolas and I take our leave of the young woman, and I go back to the house where we were welcomed for the night. I'm going to stay there for all of the rest of the day, alone, alternating between periods of meditation and writing. So moved, so turned around, I need to integrate the sensations and events that I have been experiencing since dawn, this last dawn. In this way, I remain for long hours within an immobility of body and mind, attentive to what the silence may want to tell me. Why exactly did I come here today? Do I really have to open this grave? And how would I do it? Alexander remains silent.

◆ ◆ ◆

At the end of the afternoon, I find Nicolas, and we go to say our good-
byes to Valentina and Macha. We have to get back to Valdai this evening. In twenty-four hours, my plane leaves Saint Petersburg for Paris.

A few minutes around tea. In the kitchen Nicolas is chatting, while
I am lost in thought. As I'm staring off into space, my eyes land on the
window opposite my bench. I'm motionless, drained, looking outside,
the garden, the fence. And it is then that I see, less than ten meters from
the house, directly in my line of vision, a fox sitting on his hind legs
and looking at me fixedly. The scene is so unexpected that I am dumbfounded. For three long seconds, he and I don't move. Face-to-face, eye
to eye. The moment is surreal. Then, coming out of my amazement, I
point my finger at the window.

"There's a fox . . . "

The others notice him too. And the little animal takes off through
the tall grass, like a rascal.

We depart. The car is parked in the center of the village, and
Nicolas has already started the engine. *But I don't want to leave.*

"Wait a minute . . . "

I take a few steps in the direction of Tania's house. The sun is now
very low on the horizon and lends a red tone to the front of the house.
I approach, staying far enough away so that the black dog doesn't see
me and go crazy. Then I murmur, to all the soldiers buried there: "I'm
leaving; don't come with me. There is a light for each one of you. It is
there; you can see it. Your loved ones are waiting for you. Be calm and
attentive, and they will appear. You are dead; you cannot come with me.
Seek the light—it is there for each one of you."

For a brief instant, I have a vision of all these men aligned in their
graves, so many men, so far from home.

Very sensitively, Nicolas remains silent as our car leaves Mirochny
and heads north in the warm light of dusk. I'm leaving this place. The
voyage is over.

We get back to the main road. Still no traffic. Darkness descends on the solitude of the forest. Suddenly, a form moves on my right, right at the edge of a field. A fox. Again. He's running alongside the road, and his eyes follow our passing car; then I see him veer off toward the trees. He disappears into the dense vegetation.

Several emails are waiting for me when I get back to an internet connection at the hotel in Valdai. I go through them without reading them until I discover one written by Gunther Dittmar's son, the garage man from Bad Arolsen and nephew of Alexander's wife. I had not had a single sign of life from this family since I left Bad Arolsen. A laconic sentence: "Dear Stéphane, here are the photos of Alexander and Luise," accompanied by four attachments. Nothing else. No explanation. No captions. I copy them onto my computer and open them. One photo of Luise and three of Alexander appear. I find him young, proud, and smiling for the first time. In one of them, he is dressed in a light suit and seated on a chaise longue with Tommy on his knees. Tommy was his brother's dog. Alexander inherited it after the animal had accidentally overturned Marlene's baby carriage. A little fox terrier.

Alexander smiling.

This is the first time I see him smile.

52

Afterward

Five months have passed. I'm driving to Plauen calm of mind, in the coolness of a spring night, the day before Easter. I'm coming back from another world, the inverted and invisible other side of the one that streams away in the streaks of rain flowing behind the dark windows of my car moving at a good clip on a German expressway. Another world just as present as a sound or a smell, and yet just as elusive as a breath in a woodlot.

This trip will be a determining factor: I'm going to announce to Alexander's family, to Marlene, my desire to write a book about this story. They don't know anything about that yet; the official pretext of our meeting is the account I must give them of my trip to Russia. It is they who suggested we meet in Plauen.

I need their agreement, and I can't imagine that they would refuse. But the agreement is not yet won.

Arrival, hotel. Calm night. Easter Sunday, a big sun over the town. I am happy to reconnect with Andréa and André. The three of us have dinner, and I recount for them what has happened since last we met. It feels like I'm sharing all that with old friends. As if giving me a wink, Andréa says to me that she believes in spirits. The way things came to her during these months of inquiry she still finds touching. From our first meeting on, she was extremely surprised, for example, by the

333

rapidity with which she was able to find out about Marlene. In fact, against all logic, she found in the Plauen archives the death certificate of Alfred, Alexander's brother, who died in a different town no less. Normally, this document should never have been there. And because of that, Andréa discovered Bertram and then Marlene. And it was like that all along. We were helped. For her, being used to doing genealogical research, obtaining results so quickly was really unsettling.

In fact, how many synchronicities during these months? I'm no longer keeping track of them because of the extent to which they were unbelievably present. As if everything was part of the same totality, the same musical score, a precisely orchestrated choreography. As if *someone* brought us into relation with one another, placed such and such a document on our path, inspired such and such a decisive action. What is the aim of all this? I don't have all the answers, but I understand this help to be the confirmation of the rightness of my undertaking.

We spend a pleasurable afternoon together, and then I return to the tranquility of my room. The night flows by in the blink of an eye; and in it I see that I have won serenity. In my dreams.

In the morning, Easter Monday, Andréa and André join me at the hotel for the arrival of Marlene and her husband Joachim, as well as Bertram. Heartwarming reunion. Everything is going to play out within a few moments. I am tense, even if I don't let it show. It's been more than a year now that I've been engaged in this research. And if Marlene is opposed to my doing a book, how will I react? Initially, I provide all the details of my trip to Russia. I explain to them where Alexander's body is, but curiously I have the feeling that Marlene prefers to think of him in Korpowo, even though I show her that is not the case. I see that I must not insist.

When I come to the most important reason for my traveling to Plauen, it is first of all a certain surprise that greets my desire to write. And then, spontaneously, Marlene and her husband announce that they're rather favorable.

What a relief, so happy.

Instantly, a colossal weight is lifted from my shoulders. The discussion continues, notably to work out the practical details that concern them. We agree to change their names, as well as several geographical details. I propose that they suggest some pseudonyms that they would like to bear. The exercise provokes hilarity.

In conclusion, they accept that I recount my inquiry in a book, but even more important in my eyes, they authorize me to use the real name of Alexander Herrmann. Do they realize that they are giving me an invaluable gift? In agreeing to this, they are telling me implicitly that a part of them believes in my dream.

The sun is still high when I leave the lobby of the hotel. Spring comes early in Saxony. The weather is gentle. I go out to the street and begin to walk a little, profoundly relieved.

Now I can begin to write.

Pass on this incredible adventure.

Starting tomorrow, as soon as I'm back in Paris, I will set myself to it.

In these few hours before dusk, I make my farewells to the town of Alexander's birth. I walk to his former school and then take the way he would have gone home on Neundorfer Strasse. His childhood street. I walk up it for two hundred meters and come to the building as strong feelings arise in me. Yellowed façade. Pan and Selene are still up there on either side of the fourth-floor windows. I stand motionless in front of the entrance.

A few minutes pass this way, and suddenly I remember the photo that Marlene gave me in which Alexander and his brother are playing in the backyard of the building. I take out my portable computer from my bag and display the photo on the screen. I would like to enter right now to see this spot, but the building seems deserted and unoccupied. I wait around just the same—you never know. After a quarter hour, I can make out shadows behind the glass door of the lobby. And looking through a clean corner of the glass, I see two men and a child heading toward this inner courtyard. I knock to attract their attention, and one of them comes and opens the door for me. He doesn't speak English, but by showing him the photo on my laptop and with a few gestures, he agrees to let me come in. I understand he is asking me if I want to buy the building. I tell him no and say simply "family," showing him the two brothers in the photo.

Now I'm in the backyard.

Nothing has changed in one century. The same red bricks, the same step before the entrance, the same drainpipe, the same window frame, even the same wooden door, which seems to look identical. It's really unsettling.

I had a rendezvous with this little boy.

This little blond kid who was already thinking for himself, happy and innocent. Yes, innocent. More than ninety years separate these two moments, the one in gray on my screen and the one in front of me. And a part of me is present in both of them. Straddling two worlds, bracketing a time of horror that we managed to get out of, he and I.

The little boy plays with his brother in the backyard. Laughing and happy.

I pass through the lobby, open the glass door, and go out to the street. And I walk away without looking back. I am a new man, and it's a very strange sensation. It takes some time before I realize that the weight I always had in me isn't there anymore. The inexplicable violence, the images of weapons, the brutal impulses have disappeared. I am light—almost weightless.

How strange it is, a new life is beginning . . .

Epilogue

What a strange adventure. However, at the moment of taking stock, I can see the extent to which the shadow that lived in me and haunted me since childhood was taking on a face. Then the accumulation of precise and verifiable elements led me to accept the encounter with this man who appeared in the course of a waking dream.

There couldn't have been anything worse than Alexander's life: violence, utter humiliation, shame, an epoch of blood. However, my intuition whispered in my ear that the confrontation was necessary. And that it carried within it the seed of its alleviation.

So I persevered. Doing so clarified his history, which consequently is also mine. Then, finding myself on the day of the anniversary of his death in the forgotten hamlet of Sukhaya Niva, one thing happened, the full scope and significance of which took me months to understand.

Healing the living heals the dead.

Alexander and I are not the same man, but emanations of the same consciousness. We are linked by a breath of life that moves through us both and is impregnated by the character and emotions of our two lives; and no doubt many more besides. It was given to me to measure during these months of inquiry how the lives are individual and unique, even though what animates them is eternal.

I am not Alexander *who returns*, but an individual carried by an immortal breeze that passes from eternity into mortal bodies.

The racist and impoverished thought that swept Alexander away during one life did not live on through me. It is even the exact opposite. All my life I have been the antithesis of Alexander. I am a man profoundly open to the world. I have traveled around our planet ceaselessly in order to hear and understand those who think and live differently. Without judgment, engaged in sincere active listening. I have always strived to be vigilant and kindly in what I do and in my thoughts. In becoming a journalist at the age of nineteen—the same age at which Alexander joined the Waffen-SS—I threw myself passionately into THE profession that, in the words of Dan Rather, allows you "to tell people what is attempted to be hidden from them." In my eyes a journalist is the enemy of propaganda. With his words he brings freedom and provides for each individual the possibility of being the master of his own reflections, whereas Alexander with his words or his fists brought only fear and suffering.

Discovering, verifying, and sharing information has been for me and still is today a sacred task.

In contrast, Alexander was grabbed by the Nazi verbal diarrhea. From adolescence on, he stopped thinking for himself and decided to become the armed, blind tool of an inhuman ideology. To do that he crushed his own conscience. Because *before*, wasn't he a kind, open, curious child born into a loving family?

Our relationship demonstrates in an obvious way the fragility of the thoughts that turn us against one other. The weakness of these ideas for which certain of us kill each other. Because Alexander's ideas did not withstand the transition past death. They are worth nothing; they have no strength and no future. They survive just in fear. And they did not survive in me. I offer Alexander this understanding. Through me, he realizes how frustration led him into error, and death trapped him in its fears.

Ultimately, we have only one life. We pass through a multitude of existences, of course, but each time as unique individuals. Only once will I be Stéphane Allix, just as Alexander Herrmann had only one life. Two different faces, two personalities opposed in many aspects, two lives, one single eternity.

After my return from Russia, I experienced weeks of strangeness. Autumn gave way to winter; the days became tiny and the nights interminable. I don't like this time of darkness, being one who inherited the worst of darkness. I was still inhabited by the echo of cannons. This horror that was my own. I realize now that my body, my cells held the memory of death. Death was there. Lurking. Inaccessible to my mind, to my thinking, to my reason, or to my consciousness. This fear begins roiling when I provoke it. Ordinarily, it remains below the level of consciousness, but it's certainly still present. Because I am the spokesman of the dark. I carry the voice of an army, all the soldiers forgotten and without graves. These anonymous dead, some of whom must have crossed paths with me in the forests of Russia.

And I carry as well the memory of their victims.

The innocent faces.

The women and children and men thrown into the void by the pure hatred that appeared at the heart of our Europe.

The shame *that could come again.*

And in fact, to the extent that I was on this voyage with Alexander at my side, fear was reawakened. Several times, paralyzed with shame and sadness, I wanted to give up. Abandon this book project, burn the documents, and forget everything about this story and this name.

I was carrying his downfall within me. By engaging resolutely with this voyage, I confronted the same challenges, the same temptations he did. Reconnecting with him was fraught with pitfalls and dangers. His shadow could have captured me. These tormenting demons had already approached me. I recognized them from the anger that sometimes took up residence in me. The anger of revolt, even when it seemed justified by the harshness of the world, is still anger and leads only to the void. However, this anger poured out of me from my whole being given the slightest annoyance.

Yes, so many times I wanted to give up.

And then my wife brought to my attention the admirable words of Romain Gary: "When you write a book, let's say on the horror of war, you are not denouncing the horror, you are ridding yourself of it."[1] So I accepted to go all the way, and to write, to tell all, because I so badly wanted to rid myself of this past that had always pursued me.

And to free oneself from the past, you need to look at it straight on.

Otherwise life is nothing but a cascade of repetitions.

So I pursued the voyage up to the field east of Sukhaya Niva. And I accompanied a demon toward the light.

Healing was also becoming aware of the anger that separated me gently from what makes up my life: my loved ones, my relationship with others, my ability to accept different words, to welcome the unexpected with joy.

Alexander is distant now. I feel he is freed. He is trying to win his forgiveness. Our relationship has found a good balance, but sometimes I continue to question myself. He is no longer someone unknown, however, so many mysterious points remain. Who was this person he had loved so dearly, for example? Could this lost love have left an emotion in my own life? Did he really walk along the Rue Gay-Lussac or in the Luxembourg Gardens, the stage for my childhood games? Why did he come back to France, in me? Did he love someone in my country? What happened in the village of Bailleul? At what moment, in the end, and this is the most essential question, did he perceive that he was participating in horror? Perhaps the future will bring some fragments of an answer.

There remains one last question: what to do about Alexander's remains under the house in Mirochny? Do I go back there to exhume him, or do I leave him where he is resting now? It is the guardian angel who shares my life, my wife, who, once again, found the right words.

One evening when we were with our friends Sandra and Christian Gamby, I was recounting the final developments in this story and my hesitation about returning to Russia. At that moment, Natacha looked at me and said, "Going to dig him up would be to bring him back to life and reactivate that energy in you."

And in that very moment, I knew that I would not return to Russia.

Alexander's remains will always rest there where they were first buried, in the past, under Russia's cold earth.

Natacha has just blown away the last relic of a shadow still stuck to my clothing. My mission was not to have Alexander reborn, but to heal him of his ignominy, to heal us.

And that is in the process of being accomplished.

Our metamorphosis has begun.

From now on, in front of me there are life and joy.

The light needs darkness in order to be perceived.

The light . . .

Thanks

This book is the story of a meeting, one of those moments in life that changes everything. The book grew from an accumulation of meetings, synchronicities, and intuitions. The bringing to light of this panorama of my "story" would not have been possible without the sometimes very intense involvement of the women and the men who pushed me, untiringly, to continue along my path. All of them are very dear to my heart. Sometimes even much more than that.

Thanks to Marie-Pierre Dillenseger for having initiated the trip to Peru, to *where there are stones*, and for having advised me afterward so energetically during my inquiry.

Thanks to Jan Kounen and Anne Paris, whom "chance" put on my path one autumn evening in order to advise me to meet Yann Rivière.

Thanks to Yann Rivière for having provided me with the pliant framework propitious for the emergence of that memory.

Thanks to Serge Augier for having reconnected me to my body.

Thanks to Charles Trang, whose advice and writings allowed me in grand measure to penetrate into Alexander's day-to-day life in France and Russia, and whose help in the exploration of the archival documents was priceless.

Thanks to Andréa and André Harnisch, who opened so many doors for me in Germany.

Thanks to Thomas Goisque for having recommended Nicolas Fréal to me. And thanks to Nicolas Fréal for his patient assistance on the roads of Russia. Nicolas is an ideal travel companion.

Thanks to Sylvie Baldacchino for having taken care of my body, where sometimes so much sadness played out.

Thanks to Mika de Brito for his help.

Thanks to Claus and Monika Weisbach for their warm welcome.

Thanks to Sandra Gamby, Ria Wormser, Béatrice Isner, and Pirjo for their help and their translations from German.

Thanks to Véronique Dimicoli for her patient retranscriptions.

Thanks to Antonin Dehays, Jean-Luc Leleu, Charles W. Sydnor, and Lutz Möser (Bundesarchiv Berlin) for the sharing of their historical knowledge and their logistical assistance.

Thanks to Agnès Stevenin, Florence Hubert, Patrick Manreza, Laurie Fatovic, Michel de Grèce, Robert Martin, Henry Vignaud, and Pierre Yonas for having shared their perceptions of those other realities that are so present and yet inaccessible to so many of us.

Thanks to Djohar Si Ahmed, Jim Tucker, Bénédicte Uyttenhoven, Thomas d'Ansembourg, and Arnaud Riou for having listened to my recounting of overviews of this strange story, and for their precious advice.

Thanks to my French publisher, to Michka and to Tigrane, founding pillars of the marvelous publishing house that is Mama Éditions. Thanks to both of you, as well as to Juliette and your whole team, whose involvement and enthusiasm for this book never waned in its intensity. You accompanied me with graciousness, eyes shining, at each stage of this long journey. As if you knew from the beginning where all that was going to take us, while I still had no idea.

Thanks to my first readers, whose feedback was so important: my mother, Claude Allix, Christophe Fauré, Fabrice Midal, Laurent Gounelle, Amélie Nothomb and Tom Verdier, Agnès Ledig, Matthieu Ricard, and Boris Cyrulnik . . .

Many thanks to Jon Graham, Inner Traditions • Bear & Company acquisitions editor, for your trust and appreciation of my work. Your decision to publish *When I Was Someone Else* in English is such a great honor.

Thank you to Jack Cain for this extremely well done translation of my story. Writing is like creating music, and I feel so grateful to you for the respect and the beauty of your dedication to find the melody of my words.

A particular thanks to project editor Meghan MacLean, who finalized the editing process with me with a careful attention to every detail.

Thanks to Jeanie Levitan, editor in chief, and Patricia Rydle for your work in the early stages of this English edition.

Thanks to copyeditor Sarah Galbraith, publicist Manzanita Carpenter Sanz, and designer Debbie Glogover.

Additionally, I want to warmly thank my first English readers for whom I have a huge admiration. I feel very honored and touched by your friendship and your comments on *When I Was Someone Else*—Stanislav Grof, Kenneth Ring, Dean Radin, Eben Alexander, Jim Tucker, Bruce Greyson, David Lorimer, Chris Bache, and Pim van Lommel.

Thanks to Natacha, my so beautiful and indispensable other half who was the very first to read this book and who brought me precious advice, as well as having had to put up with the presence of this *other man,* during all the long months. I love you so.

Thanks to Luna for your curiosity, your questions, and the intelligence of your take on things.

Thanks to Alexander Herrmann's family, who agreed to meet with the Frenchman with the completely crazy story. In spite of their doubts and their skepticism, they were able to see my sincerity, and the importance to me of conducting this inquiry. As well as their help and their welcome, they agreed that I would relate this story using Alexander's real name. I am infinitely grateful for that. For me it was so important to be able to speak of Alexander Herrmann, this name that emerged in my mind during the waking dream. In contrast, in order to preserve anonymity for other family members, we agreed that all the other names would be changed as well as certain other little details that could lead to their being identified. The question of the Second World War is especially sensitive, so I also wanted to respect the wishes of this family, who discovered, through me, a little about the life story of their relative who was the slave of a time of darkness.

Finally, thanks to my allies, to my masters and guides in the invisible world.

Notes

6. UNDERSTANDING HORROR

1. Pisar, *Le Sang de l'espoir*, 51.
2. Stevenin, *De la douleur à la douceur.*

9. THE MILITARY FOLDER

1. Littell, *Les Bienveillantes*, 26–27.

19. BAD AROLSEN

1. Levi, *Si c'est un homme*, 163.
2. Pisar, *Le Sang de l'espoir*, 24.

25. DREAM

1. Marlantes, *Partir à la guerre*, 104–5.
2. Marlantes, *Partir à la guerre*, 109.

26. HITLER COMES TO POWER

1. Rees, *Ils ont vécu sous le nazisme*, 86.
2. Kageneck, *Examen de conscience*, 11.
3. Rees, *Ils ont vécu sous le nazisme*, 15.

4. *Géo Histoire,* "Le nazisme," 101.
5. *Géo Histoire,* "Le nazisme," 101.
6. Lusseyran, *Et la lumière fut,* 184.
7. Pisar, *Le Sang de l'espoir,* 12.

31. MEDIUMS

1. Allix, *La mort n'est pas une terre étrangère.*

34. EINSATZGRUPPEN

1. Sydnor, *Soldiers of Destruction,* 39.
2. Rees, *Ils ont vécu sous le nazisme,* 12.
3. Onfray, "Une généalogie de guerre civile," 38.

38. LIFE'S TRACES

1. Littell, *Les Bienveillantes,* 100.

39. SAINT PETERSBURG

1. Timothy Snyder, *Terres de sang,* 13.

40. OPERATION BARBAROSSA

1. Timm, *À l'exemple de mon frère,* 42–43.
2. Trang, *Opération Barbarossa,* 24.
3. Trang, *Opération Barbarossa,* 31.
4. Vopersal, *Soldaten, Kämpfer, Kameraden,* 366.
5. Snyder, *Terres de sang,* 294.
6. Vopersal, *Soldaten, Kämpfer, Kameraden,* 455.

44. THE ORDER TO WITHDRAW

1. Sajer, *Le Soldat oublié,* 107.
2. Vopersal, *Soldaten, Kämpfer, Kameraden,* 464.

46. HAND-TO-HAND COMBAT

1. Vopersal, *Soldaten, Kämpfer, Kameraden,* 465.
2. Trang, *Opération Barbarossa,* 52.

EPILOGUE

1. Gary, *Chien blanc.*

Bibliography

Publisher's Note: A direct translation of the foreign title is provided for those books not available in English. These appear in parenthesis directly following the foreign title. Books available as full English translations are noted as such in brackets following the full foreign citation.

Allix, Stéphane. *La mort n'est pas une terre étrangère* (Death is not a foreign land). Paris: J'ai Lu, 2013.

———. *Le Test.* Paris: Albin Michel, 2015. [English translation: *The Test: Incredible Proof of the Afterlife.* New York: Helios Press, 2018.]

Arendt, Hannah. *Eichmann à Jérusalem, Rapport sur la banalité du mal.* Folio Histoire, 1991 (Paris: Gallimard, 1966). [Original English work: *Eichmann in Jerusalem: A Report on the Banality of Evil.* New York: Penguin, 2006.]

———. *Le Système totalitaire. Les origines du totalitarisme.* Paris: Gallimard, 2002 (1951). [Original English work: *The Origins of Totalitarianism.* New York: Harcourt, 1968.]

Beevor, Antony. *La Seconde Guerre mondiale.* Paris: Calmann-Lévy, 2012. [Original English work: *The Second World War.* Orion, 2014.]

———. *Stalingrad.* Le Livre de Poche, 2001. [Original English work: *Stalingrad: The Fateful Siege. 1942–1943.* London: Penguin, 1998.]

Best, Werner. *Portraits de Nazis* (Portraits of the Nazis). Paris: Perrin, 2015.

Borlant, Henri. *Merci d'avoir survécu* (Thanks for having survived). Paris: Seuil, 2011.

Chaponnière, Corinne. *Les Quatre Coups de la Nuit de Cristal* (The four strikes of the night of crystal). Paris: Albin Michel, 2015.

D'Almeida, Fabrice. *Ressources inhumaines* (Inhuman resources). Paris: Fayard, 2011.

Desbois, Père Patrick. *Porteur de mémoires* (Bearer of memories). Paris: Champs Histoire, Flammarion, 2009.

Ferro, Marc. *L'Aveuglement: Une Autre Histoire de notre monde* (Blindness: Another history of our world). Paris: Tallandier, 2015.

Fest, Joachim C. *Les Maîtres du IIIe Reich.* Livre de Poche, 1965. [English translation: *The Face of The Third Reich: Portraits of the Nazi Leadership.* New York: Da Capo Press, 1999.]

François, Stéphane. *Les Mystères du nazisme* (The mysteries of Nazism). Paris: Presses Universitaires de France, 2015.

Frankl, Viktor. *Un psychiatre déporté témoigne* (A deported psychiatrist bears witness). Éditions du Chalet, 1967.

Gablier, Miriam. *La Réincarnation* (Reincarnation). Paris: Éditions de la Martinière, 2014.

Gary, Romain. *Chien blanc.* Paris: Folio Gallimard, 1972. [Published in English as *White Dog.* University of Chicago Press, 2004.]

Géo Histoire. "Le nazisme, aux racines d'une idéologie dévastatrice 1871–1933" (Nazism, at the roots of a devastating ideology 1871–1933), 26 (April–May 2016).

Goldhagen, Daniel-Jonah. *Les Bourreaux volontaires de Hitler, Les Allemands ordinaires et l'Holocauste.* Paris: Seuil, 1998. [Original English work: *Hitler's Willing Executioner: Ordinary Germans and the Holocaust.* New York: Alfred A. Knopf, 1996.]

Goya, Michel. *Sous le feu, la mort comme hypothèse de travail* (Under fire: Death as a hypothesis for work). Taillandier, 2015.

Gray, Jesse Glenn. *Au combat: Réflexions sur les hommes à la guerre.* Tallandier, 2012. [Original English work: *The Warriors: Reflections on Men in Battle.* New York: Harcourt, 1959.]

Grossman, Vassili. *Carnets de guerre.* Le Livre de Poche, 2007. [English translation: *A Writer at War: A Soviet Journalist with the Red Army. 1941-1945.* Edited and translated by Antony Beevor and Luba Vinogradova from Grossman's wartime notebooks. New York: Vintage Books, 2013.]

———. *Vie et Destin.* (In: *Oeuvres*) Bouquins Ed. Robert Laffont, 2006. [First English translation edition: *Life and Fate.* New York: NYRB Classics, 1960. The novel was praised as a masterpiece in Chandler's 2006 translation.]

Hopquin, Benoît. *Nous n'étions pas des héros* (We weren't heroes). Paris: Calmann-Lévy, 2014.

Husson, Édouard. *Heydrich et la solution finale* (Heydrich and the final solution). Paris: Perrin, 2012.

Kageneck, August von. *Examen de conscience: Nous étions vaincus mais nous nous croyions innocents* (Examination of conscience: We were conquered but we believed we were innocent). Paris: Perrin, 2004 .

———. *La Guerre à l'Est* (The war in the East). Paris: Perrin, 2002.

Kauffmann, Jean-Paul. *Outre-Terre.* Équateurs, 2016.

Kershaw, Ian. *Hitler—Essai sur le charisme en politique* (Hitler—Essay on charisma in politics). Paris: Gallimard, 1995.

———. *Hitler 1889-1936, Tome 1.* Paris: Flammarion, 1999. [Original English work: *Hitler 1889–1936: Hubris.* London: Norton, 1998).]

———. *Hitler 1936-1945, Tome 2.* Paris: Flammarion, 2000. [Original English work: *Hitler 1936–1945: Nemesis.* London: Norton, 2000.]

———. *Le Mythe Hitler: Image et réalité sous le IIIe Reich.* Paris: Champs Histoire, 2013. [Original English work: *The 'Hitler Myth'. Image and Reality in the Third Reich.* Oxford: Oxford, 1987, rev. 2001.]

———. *L'Opinion allemande sous le nazisme, réed.* Poche CNRS éd., 2010 (1995). [Original English work: *Popular Opinion and Political Dissent in the Third Reich. Bavaria, 1933–45.* Oxford: Oxford, 1983, rev. 2002).]

———. *Qu'est-ce que le nazisme? Problèmes et perspectives d'interprétation* (What is Nazism? Issues and interpretation perspectives). Paris: Folio Gallimard, 2003.

Kressmann Taylor, Kathrine. *Inconnu à cette adresse.* Paris: Flammarion, 2012. [Original English work: *Address Unknown.* New York: Washington Square Press, 2001.]

Langley-Dános, Eva. *Le Dernier Convoi.* Albin Michel, 2012. [Original English work: *Prison on Wheels—From Ravensbrück to Burgau.* London: Bloomsbury.]

Leleu, Jean-Luc. *La Waffen-SS: Soldats politiques en guerre* (The Waffen-SS: Political soldiers at war). Paris: Perrin, 2007. [Republished in 2 volumes, coll. Tempus, 2014.]

Lepage, Jean-Denis. *La Hitler Jugend, 1922-1945.* Le Grand Livre du mois, 2004. [English translation: *Hitler Youth, 1922-1945.* Jefferson, N.C.: McFarland and Company, 2009.]

Levi, Primo, *Si c'est un homme.* New York: Pocket, 2003. [English translation: *If This Is a Man.* Original language: Italian, 1947. Published in the United States as *Survival in Auschwitz.*]

————. *Les Naufragés et les Rescapés, Quarante ans après Auschwitz*. Paris: Gallimard, 1989. [English translation: *The Drowned and the Saved*. Original in Italian.]

Littell, Jonathan. *Les Bienveillantes*. Paris: Gallimard, 2006. [English translation: *The Kindly Ones*. New York: Harper Perennial, 2010.]

Lopez, Jean et Wieviorka, Olivier, *Les Mythes de la Seconde Guerre mondiale* (The myths of the Second World War). Paris: Perrin, 2015.

Lusseyran, Jacques. *Et la lumière fut* (And there was light). Éditions du Félin, 2005.

Manstein, Erich von. *Mémoires*. Paris: Perrin, 2015. [English translation; *Lost Victories*. First published 1958. Zenith Press 2004.]

Marlantes, Karl. *Partir à la guerre*. Paris: Calmann-Lévy, 2013. [Original English work: *What It Is Like to Go to War*. New York: Atlantic Monthly Press, 2011.]

Midal, Fabrice. *Auschwitz, l'impossible regard* (Auschwitz: View of the impossible). Paris: Seuil, 2012.

Morsch, Günter, and Agnès Ohm, ed. *The Administrative Centre of the Concentration Camp Terror*. Metropol Verlag, 2015.

Onfray, Michel. "Une généalogie de guerre civile" (A genealogy of civil war), *Le Point* 2290, July 28, 2016.

Pisar, Samuel. *Le Sang de l'espoir*. Paris: Robert Laffont, 2003. [Published in English as *Of Blood and Hope*. Little, Brown and Company, 1980.]

Prazan, Michaël. *Einsatzgruppen: Les commandos de la mort Nazis*. Paris: Points Histoire, 2015. [Title of his documentary film series: *Einstatzgruppen: The Nazi Death Squads, 2009.*]

Rees, Laurence. *Adolf Hitler, la séduction du diable*. Paris: Albin Michel, 2012. [Published in English as: *The Dark Charisma of Adolph Hitler*. London: Ebury, 2012; another edition: *Hitler's Charisma: Leading Millions into the Abyss*. Pantheon Books, 2013.]

————. *Auschwitz, les nazis et la solution finale*. mini-series for the BBC, 2005. DVD then on the French Channel TF1. Book published in 2005 by Albin Michel. [*Auschwitz: Inside the Nazi State*. BBC]

————. *Ils ont vécu sous le nazisme*. Paris: Perrin, 2008. [English title: *The Nazis: A Warning from History*. London: BBC Digital, 2012.]

Ryback, Timothy W. *Les Premières Victimes de Hitler*. Équateurs, 2015. [Original English work: *Hitler's First Victims: The Quest for Justice*. New York: Knopf, 2014.]

Sajer, Guy. *Le Soldat oublié.* Paris: Robert Laffont, 1967. [English translation: *The Forgotten Soldier.* Dulles, Va.: Brassey's, 2000.]

Snyder, Timothy. *Terres de sang: L'Europe entre Hitler et Staline.* Paris: Gallimard, 2012. [Original English title: *Bloodlands: Europe between Hitler and Stalin.* New York: Basic Books, 2010]

———. *Terre noire, l'Holocauste, et pourquoi il peut se répéter.* Paris: Gallimard, 2016. [Orignial English work: *Black Earth: The Holocaust as History and Warning.* New York: Tim Duggan Books, 2015.]

Stevenin, Agnès. *De la douleur à la douceur* (From pain to gentle sweetness). Paris: Mama Éditions, 2014.

Sydnor, Charles W. Jr. *Soldiers of Destruction—The SS Death's Head Division, 1933-1945.* Princeton, N.J.: Princeton University Press, 1990.

Timm, Uwe, *À l'exemple de mon frère.* Paris: Albin Michel, 2005. [Published in English as: *In My Brother's Shadow: A Life and Death in the SS.* New York: Farrar, Straus and Giroux, 2005.]

Trang, Charles, *Opération Barbarossa. La Waffen-SS au combat* (Operation Barbarossa: The Waffen-SS at war). Heimdal, 2013.

Vopersal, Wolfgang. *Soldaten, Kämpfer, Kameraden: Marsch und Kämpfe der SS-Totenkopf-Division. Band 2A.* Biblio-Verlag, 1999. [A masterful work that appears not to have been translated into English. On page 94, Allix provides a translation of the main title as: Soldiers, fighters, comrades. The subtitle looks like: Marches and battles of the SS Totenkopf Division, volume 2A.]

About the Author

Former war correspondent, creative director and moderator for the TV series *Enquêtes extraordinaires* (Extraordinary inquiries) on Channel M6, founder of INREES (Institut de recherche sur les expériences extraordinaires [Research Institute on Extraordinary Experiences]), founder of the magazine *Inexploré* (Unexplored), Stéphane Allix has published numerous books, including *The Test* (Helios Press).

At the age of 19, Stéphane Allix began a career in journalism by secretly joining a group fighting the Soviet occupation of Afghanistan. Without telling his parents, between the spring and summer of 1988, he spent several months in the underground movement of this country that lies at the heart of the Middle East, engaged side by side with its "Freedom Fighters."

Self-taught, he became fascinated by the profession of international reporter. Becoming a war photographer was his sole aim. Being on the ground, on the spot, what better way could there be to learn? Being that he was still young, this plunge into the terrible Afghan conflict affected him deeply.

Upon his return to France, he set about writing accompanying text for his photographic reporting. He was trained in journalism thanks to the kindness of a few principal editors of daily and weekly papers who, seeing this so highly motivated young man, agreed to have his copy reworked. In the following years, he traveled again, still in Asia, through India, Nepal, and Tibet, and concentrated on the resistance movement of the Tibetan people following the Chinese invasion. In November 1989 he interviewed the Dalai Lama in his residence in Dharamshala. This was the first of a series of his meetings with this exceptional man. In 1990, covering the revolution of the Nepali Congress Party, he published his first article in *Le Monde*.* Wanting to remain completely independent, Stéphane decided on the destinations and topics he would cover. He devoted himself to complex countries and topics in order to experience, in depth, the profession of a freelance photographic reporter. Marrying photo and text allowed him to have two arrows in his quiver and, for better or for worse, to begin to convert his passion into his life. In spite of all this, lean and hungry times were frequent.

Over the years, one destination followed another, and the world unfolded before him: the Horn of Africa, Madagascar, Iran, Pakistan, the Middle East, the Caucasus, Europe, and the United States. Beginning in 1995, Stéphane specialized in researching the production of opium and the traffic in heroin coming out of Afghanistan, this country being the principal world producer. This new direction began with months of on-the-ground exploration in the role of researcher for the American writer Larry Collins, who was preparing a novel using the heroin trade as its backdrop. This immersion in the black-market economy, this exploration of the supply lines and their proximity to civil wars and terrorist movements, as well as his knowledge of the Taliban led Stéphane to publish his first book in 1998: *La Petite Cuillère de Schéhérazade* (Scheherezade's little spoonful). Larry Collins, who took him under his wing, performed, in friendship, the honor of signing the preface. This inquiry, which told the story of his travels on drug trafficking routes, from the poppy fields of the Golden Crescent right

---

*The most prestigious and respected French newspaper. —Trans.

to the doors of Europe, has been hailed as a reference work by those involved in the antidrug struggle and the provision of information about it. In parallel, Stéphane collaborated on these topics with numerous communication media, including the French monthly newspaper *Le Monde diplomatique* and the European and French TV channels ARTE, Canal+, and France 2.

In 2000 he founded in Kabul the office for the Société des explorateurs français [French Explorers Society] in Afghanistan. His two brothers, Thomas and Simon, were part of the on-the-ground team that accompanied him in this adventure. On April 12, 2001, while they were traveling in separate cars south of the capital, Thomas was killed in a traffic accident.

His brother's death was a cataclysm. Following this day that impacted his whole being, and having been plagued since adolescence by large existential questions that most of us end up learning to silence, from this moment forward Stéphane felt the absolute necessity to find answers. The idea of pursuing his life in a devil-may-care manner no longer had any meaning. The comfortable day to day was missing what is essential. What happens after death? And this question leads to another, just as critical: What are we living for?

For two years a metamorphosis worked away, and in 2003 he definitively turned the page on his fifteen years as an international reporter in order to engage in an exploration of the mysteries of consciousness, with, however, the same rigor, the same seriousness, and the same requirement for rationality.

He discovered that, far from being a citadel of established certainties, science is rocked to its core by an immense revolution that brings into question the very fundaments of our vision of the world. Nearly a century ago, physics touched with one finger the paradoxes of our definition of reality. It is joined today by some other disciplines.

The study of the research on the consequences of this scientific revolution that is in progress gave Stéphane the opportunity to meet numerous researchers around the world: physicists, biologists, medical doctors, astrophysicists, and so on. He realized that unexplained human experiences, far from being reduced to hallucinations or delirium, are, on the contrary, the innumerable echoes of what is beginning to become established in even the most rational circles: our reality is composed of an immaterial, energetic dimension—in other words, a spiritual dimension. Consciousness is not a product of our material brain; it is even no doubt what causes matter to emerge.

Since this idea is found in numerous spiritual traditions, Stéphane Allix decided to throw himself into a grand inquiry in order to bring to light the parallels between the hard sciences (quantum physics, biology, astrophysics, etc.) and the humanities (psychology, anthropology, psychiatry, etc.) as contrasted with, on the one hand, unexplained—experiences and, on the other hand, millennial traditional knowledge.

At the end of June 2006, he attended, in Iquitos in the Peruvian Amazon, an international conference on shamanism that brings together researchers from the entire world, psychologists, anthropologists, and shamans from the whole Amazon region. The encounter with shamanism was critical and marked a turning point in his life. The direct and powerful experience of altered states of consciousness became from that time forward a source of learning and practice.

The following year, in July 2007, Stéphane Allix founded INREES. The goal of INREES is to seriously look into topics that we term extraordinary or even supernatural. In these times where new fields of knowledge are emerging, INREES then offers a framework for speaking about science and spirituality, the latest research on consciousness, on life and death, while making a scientific and rigorous approach to the invisible world from the visible world. Without taboos, without prejudice, with rigor and openness. In 2008 what would become the magazine *Inexploré* (Unexplored) was launched, first by subscription, then on newsstands.

This novel approach attracted major media attention, and in 2009 the French channel M6 signed contracts for the documentary series *Enquêtes extraordinaires* (Extraordinary inquiries), which ran for two seasons. Stéphane Allix served as the concept designer and presenter. The woman who has shared his life for years, the producer Natacha Calestrémé, directed the series and produced most of the episodes. Having become within a few years a specialist in these "extraordinary experiences," Stéphane appeared regularly in the media. He also has published books in France that are among the most important on these questions, and he has directed the management of book collections on these topics for several publishers.

Stéphane Allix has today given up the management of INREES and also his editorial work in order to devote himself exclusively to writing and inner exploration.

In June 2013, upon the death of his father, he decided to proceed with an experiment designed to test the possibility of communication with the Beyond. To do this, telling no one, he hid several objects in his father's coffin and several months later visited various mediums, individuals who claim to be able to communicate with the dead, with the aim of testing them. The results were stunning. Stéphane recounted them in his book *Le Test* (*The Test*), which was a great success in France and has been translated into several languages. With *Lorsque j'étais quelqu'un d'autre* (*When I Was Someone Else*), Stéphane Allix goes even further into the exploration of relations between the dead and the living.